The Hidden Famine

The Hidden Famine

Poverty, Hunger and Sectarianism
in Belfast 1840–50

Christine Kinealy and Gerard Mac Atasney

Pluto  Press
LONDON • STERLING, VIRGINIA

First published 2000 by Pluto Press
345 Archway Road, London N6 5AA
and 22883 Quicksilver Drive, Sterling, VA 20166–2012, USA

www.plutobooks.com

British Library Cataloguing in Publication Data
A catalogue record for this book is available from the British Library

Library of Congress Cataloging in Publication Data
Kinealy, Christine.
  The hidden famine : poverty, hunger, and sectarianism in
Belfast, 1840–50 / Christine Kinealy and Gerard Mac Atasney.
      p. cm.
  Includes bibliographical references (p.) and index.
  ISBN 0–7453–1376–0

  1. Belfast (Northern Ireland)—History. 2. Famines—Northern
Ireland—Belfast—History—19th century. 3. Poverty—Northern
Ireland—Belfast—History—19th century. 4. Poor—Northern Ireland—
Belfast—History—19th century. 5. Belfast (Northern Ireland)—Social
conditions. 6. Belfast (Northern Ireland)—Church history. 7. Ireland—
History—Famine, 1845–1852. I. Mac Atasney, Gerard.
  II. Title.
  DA995.B5 K56 2000
  941.6'7081—dc21   00–008778

ISBN 0 7453 1376 0 hbk
ISBN 0 7453 1371 X pbk

09   08   07   06   05   04   03   02   01   00
10   9   8   7   6   5   4   3   2   1

Designed and produced for Pluto Press by Chase Production Services
Typeset from disk by Stanford DTP Services, Northampton
Printed in the European Union by TJ International, Padstow

We would like to dedicate this book to Rita Pearson (d. 1999) and Philip Wilson (d. 1998)

Contents

List of Illustrations

Figures

Maps

Acknowledgements

Many people have contributed directly and indirectly to the writing of this book.

Friends and colleagues have provided on-going support, especially Bernadette Barrington, Eileen Black, Pat and John Brandwood, Deirdre and Lyndsey Briggs, Ann Brownlow, Susan Burnett, Arthur Chapman, Bill Crawford, John Dallat, Sandra Douglas, Angela Farrell, Ben and Nellie Fearon, Fionnula Flanagan, Brian Griffin, George Harrison, Roddie Hegarty, Bobby Lavery, Maura and Peter Mac Atasney, Pat McGregor, Fr Kevin McMullan, Kevin McNally, Ian Maxwell, Donal Moore, Don Mullan, Monsignor Raymond Murray, Cormac Ó Gráda, Fr George O'Hanlon, Ray and Honora Ormesher, Trevor Parkhill, the late Rita Pearson, John Richie, Owen Rodgers, Peter Roebuck, Louise Ryan, David Sexton, Sean Sexton, John Shaw, David Sheehy, Alison Skilling, Teresa Stein, Thompson Steele, John Trimble, Roger van Zwanenberg, Ian Vincent and the late Philip Wilson.

We would also like to acknowledge the assistance of the staff of the Bodleian Library in Oxford, the British Library at Colindale, the City Hall in Belfast, the Craigavon Historical Society, Cumann Seanchas Ard Mhachan, Down and Connor Diocesan Archives, the History Department in the University of Central Lancashire, the Irish Linen Centre at Lisburn, the Linen Hall Library in Belfast, the National Archives in Dublin, the National Library in Dublin, the Public Record Office in London, the Public Record Office of Northern Ireland, Queen's University Medical Library and the Ulster Museum. We are particularly grateful to the Deputy Keeper of Records, the Public Record Office of Northern Ireland and to Dr David Craig, Deputy Keeper of the National Archives in Dublin. We also gratefully acknowledge financial assistance from the Belfast Society.

Special thanks are due to Arthur Luke who has provided many insights into Belfast past and present, and to Professor John Walton who read earlier drafts of the text. We should also like to express our gratitude to Sean Gill who drew the maps and Ian Briggs who scanned documents. Any mistakes and omissions are, however, the responsibility of the authors.

We are particularly grateful to those people who have lived
through the writing of this publication at various stages of its
existence. They are Daphne, Kieran, Siobhan and Robert.

Finally, inspiration and encouragement was also derived from a
Conference on the Great Famine held in Hunter College, New
York in October 1997, where the keynote speakers included Mary
Nellis of Sinn Féin and Billy Hutchinson of the Progressive
Unionist Party. Their ground-breaking contributions were a
reminder of a shared past which also offered hopes of a collective
future.

Christine Kinealy
Gerard Mac Atasney

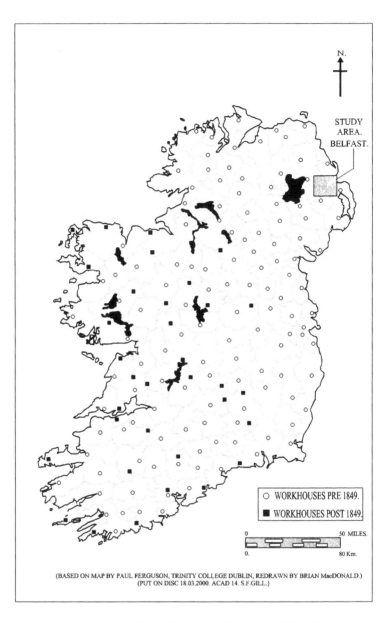

N.

STUDY
AREA.
BELFAST.

○ WORKHOUSES PRE 1849.
■ WORKHOUSES POST 1849.

0   50 MILES.

0.   80 Km.

(BASED ON MAP BY PAUL FERGUSON, TRINITY COLLEGE DUBLIN, REDRAWN BY BRIAN MacDONALD.)
(PUT ON DISC 18.03.2000. ACAD 14. S.F.GILL.)

Map 1 Poor Law Unions in Ireland, 1842–49

Introduction

Despite the outpouring of academic publications, which accompanied the sesquicentenary commemorations of the Great Famine in 1995, certain aspects of the crisis remained under-represented. One such omission was a scholarly reappraisal of the impact of the Famine in the province of Ulster. Many historical studies have tended to ignore the Ulster dimension or represent the northeastern counties as areas where the impact of the Famine was minimal. In their ground-breaking history of Guinness's brewery, Patrick Lynch and John Vaisey wrote: 'The areas unaffected directly by the Famine were the maritime economy centered on Cork, Dublin and Belfast.'[1] More recently, Roy Foster stated: 'Regions with varied local economies (notably the north and east coast) escaped lightly.'[2] And Brian Walker, a historian from Ulster, in a publication about the role of myth in Irish history, claimed: 'The Great Famine, with its enormous human toll, affected Ulster far less than elsewhere in Ireland, thanks to northern industrialization and the availability of crops other than the potato.'[3] At the same time, a collective impression was created that the impact of the crisis was confined largely to Catholic communities. This viewpoint was articulated by the economic historian Liam Kennedy, who stated: 'Ulster fared better than the average experience of the island ... The Protestant people of that province suffered less severely from famine.'[4]

Overall, therefore, the traditional orthodoxy has been that the Famine had little impact on the northeastern corner of Ireland, especially on the Protestant population. Contemporary evidence suggests otherwise. In July 1847, the Belfast Orange Lodge lamented that the recent famine had 'thinned out our local population and removed many of our Loyal brethren'. In recognition of the calamity, no music was played at the traditional Boyne commemoration.[5] The denial of the extent of the Famine in Protestant and Unionist historiography appears to owe more to political expediency than to historical reality. In 1937–38, the Unionist government of Northern Ireland refused to allow the Department of Education to participate in an all-Ireland study of famine folklore. The resultant survey, therefore, covered only the 26 counties of what was then the Irish Free State.[6] More recently,

1

a number of Unionist politicians reacted angrily when the British
Prime Minister, Tony Blair, issued a statement that 'Those who
governed in London at the time failed their people through
standing by while a crop failure turned into a massive human
tragedy.' In the same year also, members of the Democratic
Unionist Party opposed a motion by nationalist members of
Belfast City Council to erect a stained glass window in the City
Hall, as a commemoration to those who died in the town during
the Famine. Sammy Wilson, a DUP Councillor, argued that to
erect such a monument would give Sinn Féin 'the monsters of
manufacturing and media manipulation' a propaganda victory.
Moreover, 'There is no evidence that the Famine played any part
in the history of Belfast.'[7]

How can such attempts to deny a common history be explained?
Stephen Rea, one of the founders of the Field Day Theatre
Company in Derry, is a Belfast-born Protestant who is also a
Nationalist. His explanation of the Unionist view of Irish history
is that 'There is an amnesia among Protestants in this town
[Belfast] about their part in the creation and preservation of so
much of the culture of modern Ireland.'[8] His comments are
particularly pertinent to the memory of the Famine in Belfast.

The belief that the Famine had no direct impact on Belfast has
been one of the most enduring myths of Famine historiography. It
is a perception that has also been absorbed into popular traditions.
During a debate in *Dail Eireann* in 1995, one member asserted:
'My ancestors, who came from Belfast, would have been very little
affected by the Famine.'[9] The failure of historians to undertake
research on the Famine period in Belfast is difficult to understand
given the vast amounts of historical records available. However,
one Dublin historian, Mary Daly, provided an insight into the
reluctance of Irish historians to engage with certain topics when,
in a lecture in the Linenhall Library in October 1995, she stated:
'Now we are in a cease-fire situation, we can talk about aspects of
history which we may previously have felt uncomfortable with.'[10]
Despite this assertion, and a renewed commitment to the Peace
Process in Northern Ireland, even Famine publications which have
taken a comparative approach to the topic have omitted to look at
the impact of the Famine on Belfast.[11]

Three publications have helped to rectify this omission. *Death
in Templecrone* by Patrick Campbell (which was published in
America only, in 1995) provides an in-depth study of a parish in
northwest Donegal, and Gerard Mac Atasney's *This Dreadful
Visitation. The Famine in Lurgan/Portadown* (Belfast, 1997)
examines the impact of the Famine in one of the most industrialized and largely Protestant areas in Ulster.[12] A more general
overview was provided by *The Famine in Ulster* (edited by

Christine Kinealy and Trevor Parkhill, 1997) in which each Ulster county was examined by local historians.[13] A study of the impact of the Famine on the town of Belfast was not included in this collection.

The myth that the impact of the Famine did not extend to the northeastern corner of the island has its origins in the Famine period itself. In April 1846, the *Belfast Vindicator*, whilst complaining of the indifference of many of the wealthy inhabitants in the Belfast area to the increase in hunger amongst the local poor, attributed the attitude to 'the fine philosophy that would starve the poor for the honour of the rich'. Moreover, the newspaper asserted that the rich hated to be reminded of the existence of distress 'because it is a disgrace to the province, and [yet] wonder that persons will not be content to linger, sigh, and die in silence, sooner than sully the credit of Ulster'.[14]

During the Rate-in-Aid dispute in 1849, the Ulster Guardians – in an attempt to avoid paying the new tax – depicted themselves as having ridden the Famine crisis with ease. The reasons were generally related to the perceived religious and economic superiority of that portion of Ireland compared with the rest of the country. The hardships of the preceding years were marginalized and the fact that within Belfast four auxiliary workhouses were still required to meet the demand for relief was ignored. Moreover, the Rate-in-Aid conflict served to create an impression that Ulster was both different from, and superior to, the rest of the country. In February 1849, for example, the *Belfast News-Letter* cautioned that 'The sturdy men of the North will now be compelled to feed the starving masses in whom bad landlordism, disloyal teaching, a false religion and an inherent laziness have combined the share of canker of their country.'[15] These perceived differences were exploited for political advantage in the decades after the Famine.

The presence of textile production, and especially linen, within the northeastern economy is sometimes seen as having protected the area from the worst impact of the Famine. This assumption has been challenged by Mac Atasney's study of the Lurgan district, which was situated at the heart of the linen triangle. Those people involved in domestic production also had to grow potatoes in order to survive.[16] Brenda Collins has also demonstrated how, in the 1840s, the whole textile industry – both domestic and factory – was underpinned by potato production. This interdependence meant that the collapse of the latter inevitably damaged the former.[17] Successive failures of the potato crop after 1845, therefore, resulted not only in a shortfall in food but it meant that textile workers who depended on their farm income could not survive. This reduction in domestic production, in turn, had an impact on employment within the textile factories in the towns.

Collins regards the high numbers of emigrants during the late 1840s from ports such as Belfast as proof that 'domestic linen manufacture was not a prop which successfully supported the rural people when the potato crops failed'.[18]

The Famine also occurred during a period of readjustment within the textile industry, which had been accompanied by economic hardship and dislocation. Although the domestic system survived changes in technology, increasingly production became mechanized and moved to towns such as Belfast and Armagh. Ironically, in the surrounding rural areas, dependence on potatoes increased rather than decreased in the pre-Famine decade.[19] These changes were facilitated by concurrent improvements in transport. One consequence was that the economy of Ulster became more fully integrated both internally and externally with British markets. The entrepreneurs and industrial workers of Belfast saw their economic interests as lying with Britain rather than Ireland.

Visitors to Belfast in the decades preceding the Famine were impressed with the affluence and industry of the population, especially when compared with other districts in Ireland. The Halls, two Irish travellers who toured the country in 1840, commented: 'The clean and bustling appearance of Belfast is decidedly un-national.'[20] Two years later the writer William Thackeray described Belfast as being 'hearty, thriving and prosperous, as if it had money in its pocket and roast beef for dinner'.[21]

Yet, whilst Belfast was one of the most industrialized and prosperous areas of Ireland, incomes remained low. In the 1840s, much of Belfast's population was living close to the margins of survival, and poverty was endemic. In each decade since the passing of the Act of Union, the combination of food shortages and unemployment had resulted in the establishment of private soup kitchens in the town.[22] Rapid urbanization since the 1820s had also put pressure on housing and the local infrastructure, leading to overcrowding and insanitary living conditions. Not only did Belfast display many of the general features of urban living in the early nineteenth century, the social conditions within the town compared unfavourably with other urban centres. In the middle of the nineteenth century, Belfast had one of the highest death rates of any town in the United Kingdom. In 1851, due to massive infant mortality, the average age at death within the town was nine years.[23] Yet, regardless of widespread poverty, in the early nineteenth century the Protestant poor in particular had come to regard themselves as a sort of 'plebeian aristocracy'.[24] This view remained untarnished by the experiences of the late 1840s.

In 1838, a national system of poor relief was introduced which divided Ireland into 130 Poor Law Unions, each with its own workhouse. The Belfast workhouse was officially opened on 1 January 1841 and could accommodate 1,000 inmates.[25] When the potato blight appeared in Ireland, therefore, Belfast already possessed a workhouse and was integrated into the national system of poor relief. The boundaries of the Belfast Union extended beyond the traditional borders of the borough and included the industrial suburb of Ballymacarrett. During the early years of the Famine, the population of Ballymacarrett suffered intensely. Yet, repeatedly, the town authorities treated the district as separate from Belfast, and as a consequence the area was unable to avail itself of government assistance. This placed a considerable burden on private relief efforts. Yet Ballymacarrett was a predominately Protestant area and was one of the most industrialized districts in Ulster. Its experience showed that no district or religion was immune during the Famine.

The Guardians who administered the workhouse system in Ulster were regarded by government officials as being of a higher calibre than those in other parts of the country. In the opinion of Edward Senior, the local Poor Law Inspector, 'the northern Guardians are a better educated and more intelligent class and a more independent class'.[26] During the Famine years, the Belfast Union achieved a reputation for being one of the best administered in Ireland. This reputation was based on the fact that the Union was one of the few that did not receive any government loans for famine relief. Moreover, the Belfast Guardians refused to provide outdoor relief (the *bête noire* of relief provision) even after it was incorporated into the Irish Poor Law in 1847. As far as possible also, the relief officials preferred to use privately raised rather than public funds. Following the appearances of blight in 1845 and 1846, therefore, the town authorities again opened soup kitchens, funded by private contributions, as a means of providing relief in the cheapest – and most effective – way possible. Significantly, when government soup kitchens were opened in the summer of 1847, Belfast Union was one of three Unions which did not resort to relief provision. This high level of self-reliance gave the impression that suffering in Belfast was far less than elsewhere. The truth is more complex. Many of the decisions made by the Belfast Guardians were based on a reluctance to incur the additional costs of a government loan and the bureaucratic intervention that would have entailed.[27]

Clearly, by late 1846 the distress caused by the potato failure was having a major impact on Belfast. The distress was intensified by the coincidence of a trade slump in the local textile industry. Belfast was thus undergoing both an industrial and an agricultural depression. By the end of the year, the workhouse was full. Private charity was also under considerable pressure – by the beginning of 1847, the Belfast soup kitchens were feeding over 3,000 daily.[28]

A reporter with the *Belfast Protestant Journal* wrote that he 'could hardly believe that such a state of things prevailed in a place so enlightened as Belfast', and continued that the high level of misery in the town was due to the fact that the local population was too proud to seek assistance, 'unlike their counterparts in the south'.[29] The spread of fever in the town, exacerbated by overcrowding and insanitary conditions, led the *Banner of Ulster* to describe the condition of the poor in the town as one of 'starvation and misery'.[30] In 1847, parts of County Down were being likened to Skibbereen in County Cork, which had become a benchmark of famine suffering. A member of the Society of Friends, who visited eastern Down at the beginning of the year, reported: 'It would be impossible to find more distressing cases, short of the horrors of Skibbereen.'[31]

The issue of mortality in the Famine is complex and inconclusive, and the precise number of people who died is unknown. Unlike in England and Wales, in Ireland civil registration of births, deaths and marriages was not made compulsory until 1864. Independent estimates by economic historians such as Joel Mokyr and Cormac Ó Gráda have placed excess mortality in the country as being more than 1 million.[32] Local data are rare. In the place of direct evidence regarding mortality, indirect evidence and folk memory have acquired special value. In Belfast, mortality statistics are further obscured by the fact that the town was one of the few districts in the country to experience a population *increase* between 1841 and 1851 (the intercensal dates): in 1841 the census population was 75,308; in 1851 it had grown to 100,301. The population of the industrial suburbs grew most rapidly. However, the precise number of people resident in Belfast during the Famine period is not known; nor is the number of famine mortalities. By the spring of 1847, local newspapers such as the *Belfast News-Letter* were carrying daily reports of death from destitution and starvation,[33] and institutions dealing with the crisis all reported unprecedented demand for relief and high mortality. The situation created a demand which the various burial sites within Belfast were unable to meet. The fever epidemic in 1847 and the arrival of cholera in 1849 both contributed to a sharp increase in disease and death in the town.

During the Famine period, Belfast not only had to contend with the destitution of its own population, but the authorities also had to cope with the influx of paupers from the surrounding countryside in search of employment, relief or a passage out of Ireland. In addition, after 1847 Belfast became a main dumping port for Irish paupers expelled from Britain, particularly from Scottish Poor Law Unions. The system of removal not only highlighted the difference between the Poor Laws of Ireland and Britain but also demonstrated that, despite the Act of Union, Irish paupers were an Irish responsibility. This viewpoint was confirmed in 1849 when the introduction of a new tax on Irish Unions resulted in massive protests throughout Ulster. Poor Law officials at all levels, landowners and MPs all protested that Ireland was not being treated as an integral part of the United Kingdom.[34] Yet, regardless of threats of estrangement from Britain if the tax was imposed, by the end of the Famine Protestant Ulster appeared to be more deeply committed to the Act of Union than it had been in 1845.

Religion played a significant role in shaping both private and public responses to the Famine. Clergymen of all denominations initially played an active, and generally exemplary, role in famine relief. At the beginning of 1847, the nationalist paper, the *Freeman's Journal*, praised the harmony that existed between priests and ministers on various relief committees, observing that:

> The Catholic and Protestant clergymen vie with one another in acts of benevolence. They are the most active members of relief committees – they confer together, remonstrate together, evoke together the aid of a dilatory government, and condemn together its vicious and dilatory refusals.[35]

Yet, the activities of the Protestant Churches in relief provision became tarnished by accusations of proselytizing, that is, that the hunger of the poor was being used to promote a Protestant crusade in Ireland. The main perpetrators of this campaign were the Church of Ireland and the Presbyterian Church in Ulster, but it also had the tacit support of some members of the British government. The links between Protestantism and British national identity had been clearly demonstrated in the early decades of the nineteenth century.[36] For Irish Protestants, it distinguished them from the Catholic majority and unified them with the British state. The successive years of potato blight were viewed by many in both Ireland and Britain in providentialist terms, generally being seen as a judgment against the Catholic Church.[37] The food shortages also provided an opportunity for renewed attempts at proselytizing. Conversion was also underpinned by political salvation. In the words of Donal Kerr, the motivation of the missionaries was to 'rescue the people from the darkness of popery and to bring them to the pure light of the gospel. In turn, this would make the people peaceful and more open to political integration.'[38] The two main Protestant Churches in Belfast played a pivotal role in this crusade. In the wake of the second potato failure a number of charitable organizations were established in the town, which used relief as a means of winning converts. Their activities continued beyond the 1840s. And the bitter legacy lasted even longer. It contributed to sectarian clashes in Belfast and increased the hostility between the Catholic Church and the main Protestant Churches.[39] Palpably, the changes engendered by the Famine reinforced existing religious and political divisions within Ireland. In Belfast, they also paved the way for an increase in sectarianism in the latter decades of the nineteenth century.

Why did Ulster Protestants become more attached to the Union with Britain despite repeated instances during the Famine of unequal treatment within the United Kingdom? The onset of Famine in Ireland coincided with a period of anxiety for Protestants in Ireland, due largely to disillusionment with successive governments in London and administrations in Dublin over what were perceived to be unnecessary concessions to Catholics. This feeling contributed to the reinvigoration of the Orange Order and the resumption after 1845 of the twelfth of July marches (these had been banned since 1832). The renewed attempts to win repeal made by the radical Young Ireland movement confirmed and consolidated such fears. As the Famine progressed, the nationalist press blamed British misrule for the misfortunes of the country. In 1847, the *Belfast Vindicator* informed its readers:

> The work of death goes on. We are reaping the fruit of English legislation. There is scarcely anyone so foolhardy as to defend the legislation by which this country has been reduced to its present deplorable condition.[40]

The emergence of a more militant nationalist movement, with its demand for an independent government in Dublin, united Protestants who were opposed to repeal of the Union. At the same time, the revolution in France in February 1848 inflamed revolutionary feelings throughout Europe, including Ireland.

In the face of alleged government inaction, the Orange Order presented itself as the defender of Protestant interests in Ireland. In March 1848, the Grand Lodge cautioned the government that despite 'the fearful state of excitement, loyalty to the British Crown is daily decreasing'. One Belfast Protestant newspaper warned that unless immediate action was taken against the nationalists, 'the government will stand convicted of either the grossest stupidity or the most inconceivable cowardice'.[41] Overall, despite the Young Irelanders' declarations of non-sectarianism, and the formation of a Protestant Repeal Association with branches in both Dublin and Belfast, the 1848 uprising served to polarize divisions between Catholic and Protestant communities in Belfast. Significantly, it also confirmed the Orange Order's perception that they were a garrison to defend the interests of the British government in Ireland.

The non-sectarian aspiration of the Young Irelanders was forgotten as the 1848 uprising was reinvented as a conflict between loyal Protestant and disloyal Catholics. Both the conflicts of the Law of Removal and the Rate-in-Aid also raised the question of Ireland's unequal treatment within the United Kingdom. Belfast was in the forefront of both disputes. The propitious visit of Queen Victoria to Belfast in August 1849 – albeit for a few hours only – resulted in renewed declarations of loyalty.

In the post-Famine decades, the suffering of the poor in Belfast in the late 1840s was forgotten or marginalized. This collective amnesia was helped by the economic success of Belfast in the second half of the nineteenth century. However, the distress and mortality experienced in the town during the Famine was no ordinary subsistence crisis. In Belfast the calamity not only shaped the size and social composition of the population in the years which followed, it also contributed to the growth of more entrenched political cleavages, which were based on religious rather than economic divisions. Clearly, one legacy of the Famine was that religious divides within Belfast had increased and sectarian disputes became more deeply entrenched in the decades that followed.

*

The chapters that follow deal with Belfast during the 1840s – a decade which proved to be pivotal both economically and politically in the town's development. By the 1840s Belfast was on the verge of becoming a major industrial centre within the United Kingdom. However, this transformation was accompanied by social dislocation in Belfast and in the surrounding countryside. Additionally, economic success disguised the endemic poverty which had become a feature of all British urban centres. Consequently, the potato blight struck a town which contained a high proportion of people living on the margins of economic survival. 1845 and 1846 were also years of poor corn harvests. Moreover, the agricultural collapse coincided with an industrial depression not only in Belfast but throughout the United Kingdom.

The impact of the Famine on Belfast was swift and severe, yet there was a determination amongst some of the affluent groups within the town to play down its impact on the poor. None the less, by the end of 1846, the hunger in the suburb of Ballymacarrett was being likened to the distress in Skibbereen and Bantry. The strain

which the Famine imposed on Belfast was amplified by the fact
that as a consequence of the blight there was an influx of hungry,
impoverished people, not only from the surrounding countryside,
but also from further afield. This precipitated a debate about
entitlement to relief – who was more deserving, the native poor or
strangers (the population of Ballymacarrett being considered by
some to fall into the latter category)? The institutional responses to
the Famine were constrained by a mixture of ideological, financial
and practical considerations. Yet, at the same time as people were
dying daily on the streets of Belfast, and the hospitals were
crammed and the cemeteries overflowing, the relief authorities
were being congratulated for their independence in not seeking
financial support from the British Treasury. Financial probity
rather than saving lives was a measure of administrative 'success'.

Several members of the British government saw the Famine as
an opportunity to bring about long-desired changes in the Irish
economy. For a number of evangelical missionaries, it also
provided an opportunity to bring about changes in the religious
practices of poor Catholics, by using starvation as an opportunity
to convert Catholics to Protestantism. Belfast was a major centre
for this and some of the Protestant Churches acted as a conduit for
Scottish missionaries to undertake a religious crusade in Ireland.
Although the number of converts was relatively small, the activities
of the Belfast proselytizers left a bitter legacy and increased distrust
and divides between the main Churches in the town in subsequent
decades.

Despite being praised for their handling of relief provision, the
relationship between the British government and the Belfast relief
authorities was not always cordial. As the Famine progressed, the
government attempted increasingly to make the crisis an Irish
rather than a British responsibility. The Belfast authorities believed
that they were being treated unfairly in the dispute over the Law
of Removal and by the introduction of the Rate-in-Aid. Yet, as the
responses to the nationalist uprising in 1848 and the visit of the
Queen in the following year demonstrated, Belfast emerged from
the Famine not only with its loyal, Protestant and British identity
intact, but considerably strengthened.

PART I

The 'Old' Poor Law, *c.*1640–1845

CHAPTER 1

An 'Un-National Town'

The commercial and industrial success of Belfast in the late nineteenth century was both unique and extraordinary within the overall picture of Irish economic development. In the middle of the seventeenth century, Ulster had been the poorest province in Ireland. Although Belfast had been made a Corporate Borough in 1613, as a market town and port it was overshadowed by nearby Carrickfergus. By the mid-nineteenth century, however, Ulster was the most industrialized and prosperous region in the country and Belfast was its pre-eminent town. The economic transformation of the area was due largely to the growth of the domestic textile industry, especially in the east of the province.[1] Apart from Belfast's success in textile production – initially cotton but increasingly linen – the town benefited from its activities as a major port, not only for the products of the town but also as a channel for agricultural exports from other counties within Ulster. Economic expansion was matched by rapid population growth. Much of this increase was as a result of migration to the town. In 1821, the population of Belfast was 37,000, in the 1860s it had risen to 120,000, and by the end of the century to 350,000, making it larger than that of Dublin. Again, such growth was extraordinary given the overall decline in Ireland's population after 1841.

Belfast was a predominantly Protestant town. At the beginning of the nineteenth century, Catholics accounted for only 9 per cent of the town's population but within ten years, the percentage had doubled.[2] By 1861, the proportion had risen to 34 per cent, partly due to Famine migration. However, by the end of the century, it had fallen to 24 per cent.[3] As the percentage of Catholics in the town increased, antagonisms between the main religious communities became more deeply entrenched.[4]

By the 1840s, Belfast was playing a pivotal role within the economy of the north of Ireland. Its economic status was mirrored in increased civic and political awareness, which resulted in the formation of a new Council in 1840 and the election of a Mayor in January 1842.[5] Notwithstanding commercial success and rapid expansion, economic growth in Belfast was uneven and was accompanied by extensive social dislocation. Poverty and disease also remained endemic, amplified by the fact that housing and other amenities could not keep pace with the demands of a growing population. The Famine of the late 1840s, therefore, impacted on a community that was already divided, not only along religious lines, but also by sharp economic demarcations.

The Industrial Capital of Ireland

By the middle of the nineteenth century, Belfast had emerged as the industrial and commercial capital of Ireland. However, its dominant position owed much to the economic developments of the late eighteenth century, notably the introduction of cotton manufacture in 1777.[6] The subsequent expansion of cotton production in Belfast outstripped that of other parts of the country and, in its wake, created the need for innovative textile machinery. Thus, in 1798, the Lagan Foundry was established, followed a few years later by the Belfast Foundry in Donegall Street.[7] By 1811, 15 steam-powered, twelve water-powered and six horse- or hand-powered mills had been constructed. Moreover, 150,000 spindles were working in the town, employing 2,000 spinners and 11,000 weavers.[8] The success of the cotton industry can be illustrated by the fact that at the beginning of the nineteenth century, Belfast accounted for a quarter of total Irish imports of cotton wool and yarn; by 1820, that proportion had doubled.[9]

However, by the late 1820s, the cotton industry had declined in relative importance in the town's economy as a technological revolution occurred in another area of textile production. In 1825, James Kay patented the wet-spinning process by which the finest yarns could be spun by machine. As a consequence, the production of yarn was transformed gradually from a domestic to a mechanized factory industry.[10] Although cotton production continued to be significant, Belfast entrepreneurs recognized that future economic success lay in linen manufacture through mechanized flax spinning. The first steam-driven, wet flax spinning mill in Ireland was opened in 1829 by the Belfast brothers Thomas and Andrew Mulholland.[11] By the mid-1830s, over 20 mills in the town had converted from cotton to flax, making flax manufacture the most significant employer of factory labour. By 1850, there were 29 linen mills but only two cotton mills. The flax mills were concentrated in the north and west of the town.[12] As had been the case with cotton, the expansion of linen necessitated new equipment and three new foundries – Boyds (in 1834), Albert (in 1843) and Falls (in 1845) – were constructed.[13]

Although textiles were the backbone of the Belfast economy, other industries also contributed to the commercial vibrancy of the area. By the 1820s, Belfast had become the single most important centre for shipbuilding in Ulster. Between 1824 and

1854, 50 vessels were constructed in the town's three shipyards. In 1838, the first Irish-built iron steamer was launched from Coates' Lagan Foundry.[14] By 1841, the town provided employment for almost as many shipwrights as Cork and Dublin combined – 177 in Belfast compared with 91 in each of the other two centres.[15] The first half of the century also witnessed significant growth in rope and glass manufacture, tobacco processing and whiskey distilling.[16] Industrial growth was paralleled in commerce with the emergence of three Belfast-based banks; the Northern Bank in 1824, the Belfast Bank in 1826 and the Ulster Bank in 1836.[17]

Belfast's growth was facilitated by improvements in transport networks which, in turn, allowed a greater expansion of economic activities. By the 1820s, a regular steamship service had been established, which strengthened existing trade links with the northwest of England, particularly Liverpool.[18] Tonnage cleared from Belfast port increased from 91,000 in 1815 to 291,000 in 1835.[19] To allow further expansion, in 1837 the town authorities agreed to straighten and dredge the shallow, winding channel which provided the main access to Belfast. The work was completed in 1849 and as a consequence Belfast was transformed into a major port within the British Empire.[20] Communication links within Ulster were enhanced by the creation of a railway network in the 1840s which connected Belfast with Ballymena and with Lurgan, Portadown and Armagh, which were also major textile centres. The rail links with Armagh siphoned off to Belfast much of the business which would otherwise have gone to Newry.[21]

The developments in transport enabled Belfast to benefit from its close proximity to the centre of Britain's industrial heartland, the north of England and central Scotland. The technological, commercial and communication improvements ensured that the town was able to take full advantage of its links with British markets and with trading centres throughout the Empire. On the eve of the Famine, therefore, Belfast had become the undisputed industrial and commercial capital of Ireland.

The Athens of the North?

Whilst the economic expansion of Belfast in the early nineteenth century was rapid and, compared with other Irish towns, impressive, the town's development was sporadic and uneven. During the Napoleonic War, Belfast's economy had prospered. Exports of cattle, corn and textiles from the port had all increased dramatically. The postwar slump throughout Ireland after 1815, combined with the collapse of the local cotton industry, damaged the economy of Belfast.

Recovery from the postwar depression proved to be slow. For those who remained in employment, conditions were harsh and hours were long. Cotton weavers were working seven days a week from 4 o'clock in the morning to midnight in order to earn 4s 6d a week.[22] In May 1826, the *Belfast News-Letter* reported that a 'multitude of operatives' had been laid off and estimated the number to be no less than 10,000. During the trade slump of 1825–26, one-third of all cotton weavers in the Belfast region were unemployed.[23] In Ballymacarrett, unemployment was particularly high. As a result an emigration society was formed, its aim being to procure funds and assist those weavers who wished to emigrate to British North America (Canada).[24]

Following a meeting in the Town Hall in May 1826, a relief committee was established in Belfast. The remit of the committee was to solicit funds in aid of the distressed weavers' families and to apply to the government for loans to enable local employers to continue in business.[25] The relief committee raised money through a series of charity events which included a ball, a play and a 'grand sparring match' in McAllister's Racket Court in Peter's Hill. In total, subscriptions reached £2,500.[26] The demand for assistance was so great that the relief committee needed to meet daily in order to assess the 'numerous applications' for aid. To facilitate this process, they divided the town into relief districts so that the needs of each family could be evaluated. Each applicant who was deemed to be eligible received a weekly ration of 28 lb of potatoes, the same quantity of meal and a half bag of coal.[27] Able-bodied men who received relief were required to break stones in return.[28] By August 1826, the relief committee began to wind down its operations. In September, as trading conditions revived, many weavers were again able to find employment.[29] Nevertheless, even after the slump was over, the situation of the cotton weavers did not recover. In 1830, the *Belfast News-Letter* reported that cotton weavers in Ballymacarrett were 'forced to live on Indian meal unfit for cattle and ... were reduced to skeletons from overwork and lack of sleep'.[30]

The revival of the town's fortunes in the late 1820s was due largely to a reorientation of the textile industry to linen production. This shift was made possible as a result of the initiative of a number of Belfast industrialists, such as the Mulholland Brothers, who embraced the new technologies associated with factory production. It was the linen rather than the cotton industry which gained from the modernization of production techniques. Initially, the domestic out-work system based in Belfast's rural hinterland benefited from the increased demand resulting from the move to factory spinning. After 1840, however, the wages of rural weavers declined rapidly due to an abundant supply of labour and competition from England and Scotland and the increasing move to mechanized production.[31]

By the 1830s, Belfast was on its way to becoming the premier industrial location in Ireland. The pace of industrial development was helped by trade links with Britain. By the beginning of the nineteenth century, shipping routes between Belfast and Britain, and Belfast and the British colonies, were well established and were able to benefit from the expansion of steam shipping in the 1820s. The thriving port was surrounded by cotton and flax spinning mills, which employed thousands, both directly and in a variety of auxiliary trades. The local economy was also diverse. For example, Ballymacarrett, which was a major area of textile production, also contained two vitriol works, a foundry, a glass manufactory, public lime kilns, and two ropeworks.[32]

In spite of the success of the linen industry, mill wages – the major source of earnings – were relatively low; a man in constant employment would earn 5 or 6 shillings a week which, for a typical household, ensured a total weekly income of 14 shillings. The exception was Ballymacarrett where, by the mid-1830s, two-thirds of the population were employed by Glasgow linen merchants. These 'fancy weavers', as they were termed, had a regular family wage of £1 2s 0d. None the less, this advantage over their fellow local weavers was compromised by their reliance on the economic fortune of their Scottish employers who, in times of economic crisis, did not hesitate to reduce their wages or to stop production altogether.

In the rural areas, employment had become unpredictable due to a gradual process of deindustrialization as textile production became more mechanized. The accompanying emergence of the factory system meant that production moved from the countryside to Belfast and to other urban centres. This process of reorganization meant that alternative sources of income had to be sought by workers previously involved in domestic industry. In Carnmoney, for example, the poor relied increasingly on employment in public works programmes such as existed in the quarries and on the local roads. In Holywood, the decline of the domestic linen industry forced some of the local population to depend on agricultural production, notably growing potatoes, supplemented by collecting mussels on the seashore.[33]

Wages in the countryside were determined by demand for labour; thus at harvest time a man could earn 1 shilling a day without meals, or from 6d to 10d with meals. The rate varied widely. In Carnmoney wages were below average, ranging from 6d to 10d without meals, and 3d to 5d with meals. Wages generally dropped in winter when there was less demand for labour and so desperate were many for employment that they would accept a few pence a day for any job. Wages were generally paid in cash, but in Holywood and Knockbreda, a combination of cash and food was paid. A number of localities operated a system of duty labour where, in lieu of rent, a tenant worked a fixed term for his landlord – usually one day a week.[34]

Changes in industrial and agricultural production in the various sectors of the textile industry also had a detrimental impact on the earning capacity of women. Until the emergence of factory spinning, women had been able to make a small but valuable contribution to the family income. The demise of the spinning wheel in linen production meant that they were now reduced to preparing and winding yarn for their husbands and sons.[35] Like their male counterparts, country women earned most during harvest when they were employed in haymaking, reaping corn or digging, weeding and gathering potatoes. In this way, they could earn between 6d and 10d a day.[36] Although children as young as nine were employed in the Belfast mills, they were seldom required in outlying areas. At harvest, they could make 4d–6d a day working alongside their mothers.[37]

Overall, the changes taking place in the Belfast economy after the 1820s proved to be protracted and they altered working relationships, not only in Belfast, but throughout the surrounding countryside. Moreover, the transition to mechanization and the spread of factory production resulted in the emergence of a new source of poverty – unemployment or underemployment during the periodic trade depressions.

Housing and Diet

For much of the local population housing conditions were appalling. Belfast mill workers usually lived in courts, described by one observer as 'ill-ventilated hovels' with little or no sanitation. Kennedy's Entry warranted the description of being 'a nasty, dirty, unhealthy lane and entry containing a very poor, wretched set of tenants'.[38] A common concern of charitable organizations was the massive overcrowding in such localities. Donaldson's Entry, for example, contained one yard measuring 32 feet by 26 feet, which was held in common by the tenants of nine houses. McCrea's Entry, which encompassed 14 houses, had neither a yard nor a rear entrance, access being gained solely by means of a narrow passage. In Ballymacarrett, many houses were inhabited by two families often of between six and ten members each.[39]

Such conditions were regarded by one clergyman as being responsible for loose morals and a high level of illegitimacy. He warned that:

A very great number of the lower classes have never been married, except by what is termed a bucklebeggar. Many men and women live together just while it suits convenience. The man then decamps and leaves the woman and child a legacy to the community.[40]

Speaking on the 'evils of over-crowding', Dr Andrew Malcolm, a respected Belfast doctor, stated:

The great majority of the poorer class of houses in this town consist of four rooms in two storeys. These are generally occupied by two families. Each room varies from seven to ten feet square, and from six to eight feet high in the lower storey – the same dimensions with a lower storey in the upper. Each room, although not always, contains one window, the upper sash of which is almost invariably, in the older houses, made immovable. Such a house is manifestly insufficient to be the domicile of ten individuals; but we have known, and not infrequently [sic], so many as eighteen or even twenty persons sleeping within such limited apartments.

So struck was Malcolm by the plight of such families that he chastised the landlords who had allowed the situation to develop, saying: 'The tendency to crowd the poor into the smallest space is so great, that it would seem to be an understood law of nature that the indigent do not actually require as much fresh air as the wealthy.'[41]

Toilet facilities were rare in many houses, adding to the general unhealthiness of the poorest areas. A further consequence of lack of amenities was that 'nuisances are consequently left on the streets until the police carts remove them'.[42] The following examples give an indication of the conditions in which many lived in Belfast:

Hospital District
Several open drains of semi-liquid filth at the Antrim Turnpike and McFarlan's Court (off New Lodge Road) foul open grounds at Hardinge Street and south of Henry Street.

Shankhill District
Open drains at Shankhill Road, at east of McTier Street, at Hobson's Row, and south of Old Lodge Road. Foul, open commons in the locality of Gardner and Mitchell Street.

College District
Full of open drains and filthy areas – the former at Napier's
Row, Botanic Road, rear of Sandy Row, South Brunswick Street
– the latter in the localities of Institution Place, Emerson's
Entry, Cullingtree Road and Falls Court.

Smithfield District
Victimized by sanitary neglect are the localities of Gregg's Row,
Law's Lane, Upper Kent Street, Bell's Lane, Fulton's Court
(off Hercules Lane) and Lennan's Court (off Smithfield).

Cromac District
Large cesspools and open drains may be seen in the localities of
Annette Street, south of Alfred Street, north and east of Verner
Street, east of Staunton Street and north of Friendly Street.[43]

The filthy condition of such areas was exacerbated by the non-
regulation of tides. Thus, during the daily high tides, sea-water
passed up into the main sewers of the town, in Victoria Street,
High Street, North Street and Great George's Street, and
inundated low-lying districts. In this way, many streets became
channels for both animal and human refuse and consequently
posed a serious threat to public health.[44]

The interior of many houses was little better than conditions
outside. Bedding often consisted of damp straw while, more often
than not, people slept in the clothes they had worn during the
day.[45] In such conditions the local clothing societies provided
invaluable assistance by supplying families with blankets. In
country areas, the poorer classes tended to live in thatched
cottages, the majority of which were constructed of stone and lime,
although some were built of mud.[46] To a large extent, local
benevolence determined the condition of the poorest portion of
the population. In Knockbreda, for example, each house had been
supplied with a bed by Lady Bateson, wife of the local landlord,
Robert Bateson. Similarly, the local clergyman endeavoured to
provide blankets for all who required them over a period of ten
years.[47]

In the decade preceding the Famine, the diet of the majority of
the population, both in town and country, was generally poor and
monotonous. The mainstay was potatoes and oatmeal, with one
observer remarking that 'potatoes constitute the great basis of food
for all classes'. Occasionally, bread, herrings, buttermilk or fresh
meat could be afforded. In Carnmoney, many could manage to
obtain only one meal a day, while for others, their food was little
better than that fed to animals. Flummery (a type of oatmeal
pudding) made from the washings of starch was very common as
was starch sowens (similar in constituency to porridge), which was

obtained by the washing of industrial casks and the residue of the starch. The latter was sold at 1d a gallon and, with around 5,000 gallons consumed each week, constituted 'a considerable part of the diet of the lower classes'. Yet, while many of the poorest classes used sowens for breakfast and supper, some voiced concern that it was 'the lowest kind of diet, fit only for pigs'.[48]

Throughout the Belfast area such unwholesome food was regarded as a catalyst for disease. Henry Forcade of the Fever Hospital remarked: 'I am confident that actual disease has been brought on by want of proper sustenance. Had they received wholesome food, medicine would not have been required.'[49] In Ballymacarrett, Holywood and Knockbreda, the majority of illnesses, including typhoid, fever and dropsy, were ascribed by local medical officers to 'a want of proper sustenance of wholesome food and good clothing' with 'too much vegetable without the necessary stimulus of animal food'. Indeed, John Scott of the Ballymacarrett Dispensary described the food as being 'of the worst description', and added: 'The pork parings, so much in use among the poor, I believe to be the cause of common cholera, dysentery and diarrhoea.'[50]

Despite extensive poverty within the town, the diet of the poorer inhabitants of Belfast was slightly better than that enjoyed in the country's other major towns, including Cork and Dublin. In all three centres, potatoes were the staple food. While oats were equally important in Belfast, they were used on a regular basis by only 20 per cent of the Dublin poor and not at all in Cork.[51] The consumption of milk was similar in each of the three centres, with between one-half and two-thirds of the local populations consuming it. The consumption of fish was low in each area. While bread was rarely eaten in Belfast and Cork, it formed an important part of the diet in Dublin, where almost half the poor had access to it. Throughout the country, the consumption of any form of meat was a rarity; in Cork it was virtually unknown, while almost half the population used it in Belfast and Dublin. Nevertheless, Belfast medical officers described the meat consumed as being the cheapest type – invariably inferior cuts of pork or bacon.[52] Overall, the major advantage enjoyed by the poor of Belfast was their use of oats, otherwise their diet was very similar in terms of both variety and quantity to that consumed by their counterparts in urban areas throughout Ireland.

Information collated by the government for Glasgow provides an interesting comparison with Belfast. As in Belfast, the labouring classes of Glasgow relied on potatoes and oatmeal as the major components of their diet. Two-thirds also ate meat, including beef, as well as bacon and pork. The statistics for fish and milk were similar, but differences were evident in the variety of other foods consumed in Glasgow; bread, butter, tea, sugar, porridge and soup were occasionally used. Also, while cheese was unheard of in Belfast, it was eaten as regularly as oats and potatoes in half the districts of Glasgow.[53] The diet in Belfast, therefore, whilst offering regular basic food for its poorer classes, suffered from a lack of variety in comparison with similar areas in Britain. The monotony of the diet was borne out by the opinions of local doctors, who suggested a superior food intake would help improve the health of the poor. For those who existed on the economic margins – only barely able to obtain regular daily food – a period of unemployment could lead to severe distress. For the unemployed poor in the town who were able and willing to work, the House of Industry supplied wheels, reels and flax to women to spin, whilst stone-breaking was made available for men. Those so employed received potatoes, meal, soup and coals – enough to maintain them until prospects improved.[54] The totally destitute who were unable to work could apply to the Poor House where they obtained a dinner of potatoes and buttermilk or broth and bread, and a breakfast and supper of stirabout (a type of porridge) and buttermilk.[55]

Strategies for Survival

The poverty of some sections of Belfast society was due also to irregular employment in the course of the year. A government enquiry into poverty in the 1830s highlighted this problem in a number of districts in Belfast. In Carnmoney, Dundonald and Knockbreda, the enquiry found that the winter months presented the prospect of unemployment for all family members. Many observers stated that they did not know how such families survived but feared that their situation was 'very bad'.[56] Richard Blackiston, JP, made the assumption that the unemployed of Knockbreda survived on their savings.[57] This conjecture was unlikely; rather, the Belfast poor, like their counterparts elsewhere, resorted to one of the many pawnshops established in Belfast. Described as 'a lucrative business', the pawn business had increased dramatically in the town. From three shops in 1809, it had grown to 41 outlets by the mid-1830s. This increase was a testament to the spread of poverty in those years. The shops were used by a variety of groups, but especially by '[t]rades people, servants out of place, poor shop keepers and labourers'. Deposits usually consisted of labourers' Sunday clothes, which were pledged on Monday morning and released the following Saturday night – either by repayment of money or by the deposit of tools or even the Bible. One observer noted how 'The shops abound with all articles of weaving apparel

and bedding and there are many copies of the word of God.' Nor
was it unusual for clothes to be pledged which had been
distributed a short time previously by the local clothing society.
Although many of the middle classes complained that pawning
was used to obtain money for alcohol, for a significant proportion
of the population the shops represented their only chance of
survival in difficult times. The average number of tickets issued
each month was 3,000, although in periods of unemployment –
generally December to February – or of food scarcity – usually
May to July – this figure could more than double. These months
represented severe distress for those without work.[58]

Despite the lack of regular employment, especially in rural areas
in Ulster, few people chose to improve their condition by
emigration. In general, this option was limited to periods of severe
economic depression and was generally the choice of the more
skilled sections of workers, such as mechanics. The United States,
British North America and Scotland were the favoured
destinations of Irish emigrants. In Holywood and Dundonald
emigration was rare, while in Ballymacarrett, Carnmoney and
Knockbreda only a small number left each year. The majority of
emigrants from the Belfast area were described as being 'of the
bettermost description of farmers and tradesmen – stone-cutters,
shoemakers, nailers, and weavers'. Emigrants from the town were
occasionally supplied with food from the House of Industry, while
local congregations made small contributions to those leaving
their parishes.[59]

By the late 1830s, the poverty in Belfast was being publicly
acknowledged by a number of the town's leading citizens. In May
1837, in a letter to the local MPs, James E. Tenant and George
Dunbar, the Reverend Thomas Drew made the accusation that
'Many private individuals are aware of the vast extent of human
wretchedness which exists amongst us ... amid the retired lanes
and alleys of our great town.'[60] In the areas around Belfast
absenteeism and indebtedness were also common amongst the
landowning class. For example, half the landowners in Holywood
were permanently absent, their affairs being dealt with by their
agents. Similarly, the sole landlord of Ballymacarrett, Lord
Templemore, was non-resident, while Dundonald had only one
resident proprietor. One correspondent from Carnmoney
illustrated how such situations could be exploited when he
revealed that local farmers held their land from middlemen, many
of whom were 'very rapacious'.[61] The Donegall family, who
owned large estates in County Antrim, including much of the town
of Belfast, were notorious for their estate mismanagement and
large debts. The shock of the Famine, when income from rents
fell drastically, resulted in the sale of much of the estate in 1849.[62]

A Poor Law for Ireland

Despite the economic progress made by Belfast in the 1830s, widespread poverty continued to exist in the town. The collapse of the cotton industry left a large number of weavers without their traditional livelihoods or forced them to survive on a reduced wage. Employment within the newly established mills was irregular and wages were generally low, especially during cyclical trade depressions such as occurred in 1837 and 1839–42. Moreover, the rapid growth of Belfast had created a number of social problems generally associated with other industrialized centres, notably congestion and inadequate public facilities, both of which contributed to high levels of disease and mortality associated with urban poverty. Between 1821 and 1841 the population of Belfast had doubled, and housing, medical and public health provision had not kept pace with the needs of the population.

Unlike England, Wales and Scotland, Ireland did not have in place a national system of poor relief until the introduction of the Irish Poor Law in 1838. The lack of a resident landlord class in the Belfast area meant that the burden of caring for the poor invariably fell upon a small number of benevolent people. Consequently, poverty and disease in Belfast were assuaged through the efforts of private individuals and philanthropic organizations. By the 1830s, a number of charitable institutions were operating within the town. In 1775 a Poor House had been opened by the Belfast Charitable Society, which was supported by a combination of Grand Jury grants and public subscriptions. In 1809 also, a House of Industry had been established in Howard Street, again funded by private subscriptions. Some medical provision had also been made. A Fever Hospital was opened in 1797, and an asylum for the insane was established on the Falls Road in 1829. In addition to these institutions, a number of ad hoc measures, such as soup kitchens, had been devised with which to meet short-term emergencies. Soup kitchens had been used with considerable benefit during the economic crisis in the 1780s and 1790s, and in 1816–18 and again in 1826.[63] By the 1830s, the problem of Irish poverty and how it should be relieved had become a primary concern of the British government.

In 1833, the government appointed a Commission under the chairmanship of Richard Whately, the Anglican Archbishop of Dublin, to enquire into the condition of the poorer classes. The enquiry overlapped with the introduction of the 'new' Poor Law in England in 1834. The Commission spent three years, from 1833 to 1836, producing a detailed analysis of poverty in Ireland. By sending out and receiving completed questionnaires from local parish leaders they estimated that two-thirds of the country's

population were unemployed for part of each year. In their recommendations, they suggested that as Ireland was very different
from England, and poverty in the former was so extensive, it would
be inappropriate to introduce the English workhouse system to the
country. Instead, the Commissioners advocated long-term
measures to increase employment, such as the development of the
fisheries, the reclamation of land and a regulated system of
emigration to the British colonies.[64]

The government viewed such suggestions as expensive to initiate
and implement, and as being too interventionist.[65] Thus, they
looked for a second opinion in the form of a Commissioner for the
Poor Laws in England, George Nicholls. Unlike the detailed
analysis of the Commission, Nicholls toured Ireland for just nine
weeks, it being the first time he had been in the country. Nicholls
did not believe it was necessary to visit Ulster as he considered the
local population would be similar to English people.[66] On his
return, Nicholls informed the authorities that Ireland's poor would
benefit from the development of workhouses throughout the
country. He advocated a system similar to the Poor Law in
England and Wales, with one important difference – unlike in the
former system no outdoor relief was to be administered in Ireland.
In this way, Nicholls believed that only the truly destitute would
seek refuge within the draconian confines of the workhouse, where
relief would not be given as a right, but only to those who could
prove that they were without means.[67] This model of poor relief
had been intended for introduction to England in 1834, but it had
proved impossible to implement.[68] Overall, the Irish Poor Law
was closely modelled on the English workhouse system, although
it was more stringent in its provisions.[69]

On announcement of the new measure, a storm of controversy
erupted throughout the country and for the first time the question
of poor relief was elevated to a position of national debate in
Ireland. In Belfast, the new law had little support, especially as it
entailed relief provision moving from local control to central
control in London. The fact that all the Poor Law Commissioners were English added to an ideological gulf over the future of
poor relief provision in Ireland. At a meeting at the Court House
in Belfast on 2 February 1838, the middle classes of the town
voiced their opposition to the proposal. In a variety of resolutions,
those gathered announced their dissent from some of the
'fundamental assumptions' on which Nicholls' report and
conclusions were based. They argued that he had been 'misled' in
his stated opinion that outdoor relief was opposed by many.
Ironically, given the rationale of the government, one of the major
concerns of the meeting was the cost of any new initiative. Under
the proposed new measure, provision for the poor would become

compulsory, whereas contributions had previously been made on a voluntary basis. Moreover, the workhouses, their staff and the pauper inmates would be funded and maintained by the levying of a local tax – the poor rate – in each local Poor Law Union. The Belfast meeting expressed concern not only about the 'heavy expense of original buildings and repairs', but also about the salaries of those who would be appointed to administer the system.

Apart from the expense, the meeting was also opposed to making poor relief so easily available. The meeting stated: 'We repudiate the notion that society is bound to furnish all the able-bodied poor with permanent and profitable employment.' Instead, they recommended the occasional employment of the able-bodied poor within each parish in works of 'public and permanent utility'. Unease was also expressed at the lack of any requirement of settlement for those seeking aid, such as existed in the English Poor Law. It was argued that an essential requisite of 'an equitable and efficient Poor Law' should be continued residence for three years or at various periods for five years.[70]

A meeting in Holywood on 8 March echoed the sentiments expressed in Belfast, arguing that the initial expense would prove 'utterly disproportionate to the resources of the country'. In an attempt to economize, it was suggested that existing buildings could be used as temporary asylums for the aged and infirm during a 'period of experimentation'. Only after such a trial could permanent changes in the law be contemplated. It was also argued that outdoor relief should be available to the authorities in order to prevent any increase in pauperism during periods of extraordinary distress.[71]

The Antrim Grand Jury, at its Lent Assizes, recorded 'alarm' at the progress of a bill, 'many of the provisions of which are not only considered as dangerous to the best interests of this country, but opposed to the habits and feelings of the Irish people'. They agreed that any further steps should be taken only 'in the true spirit of experimental introduction'.[72] The Grand Jury of Down argued that any Act 'legislating for local interests' had to be capable of modification 'so as to adapt them to local differences by a discretion vested in local authorities'.[73]

The thread of continuity in opposition to the measure was the fear that local autonomy would be usurped by central government control from Dublin, which, to the business classes of Belfast, represented a nightmarish prospect. Similarly, many resented the implication that poor relief was now to be compulsory by means of a tax, which would probably increase its burden in coming years.[74] The groundswell of opinion was reflected in the local press, which reported 'universal excitement' on the subject. In an editorial on 16 March, the *News-Letter* criticized the 'mischievousness ... of Mr Nicholls' crude legislation' and argued that the government had been induced to introduce the measure on his 'notoriously defective information'. It continued:

> The Ministry obstinately persevere in forcing upon us Mr Nicholls' absurd law. All the Poor Law we want is one which will enforce contributions from absentees and heartless possessors of wealth who are content to enjoy their own temporal comforts without bestowing a thought upon the necessities of their less fortunate fellow beings.[75]

A significant source of opposition emerged in April when the committee of the Fever Hospital – also representing the fears of other publicly supported bodies – suggested that any compulsory Poor Law would end private subscriptions to their institution and 'destroy that public confidence which we have hitherto enjoyed'.[76]

Regardless of widespread dissatisfaction, as the weeks progressed it became obvious that Nicholls' recommendations were to receive government sanction. The *News-Letter* maintained its trenchant position, warning: 'Never was any former measure introduced on more bungling one-sided principles of legislation than the Poor Law measure intended for this country.' Realizing the inevitability of the enactment, the paper resorted to calls for its postponement amidst the realization that its opposition, and the dissatisfaction expressed throughout the country, had been ignored by a government determined to proceed with domestic provision for the poor.[77]

A common criticism of Nicholls' recommendations was that he had proceeded on flawed principles and was ignorant of the nature of poverty in Ireland. In relation to Belfast, Nicholls displayed a disregard for the findings of Whately's Commission. Whately's report had included evidence from some of the most influential people of the locality as well as from small farmers. Both groups had expressed strident hostility to the concept of workhouses for the poor. Opponents cut across religious and political divides. The Catholic Archbishop Crolly strongly advocated outdoor relief, claiming that fraud could be overcome by a system of regular visits to the poor. Dr Henry Cooke, an outspoken Presbyterian minister, stated that he had 'decided objections to charitable aggregations', alleging that they were attended with 'immoral effects'. A more informed opinion came from Dr Tennant of the House of Industry who warned:

> I think the collecting of a number of persons together has a very bad effect. We even find difficulty in keeping the aged and infirm people at the Poor House in any kind of regularity or order with regard to their moral conduct; and as to

contentment, still more so, with the very best and most assiduous attentions to their wants and necessities.[78]

Regardless of widespread opposition in Belfast and other parts of the country, the Poor Law bill became law on 1 July 1838.

In the period that followed, the Poor Law Commissioners, the government-appointed body responsible for the implementation of the new measure, attempted to address the many concerns of the local population. The vital issue in Belfast centred on the future of the Poor House, run by the Charitable Society. Rumours had circulated that the property would have to be given up to the Poor Law Commissioners, a fear voiced by the Marquis of Donegall, who stated: 'My opinion is that the Commissioners intend to take possession of the Poor House, its properties and its revenues, without giving a sixpence remuneration for them.'[79]

Throughout September and October there was general conjecture about the future of the Poor House once the Poor Law became operative. A positive aspect of the demise of the institution was that if the Poor House was acquired by the Poor Law Commissioners, it would ensure a saving for the newly created Belfast Union as no new workhouse building would be necessary. On the other hand, if such a situation arose, the committee of the Poor House would lose its power and be replaced by a Board of elected Guardians. Similarly, anyone entering the Poor House under the new administration would have to adhere to the regulations approved under the Poor Law. These rules, as Assistant Poor Law Commissioner Gulson outlined in November 1838, stipulated that there was no right to relief, such aid being at the sole discretion of the Guardians. The only condition for seeking admission to the workhouse was that applicants had to prove themselves to be in a condition of destitution.

The committee of the Poor House felt aggrieved by the fact that they had so little control over the future of their institution. Various committee members resented the interference in an independently run establishment and stated their intention to remove all furniture from the building and leave a healthy debt to the Poor Law Commissioners if the latter attempted to gain control. The debates concerning the future of the Poor House demonstrate that much confusion followed in the wake of the Poor Law being enacted. The Society was also unclear about its legal position even if it was left untouched by the Commissioners. Dr Henry Cooke demanded to know if, in such a situation, the committee would still retain control over its affairs or if they would be rendered 'merely puppets' under the control of the Commissioners. Eventually, a decision was taken to obtain a legal ruling on two points: first, how far the property and rights of the Charitable

Society were affected by the Poor Law; and second, how far the control of the Commissioners extended over the Poor House and the property connected with it.[80] On 19 February 1839, the General Board of the Society learned 'with satisfaction' that the property and management of the charity were not affected by the Poor Law Act. Thus the Poor House was free to operate as it had for the previous 65 years.[81]

While the debate over the future of the Poor House raged, the mechanism of the new Poor Law had been established throughout the country. To this end, Ireland was divided into 130 Poor Law Unions, each Union to be administered by a Board of Guardians. The boundaries of the Belfast Union, covering an area of 74 square miles, had been announced officially by Mr Gulson on 21 December 1838.[82] The Belfast Union included areas such as Ballymacarrett, which had been outside the boundaries of the town but which were increasingly included in its administrative structures. In the Belfast Union, there were to be 22 elected and seven *ex-officio* (non-elected) Guardians, the latter being chosen from amongst the ranks of the resident magistracy. On 1 January 1839, the Union was divided into administrative units known as electoral divisions (see Appendix I). Each division was to be represented by an elected Guardian, in proportion to its size and ratable value. The electoral divisions in Belfast, together with the number of Guardians, were as follows: [83]

Electoral Division	No. of Guardians	Population in 1841
Belfast	10	77,447
Ballygomartin	1	2,577
Ballyhackamore	1	1,979
Ballymacarrett	2	1,105
Ballymurphy	1	1,329
Ballysillan	1	1,811
Carnmoney	1	2,380
Castlereagh	1	8,221
Dundonald	1	1,151
Greencastle	1	1,941
Holywood	1	3,066
Whitehouse	1	3,985

The Belfast Guardians were duly elected, all without contest, on 10 January 1839, and the new administration moved swiftly to procure building land for a workhouse.[84] On 7 June a contract was signed to construct a workhouse for 1,000 inmates. The house, which cost £700, was completed in March 1841.[85]

The Poor Law was financed by the levying of a compulsory tax on each electoral division for the maintenance of the poor. The valuation of the Belfast Union was estimated at £271,915, making it one of the highest valuations in the country. The first rate on the Belfast Union was levied on 15 December 1840. The committee of the Fever Hospital and other voluntary institutions feared that the imposition of a compulsory tax would severely diminish subscriptions to their charities. At the commencement of building the workhouse, the Charitable Society also stated its concern that people were unlikely to make both voluntary contributions and to pay a compulsory tax. Indeed, when seeking assurances from the Commissioners, they informed them that many charitable people were withholding their subscriptions for 1839 in the belief that a poor rate would be levied within weeks.[86] The Commissioners replied that no rate would be struck until the new workhouse was almost completed, which would not be for at least 18 months.[87] Thus the Society obtained its usual quota of subscriptions. None the less, the opening of the workhouse witnessed the demise of the House of Industry. Subscribers to the latter felt that its role – providing work for the distressed – was superseded by the workhouse; as a consequence between 1839 and 1841 donations fell rapidly. By February 1841, the committee reported that its funds were 'exhausted' and threatened to close the institution unless money was forthcoming. Even at this stage, and in considerable debt, the House was supplying 900 families with food, coal and straw. The high demand for private relief was an indicator of extensive poverty within Belfast. The growing indifference of subscribers was demonstrated in a number of poorly attended 'Crisis Meetings' called by the committee.[88] Until May 1841, any contributions received were used to liquidate the debts of the House. On 31 May, it was decided that the establishment should be closed on 6 June, with all remaining property being transferred to the Surgical Hospital for its use.[89]

The closure of the House of Industry was preceded by the opening of the workhouse on 11 May 1841. The establishment of the Poor Law in Belfast marked a new era in poor provision in the town.[90] The following examples represent some of the paupers who entered the workhouse in the early years of its existence.

Biddy Carr, aged 67 – Catholic – widow – no children alive – ill clothed and dirty.
Admitted 16 January; died 1 February.

Thomas Shannon, aged three – Protestant – both parents in the Belfast Fever Hospital – in rags, hungry and dirty.
Admitted 9 February; died 12 March.

Jane Oakley, aged 20 – Protestant – mendicant – single – bodily infirm – in rags – very dirty and hungry.
Admitted 13 February; died 19 February.

John Corr, aged 30 – Catholic – painter – single – bodily infirm – ill health – dirty and hungry.
Admitted 20 February; died 2 March.

Rose McGarrell, aged 22 – Catholic – servant – clothing destroyed being so filthy, hungry.
Admitted 5 March; discharged 20 March in good health.

William Hanna, aged 50 – Protestant – labourer – widower – no children alive – ill clothed – infested with vermin.
Admitted 8 March; died 13 April.

Mary Fleming, aged 70 – Catholic – servant – widow – no children alive – bodily infirm – very dirty looking – clothes bad.
Admitted 12 March; died 2 April.

Anne Dixon, aged 37 – Protestant – winder – widow – three children alive – in rags – dirty and hungry.
Admitted 13 March; died 1 April.[91]

Such a catalogue of misery emphasized that only those in severe distress, in many cases on the point of death, sought admission to the workhouse. In Belfast, as elsewhere, on the eve of the Famine, the local workhouse was underutilized by the local population despite the existence of widespread destitution and disease.[92]

Although the Belfast workhouse was built to accommodate 1,000 paupers, a number of inhabitants believed that the institution alone would be insufficient to meet the town's needs. Consequently, on 1 January 1841, a meeting had been convened in the Police Building for the purpose of establishing a Night Asylum. Those in favour of the proposal argued that this auxiliary provision was necessary as Belfast received a large number of people who either travelled there for work or passed through on their way to England and Scotland. Few were destitute and thus they were not eligible to enter the workhouse. Nevertheless, many did require temporary assistance, usually in the form of shelter. Since May 1839, six people had been reported as dying from 'exhaustion' on the town's streets due to a lack of accommodation, whilst a number of others had been forced to sleep in ditches, fields and lanes. Those present at the meeting also heard that similar asylums had been established with great success in Dublin, Glasgow and Liverpool. As a result of the meeting, a committee was established to raise funds for a suitable location.[93] Initial interest in the House of Industry building waned when, on inspection, it was deemed to be unsuitable for the purposes required.[94] Such delays dogged the committee until November, when the Night Asylum finally opened.[95] At this stage, the workhouse had been in operation for six months, providing relief to a weekly average of 412 inmates. In the new year, the number of inmates increased substantially as a consequence of an economic slump in some sectors of the weaving industry.[96]

The Hungry Forties?

Despite endemic poverty within sections of Belfast society, by the early 1840s the town was basking in its economic success, which appeared to be all the more remarkable when compared with the economic stagnation of other parts of the country. The affluence and progress of the town was commented on by both inhabitants and visitors. Mr and Mrs Hall, travellers and social commentators who visited Belfast in 1841, observed that the high levels of industrial output and cultural pursuits in the town made it distinctly 'un-national' in its feel.[97] In the same year, Dr Henry Cooke, the controversial Presbyterian Minister, angered by a visit of the nationalist Daniel O'Connell to the town, boasted:

> Look at the town of Belfast. When I was a youth it was almost a village. But what a glorious site it does now present! The masted grove within our harbour – our mighty warehouses teeming with the wealth of every clime – our giant manufactures lifting themselves on every side, and all this we owe to the UNION.[98]

Proximity to the Belfast market had also benefited the surrounding rural areas. A visitor who travelled from Larne to Belfast in 1840 commented:

> I missed the wretched cabins of the peasantry, and found instead neat lime-washed slated cottages, large farms in the place of small ones, good hedges and brick walls for fences, instead of a few loose stones piles up ... and a state of cultivation resembling the best parts of England, rather than anything I had previously seen in Ireland.[99]

In 1842 William Thackeray described the town as being 'hearty, thriving and prosperous'.[100]

Notwithstanding the achievements of the Belfast economy, the growth of the town was uneven and the 1840s were marked by a number of trade and industrial depressions, even before the appearance of potato blight in 1845. On 15 April 1842, Dr Henry Cooke published in the *Belfast News-Letter* figures of those unemployed in and around Belfast due to the trade depression. He stated that some weavers in Belfast had been reduced to a state of total destitution. The situation was worse in Ballymacarrett, where he estimated that half the weavers were out of work, the problems originating in the Glasgow region where a severe depression had taken place. Such was the reliance of the Bally-macarrett weavers on the Scottish employers that the *News-Letter* likened it to being 'but a suburb of Paisley'.[101] The unemployment in Ballymacarrett was exacerbated by an industrial dispute between the weavers and one of their employers, Gilbert Vance. The weavers alleged that Vance had reduced wages to a pittance and they refused to work for him. Vance in turn claimed that the only alternative to lower wages was to make the men redundant.[102] The strength of feeling was such that the weavers announced their determination to emigrate to Canada and, on 19 April, a committee was appointed at a public meeting to obtain subscriptions for their support.[103] By June, the cotton industry was in difficulty, with 600 weavers in Belfast, representing 2,500 family members, reported as unemployed.[104] Many of those who could obtain work were being paid 4d for a 14-hour day.[105] In early July, a town meeting sanctioned the formation of a relief committee to raise subscriptions and 'adopt the most desirable means for relieving the distress'.[106] With over 1,500 people out of work, the *News-Letter* used the situation to lambaste the workings of the Poor Law:

> Is not the insufficiency of the Poor Law system clearly seen, when so much distress prevails throughout the country and it can do nothing to relieve it? Of the thousands of pounds which are levied off the people under the Poor Law, not one penny can be made available to relieve the prevailing distress! This is prevented by the absurd regulation against outdoor relief and against receiving a poor person into a workhouse until he has parted with all he possesses in the world and determines to continue a pauper for life.[107]

Ignorance of the rigid regulations of the Poor Law appears to have been widespread. In their early deliberations, the relief committee had proposed sending some of the unemployed temporarily to the workhouses in Newtownards and Lisburn. Yet, as Cooke later admitted, 'We had failed to understand that before any of the poor could obtain admission to a workhouse they must sell all their property and enter as absolute paupers.'[108] On 28 July, public meetings were held in Short Strand School, Ballymacarrett, Course Cross Roads, Ballyhackamore and the Town Hall in Belfast. All were convened to take into consideration proposals to apply to the Poor Law Commissioners for the raising of a rate in the various electoral divisions to assist emigration. The suggestion was opposed by some, including local shopkeepers, who claimed that they were already oppressed by rates and could not afford any additional taxation. They also argued that the crisis, although severe, was temporary, and with harvest approaching, much hardship would be alleviated.[109]

The most significant opposition to emigration came from those who believed that it was not safe. Advice had been sought from the Colonial Secretary in London, who stated that it was now too late in the season to sail and pointed out how a vessel packed with labourers had recently set out from Limerick, only to perish with the loss of many lives.[110] One of the most vigorous opponents of the emigration scheme was Dr Drew, who pleaded: 'We must not let these poor men with their helpless families, find a certain death in the Canadian wilderness and a shroud in the snow-wreaths of that fearful climate.'[111] The relief committee responded to these concerns by making preparations for the establishment of soup kitchens in the town. This decision was not without controversy and at a subsequent public meeting a row erupted between Dr Cooke and Dr Drew, with the latter expressing his opposition to the use of soup kitchens. He argued that work should be provided before soup.[112] Cooke dismissed the suggestion as 'nonsense', and stated that they would be 'better to give soup to the poor than to physic them in the hospital'. The outcome was that the committee proposed to put as many men as possible to stone-breaking in and around the town.[113]

With a subscription totalling almost £1,000 by the end of July, soup kitchens were opened in Smithfield and Ballymacarrett; the former assisting 1,600 daily, and the latter, 900 – almost 90 per cent of the local population.[114] In addition, more than 500 men were employed at a maximum of 9d a day breaking stones on Corporation Island and the Lagan Bank.[115] Assistance was received from 'country gentlemen' who, upon being requested to do so by the relief committee, forwarded 'such vegetables as they could spare'.[116] Illustrating the extremely variable nature of the weaving business was the fact that amongst the subscriptions to the relief fund were two from local weavers – £5 from the Falls Mills and £2 3s from the Ardoyne weavers.[117]

An indication of the suffering of many was the rising level of admissions to the workhouse. In July 1842, the number of inmates had reached almost 900, twice the average of 1841.[118] By January 1844, the capacity of the workhouse had been exceeded. This growth in demand for Poor Law relief illustrated both a rising level of destitution and a growing awareness that, apart from the Charitable Society, with its limited capacity, the workhouse offered the only hope of a meal and a roof to many in the Belfast Union.[119] Having been stretched by limited, periodic crises in the early part of the decade, it remained to be seen how the new Poor Law would cope in the midst of the calamitous years of 1845–50. Within six years of the Belfast workhouse being opened, the town was to face a crisis which put pressure on the existing poor relief provision and forced radical, additional measures to be introduced. The crisis caused by the Famine changed both the nature of poverty within Belfast and the way in which poor relief was subsequently administered.

PART II

A National Crisis, *c.* 1845–47

CHAPTER 2

A 'Man-Made Famine'

In the summer of 1845, reports were received from Europe of the appearance of a mysterious disease or blight on the potato crop. When it reached England in August 1845, there was concern about the possibility of the disease reaching Ireland.[1] By early September there were isolated reports of the blight on the potato crop in Ireland. Within a few weeks the disease had spread to other parts of the country, especially the east coast. The blight was reported to be particularly virulent in County Antrim.[2] But because of its late arrival in Ireland, approximately 60 per cent of the potato crop remained blight-free.

The British government, under the leadership of Sir Robert Peel, responded quickly to the news of the impending food shortages in Ireland. The main impact of the deficit would not be felt until the following spring, which meant that Peel's administration had time to set in place a comprehensive programme of relief measures. His response included the establishment of a Scientific Commission to ascertain the extent of the damage to the crop, and a Relief Commission to oversee and coordinate the work of local relief committees. Peel also secretly arranged for Indian corn to be imported into the country. These relief measures were traditional responses to what was viewed as a serious but short-term crisis. However, despite the recommendations of the Lord Lieutenant and a number of local corporations, including Belfast's Town Council, Peel refused either to limit the export of food or prohibit distillation in Ireland – both of which restrictions had been employed in previous periods of distress.[3] From the outset, therefore, tension was evident between the local and central administrations over the approach to relief provision.

A feature of the domestic textile industry was the fact that it was underpinned – and sustained – by the availability of nutritious and readily available food, in the form of the potato. Despite changes in textile production, in the mid-1840s there was a high level of interdependence between the textile industry in Belfast and domestic production in the surrounding counties. The delicate equilibrium of this system meant that any scarcity could undermine the whole of textile production, in both the home and the factory.[4] The failure of the potato crop, therefore, quickly impacted on the Belfast market. Moreover, the destruction of the potato crop by blight meant 'not only food shortages but also the beginning of the collapse of this way of life'.[5]

The appearance of blight coincided with the onset of a trade depression in the Belfast area, which had its origins in Britain. The consequent reduction in wages and employment opportunities added to the vulnerability of the poorer classes. Significantly, one of the first areas in Belfast to suffer from the combination of crop failure and trade depression was the highly industrialized – and largely Protestant – district of Ballymacarrett. Although the townland was part of the Belfast Union, it was separated from the town by the River Lagan and was situated in County Down. Consequently, there was reluctance to acknowledge that distress in Ballymacarrett was the responsibility of the town authorities in Belfast. At the same time, despite evidence of comprehensive suffering in the Belfast area, some of the local taxpayers were determined to minimize reports of the poverty and suffering in the town. This was attributed by some of the press to a general desire to prove that Ulster, and Belfast in particular, was different from the rest of the country.[6] As a consequence, local relief measures were slow to materialize. By the summer of 1846, Belfast – in common with the rest of the country – appeared to have survived the combination of blight and unemployment. But as the harvest of 1846 approached, there was apprehension that the crop would be a small one. Moreover, the trade depression was intensifying. When there were reported sightings of the blight as early as July 1846, a second year of distress appeared inevitable.

An Unusual Blight

On 10 September 1845, the *Belfast Vindicator* reported a partial failure among potatoes close to the coast. Nevertheless, it confidently predicted that, due to the general excellence of the crop elsewhere, there would be a 'very abundant' harvest.[7] This prediction proved to be unfounded. Within the space of one week, all the Belfast newspapers were carrying accounts of the 'alarming progress' of the potato disease throughout Europe and in Ireland. *The Belfast News-Letter* on 12 September commented on how the crop 'appears to be far short of what was expected from its appearance in July'. Four days later, the *Northern Whig* described how a blight of 'unusual characteristics' had 'almost universally' affected the potatoes on the Isle of Wight.[8]

The rapid spread of the disease was evident from the marked change of tone of local newspaper reports in late September and early October. On 27 September some disease was acknowledged but was described as being 'not to any considerable extent', but by 14 October, the state of the crop was said to be 'particularly alarming'.[9] During the early stages, there was much confusion about the incidence of disease. The *Northern Whig* stated that along the coast, near Holywood, it prevailed to a small extent, increasing gradually as it moved inland.[10] This assessment was a contradiction of the *Vindicator*'s report of one month earlier. Indeed, as the crisis gathered momentum, conflicting attitudes and reports among the local press were to become a common feature. Both the *Banner of Ulster* and the *Whig* were sceptical of reports of large-scale crop failures. Whilst the former opined that many were simply 'exaggerated', the *Whig* cautioned against 'needless alarm' in the belief that this would only 'operate injuriously upon the commercial interest of the country'.[11]

The *Vindicator*, which was a supporter of O'Connellite politics, swiftly published its solutions to the problem. It recommended that companies should be established by the wealthier classes in all major towns to purchase meal with a view to selling it at a moderate price to the poor during the ensuing summer, when the shortages would be most severely felt. The paper also advocated the closure of every distillery in the country and added that 'The sliding scale and every other impediment to the free ingress of food should be at once removed for, if famine be added to the inflictions of bad laws, the result may be dangerous indeed.'[12]

The press was not the only arena in which contrasting opinions were to be found. Estimates of losses of the potato crop varied widely, with one of the first coming from Dr McKittrick of Holywood. In his capacity as secretary of the local Farming Society, he commented on 15 October that a failure of one-eighth to one-sixth of the crops would be 'a very moderate calculation', and concluded gloomily: 'I do not know of any successful attempt to arrest it. All soils and all situations, and the late and early crops, are suffering.'[13] A contrasting opinion was offered by Walter Lowry, a Belfast resident magistrate, who argued that the 'alarming statements' in relation to the local crops were 'greatly exaggerated'. He estimated a loss in the region of one-tenth of the crop.[14]

Lowry's opinion was, in turn, contradicted by statements forwarded by two new relief bodies in Dublin. The first, the Mansion House Committee, had been established on 31 October 1845 following a public meeting in the city. Amongst its objectives was an enquiry into the 'extent of the calamity' and, to this end, estimates were sought from local clergymen, prominent individuals and Poor Law Guardians. The replies received from County Antrim reflected the amorphous spread of the disease; 14 replies stated that the crop was above average; 18 stated it was average, while 16 said that it was below average. In relation to the proportion lost, 17 estimated this to be one-third of the crop, 14 said one-half, whilst seven believed the figure to be more that one-half. Finally, eleven respondents expected that the remainder of the crop would not be saved.[15] Although the answers referred to loss by county and not by Poor Law Union, they provided an indication of the divergences in public opinion as to the extent of the disease in late 1845.

The second body to be established was the government-appointed Relief Commission. The Commission was based in Dublin Castle and its main purpose was to coordinate relief projects throughout the country. Within weeks of its creation, it had received hundreds of letters seeking assistance, including a number from Belfast. Their contents included estimates of loss, suggestions for the remaining crop and proposals to obtain benefit from potatoes already diseased. Writing from Bunker's Hill House near Belfast on 5 November, William Radcliffe estimated that by the following March at the latest, there would not be 'a sound potato in the country'.[16] Letters from Lord Donegall, a local landlord, warned against recommendations for the housing and pitting of potatoes – a protection against rot advocated by many agriculturists. He remarked that those which had been so treated 'apparently in a perfect sound state' had, within weeks, 'decomposed by one or two-thirds'.[17]

One of the most unusual correspondents from Belfast was the artist James Burns, of Henrietta Street. He wrote long, detailed letters to the authorities in Dublin Castle warning, in graphic terms, of the calamity about to engulf the country. The following letter is typical:

It leaves us in complete uncertainty whether a single tuber shall remain in the island by the end of three months!!! The rate at which the destruction proceeds has not and probably cannot be ascertained. But the concurrent testimony of great numbers shows it to be accelerating. This increases the probability of a speedy destruction of the entire crop. If this accelerating progress continues, and no means available on a large scale have yet been found to check it, the speedy annihilation of the general crop is inevitable!!! What would be the consequences? – Horrible! beyond all human conception!!! – sweeping – overwhelming ruin and death and boundless confusion such as never befell any European country!!! Millions of Irish peasantry have nothing to depend on to sustain life – absolutely nothing – save the *potatoes* they grow! If they decay before the next crop is available, nine months hence, they must die by millions!!! It is no exaggeration to say millions as no efforts of mere benevolence could be felt in a calamity of such unheard of – such stupendous, magnitude!!![18]

In a further communication, Burns stressed the necessity of immediate action to counter the effects of the disease, warning:

> There is not a moment to be lost. Nothing short of a united and simultaneous effort by all classes can save us and no such unity and quickness can possibly take place but through the authority of the Government. The fate of the country is this moment in the hands of the Government.[19]

Burns' concern resulted from the fact that, due to the almost total reliance of millions of people on the potato, when this crop failed, the lives of the people could be saved only through government intervention. His comments, however, were less directly applicable to towns such as Belfast where the economy was more diverse and commercialized. Nevertheless, the lives of the urban poor in Belfast were affected. Increases in the prices of basic foodstuffs added to the vulnerability of those already existing on the economic margins and decreasing the purchasing power of all workers. Moreover, migration from surrounding rural areas transferred both poverty and disease to the town. Consequently, the survival of the poorest groups in Belfast, and those who became economic refugees within the town, was also dependent on relief provision.

Local Responses

Some of the business classes in Belfast were also aware of the need for immediate action to counteract the impact of the potato disease on the population. At the end of October, a petition signed by almost 200 of the town's most prominent individuals was sent to the Mayor, Andrew Mulholland, requesting a public meeting to debate the situation.[20] The subsequent assembly discussed two matters which were regarded as being equally important to the welfare of the population. First, the subject of prohibiting the use of grain for distillation was addressed, with one of the main proponents of the move being Dr John Edgar, a leading Presbyterian advocate of temperance. Edgar's concerns for the local poor became conflated with his more general condemnation of the evils of alcohol. He estimated that the grain used in the distilleries was equivalent to 150 shiploads of meal – each ship containing 500 tons. He suggested the use of wine for those who wished to continue drinking and concluded, 'I beseech you not to suffer the handful of meal ... to be converted into poison by the distiller.'

The second proposition referred to the import and export of foods from local ports. In a strongly worded speech, William

Sharman Crawford, a liberal Ulster landlord and radical MP, concluded that one measure was essential:

> The question is clear. The people are in danger of starvation – the existence of our fellow-creatures is in jeopardy and it is the duty of every man in his sphere to use every means in his power to mitigate the suffering likely to arise, both by his individual exertions and by calling on the government to open the ports and cheapen provisions.[21]

The town meeting sent a memorial to the Lord Lieutenant advocating the closure of distilleries and the opening of ports to the free admission of food. Nevertheless, the sentiments of the meeting met with strong opposition from the *Northern Whig*. In a lengthy editorial, it claimed that only 'in very strong cases' could any interference with 'legitimate trade' be warranted. At the same time, it dismissed the opinions of many of those advocating closure of the distilleries on the grounds that the temperance speeches were 'applicable not merely to the present case but to all times'.[22]

Similar proposals for an end to distillation came from Dublin Corporation, the Mansion House Committee and an assembly of operatives in Glasgow.[23] Each resolution received a courteous reply from the office of the Lord Lieutenant, but nothing else was heard of the matter. Ironically, only a few weeks earlier Lord Heytesbury, the Lord Lieutenant, had urged the Prime Minister to forbid distillation, saying that 'this is demanded on all sides'. Peel, however, had determined to avoid this traditional relief measure despite the gravity of the situation.[24] Increasingly, Peel viewed the potato failure as an opportunity to repeal the Corn Laws and thus complete a free trade programme he had commenced in his 1842 budget.[25] Writing to the Home Secretary, Sir James Graham, he explained: 'I have no confidence in such remedies as the prohibition of exports, or the stoppage of the distilleries. The removal of impediments to import is the only effectual remedy.'[26]

The *Northern Whig* also remained trenchant in its opposition to such demands. Referring to the resolution of the Dublin Corporation, which was known to support repeal of the Union, the paper claimed that it was both 'blindly absurd' and 'most objectionable'. Moreover, it stated its belief that the move was precipitated by 'some narrow-minded Repealer'.[27] For the most part, the demands for additional relief measures were kept separate from demands for repeal, although, as the Famine progressed, the two issues became coupled by the radical Young Ireland movement. From the outset, the Belfast Repeal Club considered such governmental indifference as being indicative of 'the total inefficiency of foreign legislation'.[28]

The potato disease continued to spread throughout November. At the end of the month, the Rev. Dillon of Dundonald Glebe estimated that the loss in his district amounted to one-half of the crop, although in some parts it was as much as two-thirds.[29] Dr McKittrick alleged that rotting potatoes were being emptied 'by the cart-load' into the sea near Holywood. He, in common with others, regarded this action as a waste, believing that some edible remnants could be retrieved.[30] Robert Patterson of College Square North, a member of the Belfast Society for the Amelioration of the Condition of the Working Classes, estimated a waste of 3 lb of potatoes for each house in the town. He suggested a daily collection from the affluent of diseased potatoes which otherwise would have been thrown away. Patterson believed that the rotten potatoes could be mixed with oatmeal and converted into cakes, and could then be sold to the poor at a low price. He also advocated the establishment of depots to which the poor could bring their rotten potatoes and receive an equivalent amount of bread in return.[31] Patterson's main proposal centred on the conversion of diseased potatoes to starch by the poor themselves. In this belief, he echoed the sentiments of James Burns, who maintained that 'fifty-nine sixtieths of the entire nutriment' remained sound within diseased potatoes.[32] Indeed, so convinced was Burns of the value of his suggestion that he urged the government to supply every family in the country with 'three tin grates, two tubs and three yards of cloth' for the purpose of obtaining starch.[33]

Patterson also exhorted the Society to print and distribute to the poor the instructions of the Relief Commissioners for converting potatoes into starch. Consequently, on 25 November 1845, thousands of leaflets were circulated throughout Belfast, which contained the following instructions:

Plain Directions for making Good Bread from Unsound Potatoes

1. Clean the potatoes well, either by washing or scraping.
2. Rub them down to a pulp on a kitchen grater, such as can be had at very trifling cost from any tin smith.
3. Pour water on the pulp; change it at the end of ten minutes; change it again, and after ten minutes have passed, change it a third time. The water which at first came away, of a dark brown colour, will now, on being poured off, be nearly clear. All that is bad in the potato will, by this plan, be separated from what is good and washed away.
4. To every three pounds of the pulp now add one pound or about two handfuls of meal and a little salt. Roll it out into

cakes about three-eighths of an inch thick and bake them on
a griddle.

Observe – let no-one throw away potatoes which can thus be
made into wholesome and nourishing bread; but try to prevent
any from being wasted – 'Gather up the fragments, that nothing
be lost'.[34]

Evidence that the plan was having an effect was illustrated by
an advertisement in the local papers. The Belfast Wire Works,
based in Church Lane, stated that it had prepared 'a large quantity
of wire web' together with 'fine silk sieves suitable for the
manufacture of starch from potatoes'.[35]

'Absolute Danger of Starvation'

The various schemes to redeem some benefit from the diseased
potatoes met with little success. The *Belfast Vindicator* viewed the
attempts to utilize diseased potatoes as a means by which the
government was protecting the corn export trade and warned:

From North to South the sad news is ringing in the ears of the
authorities, while nothing can be seen in that direction but
listless moping over vain theories and plans to qualify rotten
potatoes for human use, so that the grain, as usual, may be
shipped out of the country.[36]

By 1846, the shortfall in the potato crop was being keenly felt
in local markets. From 3½d per stone in early 1845, potatoes
almost doubled in price to 6¾d in March 1846.[37] This increase
added to the hardships of many families who ate nothing but
potatoes and oatmeal. Their vulnerable position was exacerbated
by a further downturn in the cotton industry. One local newspaper
described the impact thus:

All branches of the cotton manufacture ... are in a state of
inactivity or stagnation as compared with their condition three
months ago. Both the Scotch Commission houses and our own
manufacturers are restricting the make and finish of cloth; and
in the town as well as in the country districts, many hundreds
of weavers and of females who earned a livelihood by
needlework are out of employment and consequently beginning
to feel privation.[38]

The reference to Scotland was significant. In 1845, the blight
had reached the Highlands of Scotland, where dependence on
potatoes was high. The crop failure coincided with a deepening
trade depression within the Scottish textile industry. In September
of that year, the cotton spinners of Glasgow had gone on strike in

an attempt to resist wage reductions.[39] Significantly also, in November the Glasgow Town Council had demanded the opening of the ports in order to allow cheap food to enter the country 'under the present appalling crisis'.[40] The situation within Scotland was of interest to many workers in Ballymacarrett who were employed by Scottish industrialists. A downturn in production in Scotland resulted in hardship in the district such as had occurred during the economic crisis of 1842. In 1846, with a poor potato crop and food prices rising dramatically throughout Ireland, the situation was much more serious than it had been four years earlier.

On 27 March, the *Banner of Ulster* carried an account which detailed the situation in Ballymacarrett. Out of 411 looms in operation between Queen's Bridge and Conn's Water Bridge, 206 were inactive, while the remainder, they estimated, would be so within one week. The paper calculated within a small area of Ballymacarrett, 194 families – a total of more than 1,000 individuals – were unemployed and 'experiencing the most severe privations'. Many were subsisting on one meal a day and had not lit a fire in their houses 'for days and nights together'. The report concluded with the following observation: 'The people are in positive want, in absolute danger of starvation, perhaps before another week, unless effective relief be procured.'[41]

Attempts to portray such accounts as exaggeration were countered by many individual tales of hardship. A number of women had been left to fend for themselves as their spouses went to seek work. The following account was published in a local newspaper in order to provide an insight into the privations of many families:

> One woman, with four young children, has had no work nor money coming in for nine weeks. Four weeks ago her husband went to England to seek employment, but he has not yet fallen into work. She is nursing one child and does not know how the other three live other than that the neighbours give them a potato or a bit of bread now and then.[42]

Such cases were continually recounted, with the vast majority of weavers reporting unemployment since the Christmas period. In some instances, men had travelled to England and had either returned without gaining work or failed to send any word or money back home. In lamenting the hopelessness of the situation, the *Banner* stated:

> We think that the poorest and most destitute may obtain a meal today and some of them tomorrow; but unless there are immediate and urgent means adopted, we know not how or

where from many of them will be fed next week. We have seen deserving families reduced to complete destitution and starvation and their case must be made known that they may be relieved in the way they wish – by work and wages.

Such descriptions of absolute misery resulted in small donations being sent to the newspaper's offices. By the end of March 1846 a relief committee had been established by the Rev. Charles Courtney and George Troup, proprietor of the *Banner of Ulster*.[43] With the donations received, they were enabled to feed and clothe 90 families. Because this aid was only temporary, a delegation was formed with the intention of organizing a public meeting in Belfast. A first step involved gaining the support of the Town Council; however, many members were unenthusiastic about providing relief to Ballymacarrett which, although it fell within the Belfast Poor Law Union, was regarded by some as lying outside the town proper. A number of councillors argued that provision for those in distress was the responsibility of the landowners of the district, whilst others alleged that the initial problems had arisen as a consequence of a combination (trade Union) which had been organized by the weavers against the manufacturers who had responded by moving the work to Newtownards.[44] This charge was dismissed by the *Banner of Ulster* as being 'preposterous', the sympathies of the paper reflecting the personal involvement in the Ballymacarrett committee of its owner.[45] A major concern of the council centred on the impact that a public meeting concerning distress would have on the general population of Belfast. It was argued by many council members that 'great care' had to be taken to avoid creating 'undue alarm'. Thus it was decided to support a private subscription fund 'sufficient for the purpose'.[46]

The cautious attitude of the Town Council was supported by both the *Belfast News-Letter* and the *Northern Whig*. The latter mentioned the distress in Ballymacarrett on just one occasion, while the *News-Letter* scarcely referred to it at all.[47] If it had not been for reports in every edition of the *Banner of Ulster* the situation might have gone unnoticed. The *Vindicator* had no doubt as to the reason both for the rejection of calls for a public meeting and the apparent apathy evident within the town, giving its opinion that:

> The distress in Ballymacarrett was the first cry of want that unhinged the fine philosophy that would starve the poor for the honour of the rich ... to disturb the composure of those who hate distress because it is a disgrace to the province, and wonder that persons will not be content to linger, sigh and die in silence, rather than sully the credit of Ulster.

The paper, which had an almost exclusively Catholic readership, resented the notion that Ulster was somehow superior to the other three provinces and claimed that any attempt to disguise the severity of the situation would only exacerbate it, warning:

> This covering will not conceal the disease. Hunger breaks through stone walls, and will not be restrained by the flimsy veil of would-be Ulster honour. It would be more to the honour of Ulster to search out and relieve distress than to hound its victims over to silence and death; at least, such is our opinion of what should be considered honour in Ulster.[48]

'A District Distinct from Belfast'. Suffering in Ballymacarrett

Faced with a deepening crisis in Ballymacarrett and the apparent indifference of the authorities in Belfast, the local relief committee continued to meet throughout the spring of 1846. The committee was comprised of wealthy inhabitants of the townland and clergymen from each of the three main churches. At the end of March, the committee ordered 1.5 tons of Indian corn for distribution 'in order to prevent downright starvation'. The committee, with the support of the Presbyterian minister Henry Cooke, also petitioned the Mayor of Belfast, John Kane, asking him to organize a town relief committee for Belfast which would incorporate the Ballymacarrett Board. They believed a body which represented the whole of Belfast would be better placed to ask for government aid. They argued that this action was necessary due to 'the great distress and destitution at present existing, and which has existed for a considerable time past, in that portion of the borough called Ballymacarrett'. This request was refused on a territorial point. The Mayor explained that Ballymacarrett was situated in County Down, whereas the greater part of Belfast lay in County Antrim, and the level of distress in the latter area did not warrant such action. Without the involvement of the Belfast Council, the Ballymacarrett Committee felt unsure of how to secure government assistance. Until they could enlist outside support, they decided to keep collecting subscriptions. At the same time, they warned that the situation in the area had deteriorated so rapidly that unless immediate action was taken 'many families would starve'.[49]

In sheer desperation, and aware of the lack of interest in their situation, the local relief committee in Ballymacarrett placed advertisements in all of the Belfast newspapers. Attesting to their personal familiarity with the 'extreme destitution' in the district, local clergymen, doctors and George Troup, signalled their intention to appeal to the 'benevolent and wealthy inhabitants of Belfast and its vicinity' for support in establishing a soup kitchen to supply food to those in need. Pre-empting any suggestions about the dangers of providing gratuitous relief, the committee promised to place able-bodied men and women in employment, 'so that none may be permitted to eat the bread of idleness'. The distress in Ballymacarrett also resulted in the formation of an Emigration Society among local workers. They stated their determination to leave a district where they were unable to 'live independently by the product of their labour'.[50]

The palpable suffering of the poor in Ballymacarrett and in other parts of Belfast led to a public meeting being held in the Town Hall on 18 April 1846.[51] The opinions voiced at the assembly in relation to gratuitous aid, the responsibility of landlords, Poor Law expenses and the culpability of the distressed were to be repeated over the following months. The debates in the first meeting to be held in Belfast illustrated what was to be an unresolved conflict between the ideological concerns of those organizing relief with the practical needs of those groups who required assistance. Concern was again expressed on the geographical position of Ballymacarrett, some arguing that it was 'a district distinct from Belfast'. When Rev. Courtney announced that the Ballymacarrett Committee had applied independently for government aid, there was apprehension that this would result in a debt being foisted on the ratepayers of Belfast, rather than just those residing in Ballymacarrett. A particularly unsympathetic view was expressed by Dr Drew. Apart from warning about the increased tax burdens which would result from asking for government aid, he alleged that the distress was the fault of the weavers as it had been precipitated by industrial unrest. In support of this, he pointed out that the weavers in Sandy Row were not in a similar position. When George Troup defended the Ballymacarrett weavers by pointing to their unique position vis-à-vis their Scottish employers, Drew grudgingly backed down. Nevertheless, he advocated that the meeting 'voice their disapproval of any improvidence which has contributed to some degree to the distress'.

Despite the hostility voiced by a number of people present at the town meeting, and the reluctance of others to become involved in actions which might involve the town in additional taxation, the assembly agreed to establish a relief committee in the Belfast Union, consistent with the resolutions of the government's Relief Commissioners. Thus the original ad hoc grouping was reformed and joined by the Mayor, local clergymen, the district medical officer and the Poor Law Guardians.[52] Yet, the establishment of the Belfast Relief Committee did little to alleviate the situation of the poor in Ballymacarrett. The Belfast Committee was immediately approached by the Ballymacarrett Emigration Society, which represented 150 people. They requested assistance to be sent to Upper Canada, having received letters and remittances and heard of the success there of friends and relatives. This appeal was refused, on the grounds that the committee did not possess the financial resources to aid those wishing to emigrate.[53] In the ensuing weeks, the *Banner of Ulster* continued to highlight the distress in Ballymacarrett, whilst criticizing the relief policies of the government. The paper was also critical of the apparent indifference of many to the suffering of their fellow townspeople and countrymen. On 21 April, the paper reported that, despite repeated requests, the distilleries were still operating to capacity. The editorial added the following scathing comments:

> The failure in the crop – by politicians in parliament, public writers and speakers out of parliament – is variously attributed to Providence. The remark is true in one sense, for man could not put the rot into the potatoes, but it is false in another, for the harvest was sufficiently abundant to give food for man and beast. The famine – if there be a famine – is man made. We have malted and distilled the famine. That fact must never be forgotten – unless we would lose the lessons that this judgment should teach.[54]

Such opinions were, no doubt, inspired by the distressing scenes in Ballymacarrett and elsewhere. Unlike the cautious approach of the *Belfast News-Letter* and the *Northern Whig*, the *Banner of Ulster*, which represented the Presbyterians of Belfast, expressed unequivocal and forthright views on the situation. Unlike the majority of other Belfast newspapers, the *Banner* was critical of the economic policy of the government in Ireland. The paper saw itself as a defender of the rights of workers and small tenants against the encroachments of greedy employers or landlords. By 1847, the paper had also become a vociferous supporter of the tenant right movement.[55]

Regardless of ideological differences, the various organs of the press agreed on one matter – that the town was undergoing an economic downturn, which was transforming into a trade depression. With demand for cloth described as being 'excessively dull', the *Northern Whig* remarked how 'every day brings accounts of further startling reductions in the already ruinous prices of yarn'.[56] Many commentators reported that prices were lower than at any former period. This worrying development was offset to some extent by news of the forthcoming harvest, with initial indications being promising. At the end of May 1846, the *Northern Whig* reported that oats were 'the finest we have seen for years', and that the potato crop appeared in good health with no reappearance of the blight.[57] A month later, the paper proudly boasted: 'There can be no doubt that the crops of every description in this neighbourhood are looking extremely well and that we should be favoured with a most abundant and early harvest.'[58]

Such accounts were naively optimistic, especially as they failed to consider that, due to the losses of 1845, there had been a shortfall in the number of seed potatoes. Consequently, as the following table illustrates, a smaller area of land had been planted with potatoes and alternative seed crops were not readily available:[59]

District	1844	1845	1846
Dundonald	One sixth	One sixth	One twelfth
Holywood	One sixth	One fifth	One seventh
Ballymacarrett	One twentieth	One twentieth	One thirtieth
Knockbreda	One seventh	One sixth	One tenth

Thus, even if the new crop were totally undamaged, it would be significantly smaller than in previous years. This fact, together with continuing industrial problems, meant that some degree of distress was likely to continue.

In June 1846, the Ballymacarrett Relief Committee received a grant of £100 from the Relief Commissioners in Dublin, but within a month their funds were exhausted. Since early April, the committee had been employing approximately 200 families – representing more than 1,000 individuals – in stone-breaking. This figure accounted for the vast majority of the population of the area. Relief work was supplemented by the distribution of food and coal as follows:

Aid Provided by Ballymacarrett Relief Committee, 25 March to 10 June 1846[60]

Item	Amount of Rations
Meal	39,055
Soup	3,017
Bread	16,887
Coals	4,710

The committee treasurer, Edward Clarke, noted that aid was provided chiefly to those 'without any means of subsistence or any prospect of getting employment'.[61] The prospects for alternative

income disappeared when the County Down Grand Jury refused
to sanction repairs to the main road through the district and thus
provide employment. This refusal prompted the Rev. Courtney to
comment that in so doing the Grand Jury had 'acted a very
unfeeling part'. Further resentment was engendered by the public
response from the citizens of Belfast whose contribution of £100
to the Ballymacarrett Committee was considered inadequate in
view of 'the exigencies of the case'.[62] The committee expressed
the determination to continue relief efforts until August, with
Clarke stating, 'There is still considerable distress in the district
but I think that the prospects of work are improving and that there
is some appearance of a revival of the weaving trade.'[63] Given the
evidence of a lacklustre market, not only in Ireland but also
throughout Britain and Europe, this view appeared optimistic.

A Divided Society

The year that the potato blight first appeared in Ireland coincided
with a number of events which were to influence the political
development of Belfast. In 1845, the Grand Orange Lodge was
reconstituted. In the same year, the legislation banning political
marches was not renewed, which resulted in an immediate
increase in party processions. Political marches had been banned
in 1825 in an attempt to curb sectarian clashes in many parts of
Ulster, including Belfast. The twelfth of July commemorations in
particular, the day chosen by the Orange Order to commemorate
William III's victories at the Battle of the Boyne, had become
occasions of conflict between Catholics and Protestants. Despite
the ban, the local Orange lodges continued to commemorate the
twelfth anniversary in other ways. This forum for Protestant unity
was regarded by their members as being especially important in
the wake of the granting of Catholic Emancipation in 1829. In
1836, in face of growing censure about its role in religious
conflicts, the Grand Orange Lodge of Ireland voluntarily dissolved
itself, although local Orange lodges continued to meet. The Grand
Orange Lodge expected that in the wake of their dissolution, the
government would outlaw all Catholic societies, but this did not
occur. Instead, the dismembering of the Orange Order coincided
with a more liberal phase in Irish politics. The new approach was
due partly to the Lichfield House Compact in 1835 which forged
a closer political alliance between Daniel O'Connell and the Whig
government.[64] At the same time, a more progressive group of
administrators was put in charge of the government of Dublin
Castle. A number of Protestants viewed these changes with deep
suspicion.[65] Accusations were made in the Protestant press that

the administration in Dublin Castle was showing preference to
Catholics, especially when making appointments in the judiciary.
Other grievances included the recent curtailing of the position of
the Church of Ireland, the constant criticisms of the Protestant
landlord class and the on-going grant to Maynooth College, the
Catholic seminary.[66] The Castle administration was criticized for
'[t]heir breach of faith with the Orange Party, their flagrant,
dishonest breach of faith'. They were also accused of being a
'partisan and anti-Protestant ministry' which rested its power on
'the affection and immunity of these savages'.[67] The revival of the
repeal movement under the leadership of Daniel O'Connell in
1840 convinced a number of Protestants of the need to unite in
order to protect their interests.[68] To counter the perceived threat
of the growth in Catholic power and ambition, a number of local
lodges suggested that the Grand Orange Lodge should reorganize.
The policies of the government were blamed for making this
revival necessary.[69]

The decision by Peel's government to increase the grant to
Maynooth College in 1845 and to establish a number of non-
denominational university colleges fuelled the belief that
Protestantism was under attack. Whilst the threat from
O'Connell's followers diminished after 1843, a more radical group
of nationalists known as Young Ireland had emerged. Many of the
leaders of this group were Protestant. They argued for a non-
sectarian approach to politics, thus reviving memories of the events
of 1798. One Belfast newspaper warned its readership: 'We live in
days of peril ... We regard the Orangemen of Ulster as the savers
of the country.'[70] The sectarian tension was manifested in a
number of clashes between Catholics and Protestants, the most
serious incident occurring in County Armagh where one Catholic
was killed by three Orangemen.[71]

The return to power of a Whig government – the traditional
allies of O'Connell – in June 1846 was also regarded with dismay
by some Protestants.[72] Consequently, the twelfth anniversary in
1846 was viewed by some members of the Orange Order as an
opportunity to demonstrate their strength and unity. The decision
to resume the tradition of marching caused some dissent within
the Protestant community in Ulster, with the higher classes
generally dissociating themselves from the event. The majority of
the press in Ulster also urged the Orangemen not to march. The
Dublin Evening Packet asked the lodges to use their energies instead
to mend their breach with Catholics. The *Belfast Protestant Journal*,
which was one of the few supporters of the marches, was
unequivocal in its support for the resumption of processions,
despite the possibility of religious clashes. It responded to the
suggestions made by the *Evening Packet* by saying: 'As well might

you endeavour to reconcile light and darkness, God and Bestial, as Protestantism and Popery.'[73] The paper maintained that 'The Protestants of Ireland have lost much by their own supineness', but pointed out that despite the Orange Institute being '[p]ersecuted, maligned, abused, misrepresented and betrayed, it still survives'.[74] In relation to the forthcoming marches, they predicted that '[i]n Belfast, the capital of Protestant Ulster, the procession will be the most magnificent that ever was witnessed in the north of Ireland'.[75]

Because the twelfth of July fell on a Sunday in 1846 it was decided to hold the marches on the Monday. On the twelfth, a special religious service was held in St George's Church in Belfast. The minister, the Rev. M'Ilwaine, was renowned for his anti-Catholic views. He reminded the Orangemen of their loyalist legacy, especially the events of 1641, when Catholics had attempted to kill their Protestant neighbours. He also attacked the system of national education for being based on 'infidel features'.[76] On the next day, the Belfast lodges assembled at York Street Railway Station at 8 o'clock in the morning. They then travelled to Brookehill near Lisburn, where a number of local lodges had been invited to congregate on the estate of James Watson Esq., the Grand Master of the County. To ensure that the Belfast Orangemen were not criticized by their opponents, John Johnson, the district master, warned them that they had to demonstrate 'sobriety, decorum and regularity'.[77] At the meeting, addresses were read from overseas Orange societies, including ones in Toronto, Adelaide and Calcutta. Many of the speeches were hostile to the recent policies of the government, one speaker accusing them of being 'hostile to the interests of the Protestants of Ireland'.[78]

A number of lodges had special scarves made for the day, and orange and purple ribbons and tassels were on sale in many shops in Belfast. Flags were also available, many carrying images of William III, 'The Man who set us Free', or indicating the origin of the lodge, such as 'Sandy Row Heroes' and 'Loyal Inhabitants of Sandy Row and Durham Street'. A new addition to the commemoration was a brass band, which was regarded as a valuable addition to the traditional fife and drums.[79] The day was not without controversy amongst the Protestant community. A number of mill owners were castigated for refusing to allow their workers to have the day off in order to participate in the processions. There was also some criticism of Ulster landlords who had distanced themselves from the Orange Order, leaving the rest of the population 'unprotected'. The *Belfast Protestant Journal* was also scathing about Protestants who chose not to participate in the day's activities, saying that the day should 'put to shame the coolness and

indifference of many nominal Protestants'.[80] Estimates for the
number of people who attended the meeting in Brookehill varied,
reflecting the political sympathies of individual newspapers – the
Chronicle calculating an attendance of 25,000, whilst the *Northern
Whig* (which had opposed the marches) estimated an attendance of
14,000. The *Belfast Protestant Journal*, in contrast, stated that
85,000 people were present at the meeting.[81]

In the evening the marchers returned to their individual lodge
rooms in Belfast. In the town they encountered a Catholic group
parading through the streets with drums and green branches,
several of whom were armed also with pitchforks, spades and
clubs. A number of clashes took place, which resulted in the arrest
of some Catholics but no Orangemen. Despite this confrontation
the passing of the Boyne anniversary in Belfast was regarded by
the local Orange lodges as a triumph. The Orangemen were also
congratulated by a Belfast newspaper for having spared 'no
expense or labour' in their effort to do credit to 'the centre of
Ulster's civilization'. As a result of the success of the day, the
Protestants in the town were said to have acquired 'a new energy
and fresh enthusiasm'.[82] Overall, throughout Ulster, the day was
regarded as having been a success and was deemed to have been
the largest in recollection.[83] Moreover, in its wake, the Grand
Orange Lodge began to reorganize under the presidency of the Earl
of Enniskillen. One consequence was that a large number of new
lodges were created, especially in the Belfast area.[84] In recognition
of its growing membership, in November 1846, Orange officials
met in Belfast and created a Grand Lodge for County Antrim
which included lodges from Belfast, Lisburn and Derriaghy.[85]

The onset of the Famine in Ireland, therefore, coincided with
the emergence in Belfast of a more militant form of Orangeism,
which was highly organized. The twelfth of July was again revived
as an occasion for displaying the society's strength and solidarity.
During the summer of 1846, however, a major concern of the
town's population was the prospects of the approaching harvest.
The experience of the previous few months had demonstrated that
the welfare of many people in the Belfast Union was dependent
on a successful potato crop in the coming months. The
reappearance of blight in July – earlier and more extensive that in
the previous year – again left the people without food security. The
deepening trade depression also meant that unemployment would
continue. In the second year of distress, therefore, the survival of
the poor in Belfast would depend on the response of both local
and central relief agencies to the deepening crisis.

CHAPTER 3

'All the Horrors of Famine'

The second, more extensive, failure of the potato crop in 1846 marked the onset of famine in Ireland. Unlike the localized appearances of disease in the previous year, in 1846 the blight was universal, with no part of the country remaining untouched. The corn crop was also below average. Moreover, the economic recession in Britain was starting to have an impact on Irish industries. Clearly, the demand for relief was going to be higher than in the previous twelve months. Yet, whilst there was consensus regarding the effectiveness of the traditional relief measures adopted by Peel's government in the previous year, they were also regarded as having been unnecessarily expensive and generous by the incoming administration.[1] In June 1846, Peel's government had fallen as a result of its controversial decision to repeal the Corn Laws. The incoming Whig administration, led by Lord John Russell, came into office as a minority government.

In general, the change of government was welcomed in Ireland as the Whig Party had been a traditional ally of Daniel O'Connell, the Irish nationalist MP and the leader of the Repeal movement. The new administration, however, believed it was necessary to introduce relief policies which were more economical and accountable than those of their predecessors.[2] This change of policy was due to a combination of British public opinion, electoral pressure and an ideological commitment to the efficacy of the market.[3] Consequently, public works were made the main method of alleviating distress after the 1846 failure. At the same time, financial support for landlords and relief committees who established public works was reduced. Conditions upon which employment could be obtained were also made more stringent. The combined effects of food shortages, unemployment and inadequate relief provision proved to be fatal. The sharp increase in disease, emigration and mortality in all parts of Ireland in the winter of 1846–47 demonstrated that the localized distress of the previous years had been transformed into a national famine.

Belfast in Crisis

For a brief period in July 1846 it had appeared that a successful potato crop would be harvested. In the middle of the month, the

Banner of Ulster remarked that 'there are no real grounds for anticipating the recurrence of the pestilence which was so destructive in the past season'.[4] However, on 21 July reports had been received that the crop in Killinchy and Killyleagh was 'tinged with the plague of last year'.[5] At the beginning of August, the *Northern Whig* commented: 'Accounts of the worst kind reach us from various quarters respecting the state of the potato crop; and we have ourselves seen enough to cause the greatest apprehension.'[6]

Corroboration of the press reports was obtained in replies to a circular sent out by the Poor Law Commissioners in August. In response, the clerk to the Belfast Union stated that the entire crop had failed in every electoral division with all potatoes being unfit for human consumption.[7] The *Whig* observed that 'not one field has escaped the ravages of the blight' and described how the stalks appeared to have been 'blasted with lightning'.[8] Unlike in the previous year, there was no disputing the impact of the blight which, in addition to being more widespread than before, had occurred two months earlier. Significantly, and unlike in 1845, the yield from other crops was poor, especially that of oats, carrots, turnips, onions and flax. In noting that the failure of the new harvest was 'more generally fatal' than in the previous season, the *Belfast News-Letter* predicted that unless sufficient relief was 'speedily forthcoming', the area would be afflicted by 'all the horrors of famine'.[9]

The newspaper's concern stemmed from the fact that many of the labouring classes in Belfast had already suffered a fall in their living standards due to the initial potato failure. The fear was that a second year of food shortages and high prices would increase their vulnerability. Moreover, prolonged distress would increase the likelihood of an outbreak of disease in the town. In early September, the local press reported the prevalence of disease amongst those residing in 'narrow filthy streets' who were living on 'unwholesome and scantily supplied food'.[10] Even before this crisis, the lack of a proper public health policy had been lamented by the local medical fraternity. Typical of such problems was what had been termed the 'Blackstaff nuisance'. In late September, a memorial was presented to the Town Council from the inhabitants in Durham Street, an area that was regularly flooded, due to the technical inability to control the level of the Blackstaff river. Open sewers also ran through the locality. A similar petition, from 200 families, had been sent in January 1845 yet no effective measures had been taken to counter the problem. In the intervening period, the local population had almost doubled due to an influx of paupers from outside the town. This pattern of immigration into urban areas was repeated in other towns in Ireland. In Belfast, the

News-Letter warned that the inflow of the rural poor was making the risk of fever and disease 'most alarming'.[11]

Indicative of the unhealthiness of many areas of the town was the number of manure heaps left on the streets. In one week, the *Banner of Ulster* counted almost 1,400 such 'nuisances' and commented how 'many of our streets are literally blocked with heaps of manure'. On Donegall Street alone, in the centre of town, 341 dung heaps were recorded (see Appendix II). Ironically, the local Police Committee, the body responsible for cleaning the streets, argued that the amount of manure was directly attributable to the potato failure in that the farmers were 'not disposed to purchase the article as before'.[12]

In spite of the obvious problems within Belfast, much of the local and national press coverage centred on harrowing stories from the west and south of the country. This focus was undoubtedly to the detriment of the poor within Belfast, whose need was judged to be less than that of paupers elsewhere. The *Northern Whig* and the *Belfast News-Letter*, in particular, initially provided little coverage of the distress in the town. However, both the *Banner of Ulster* and the *Vindicator* lambasted the indifference and selfishness of some groups within Belfast, the *Banner* stating:

> Long lines of splendid mansions have been run up in front of miserable hovels, or closed cellars, as if to hide from public view the wretched haunts, always of poverty, but often of honest, struggling, industrious, and sorely-tried poverty.

In an attempt to apprise its readers of the reality of life for many in the town, the paper described a visit by a member of the Town Mission to the district bounded by York Street on the south and part of Donegall Street on the west. The report stated:

> One home consisted of two little rooms ... There were eight persons living in this miserable place. The woman had been the mother of 13 children – five were dead. In another street – Drake's Lane – we found a family living in a similar place. Two bundles of straw served for beds. They were both in one little room. The family consisted of the father, mother, an old woman, five boys and a girl. These nine persons slept night after night on two bundles of straw in that wretched place. There were no chairs in the house as there were none in the others. The old woman said she had not tasted food for 24 hours.[13]

Initially, the increase in poverty remained confined to the poorest districts in towns such as the Pound and Smithfield (which were predominately Catholic areas) and parts of Bally-macarrett (which was predominantly Protestant). However, the deprivation rapidly spread into other areas of Belfast. For many of the town's merchant and gentry class, the distress only began to manifest itself towards the end of 1846 when, in desperation, multitudes descended on the town in the hope of obtaining work or charity, or of emigrating. Their presence put immediate pressure on the existing relief facilities and, at the same time, made the impact of the food shortages more visible. As a consequence, the Belfast press began to report on the crisis within Belfast. The *News-Letter* reported that the streets were 'crowded with a greater number of paupers than at any time within our recollection'.[14] A correspondent to the *Vindicator* stated that the large numbers of people going about the town who appeared to be starving was 'truly distressing'.[15]

The fact that poverty was openly displayed on the streets of the town acted as a catalyst for private efforts to alleviate the suffering. Soup kitchens, similar to the one that had been operating in Ballymacarrett, were regarded as the most economical and effective form of relief. At the end of October, the butchers of Hercules Street established their own soup kitchen to which they contributed meat and vegetables in addition to financial support. Within days, hundreds of people were obtaining a daily meal by this means.[16] On 9 November, a meeting with the aim of establishing a further soup kitchen was held at the offices of J. & J. Sinclair in Tomb Street. The meeting discussed the relative merits of selling food cheaply to the poor as opposed to providing rations free of charge. One speaker recalled the situation in 1800 when the sale of Indian and oaten meal at cost price had successfully alleviated much destitution. Other speakers emphasized the need for food to be sold because, if it was given gratuitously, 'they would have all the poor of the North of Ireland coming to them, with disease of all kinds'. The meeting was adjourned with an agreement to convene a more representative assembly of the inhabitants in the Town Hall.[17] The response of the butchers and other concerned bodies was in contrast to the avarice of a number of merchants in the town. At the November Quarter Sessions, a judge commented on how certain dealers had succeeded in adulterating Indian meal – which was increasingly becoming the staple diet of the poor – with ingredients that were not only unwholesome but, in many cases, poisonous.[18]

As the situation of the poor in Belfast continued to worsen due to food shortages, local industry entered a slump. One prominent industrialist remarked how 'All kinds of matters – political and commercial – are in a stagnant state. The flax mills are working short time from scarcity of flax.'[19] In fact, the mills had reduced production by one-quarter, a loss which was costing the local economy an estimated £2,000 each week.[20] In such deteriorating circumstances, the meeting at the Town Hall at the end of

November acquired a new significance. All those assembled lamented how, by a 'visitation of a mysterious Providence', the working classes had been deprived of their staple food – a situation exacerbated by 'diminished employment and wages'. They acknowledged that, in such circumstances, it was 'a duty of the opulent to contribute to the comforts of their suffering neighbours'. The meeting also agreed that the wants of the largest numbers could be supplied at the smallest expense by the establishment of soup kitchens. A further advantage of soup kitchens was that the committee administering them would be eligible to apply to the Relief Commissioners in Dublin for a grant. In order to reduce the possibility of fraud and in the interests of economy, it was suggested initially than one kitchen would suffice. Such concerns were quickly dismissed.

In recognition of the 'very great distress' prevalent in the town, two soup kitchens were opened – one in the old House of Correction in Howard Street and the other in an unoccupied house in Great George's Street, where a boiler with a capacity of 1,100 quarts was put to work. It was envisaged that most of the bread and soup would be sold at a reduced price, the tickets to be purchased at the kitchens. Gratuitous relief was to be given in extreme cases only and its administration was to be stringently monitored. Each applicant for the latter had to produce a recommendation from a clergyman, a manager of a charity or from a subscriber to the soup kitchen fund. These recommendations would then be scrutinized by a committee, which was to meet daily at the House of Correction. People purchasing their food were to be supplied at 1 o'clock, while those claiming gratuitous relief were dealt with one hour later.[21]

The shortage of food resulted in a rise in food prices, which benefited those in a position to supply the market. The *Banner of Ulster* noted: 'Farmers are asking and holding out for most exorbitant prices and their terms are accepted.'[22] By mid-December oatmeal had become scarce in the grain markets: on one day, only two sacks were available for sale – at 21 shillings per cwt, an increase of 50 per cent since the end of August. As a consequence 'several of the retail grocers declare that they find it impossible to find purchasers among the poor at the present high prices'.[23] A number of merchants were also finding it difficult to import sufficient supplies of food into the country. The Belfast-based company, Richardson Bros, who were the largest importers of Indian corn into Ireland, informed the government that they would be unable to bring large supplies of corn into the country due to 'either lack of vessels or the extravagant rates of freight demanded'. They urged that government steamers be made available to them which would 'be constantly employed in the transmission of grain to Ireland'. Their request was refused.[24] Clearly, the free market was not working in the interests of the poor people of Ireland.

The problem of expensive and scarce food was exacerbated by the policy constraints imposed on the local relief committees. Moreover, there was an ideological clash concerning the right of local committees to sell food at below the often inflated market price. On 19 December, the Relief Commissioners in Dublin received an application from the soup kitchen in Ballymacarrett. In the kitchen, food was either sold at a reduced rate or distributed gratuitously.[25] The purpose of the correspondence was to receive a government grant equivalent to the amount raised locally. In order to qualify, local relief committees had to adhere to certain guidelines, one of which stipulated that no gratuitous relief could be given, apart from in exceptional circumstances. In response to the application, the Ballymacarrett Relief Committee was informed:

> Gratuitous relief, whether partially given in provision, sold under cost, or wholly given in food without charge, cannot be sanctioned where the fund is augmented by a grant from Government, except when limited to the actually infirm poor where the workhouse is full.[26]

The policy constraints which restricted access to food were frequently at odds with the way in which local relief committees and charitable bodies wanted to act and, more importantly, with the needs of the people who were suffering. Unlike government-appointed officials, those witnessing large-scale suffering on the streets did not attempt to discern between 'infirm' and 'able-bodied' poor. An example of such was the contribution of the Master Bakers who announced, on 17 December, that:

> Considering the present distress among the poor and the high price of provisions, we will defer giving the usual Christmas loaves or any gratuities as in previous years and instead will hand to the Belfast Relief Committee the sum of £111.[27]

Protest and Riot

Regardless of the attempts by a number of merchants to provide aid, several bakers' shops were assailed on 18 December by approximately 200 men, demanding food. Extreme cold, 'more severe than it has been known for a long time at this season', had resulted in their being discharged from employment on the Belfast to Ballymena railway. The men then marched to the bakery owned by Bernard Hughes in Donegall Street, where they demanded bread. Their request was refused. They moved on only when two 'gentlemen' bought some bread and distributed it among them. The protesters then proceeded to the public bakery in Church Street, where they threatened to take bread from the shelves by violence. After a brief stand-off, bread to the value of 20 shillings was distributed. Inevitably, the appearance of such a large crowd in town attracted attention and when they proceeded to surround Elliott's Bakery in North Street, the police arrived. The leaders were arrested, causing the rest of the crowd to disperse. In their defence, the protesters claimed that they acted through hunger and not from any disrespect of the laws.[28] Indeed, their actions illustrated that those in need in Belfast were prepared to go to extreme lengths to feed themselves and their families. In this way, the poor in Belfast were no different from the many groups throughout the country who participated in similar food riots. At the same time, this public demonstration of need indicated that existing relief measures were regarded as inadequate. Moreover, the protest was a sign that social relations within the town were starting to fracture.[29]

The motives of the Belfast rioters were regarded with contempt by the *Northern Whig*, which labelled the event as 'an exhibition calculated in great measure to make the belief current that there is a number of persons destitute in the town'. The editorial policy of the paper continued to deny that there was any real suffering within the district. This attitude of the paper was evident in the following comment about the riots: 'Their behaviour was the more unexpected inasmuch as no person in touch in the town had been informed that destitution, to any alarming extent existed in it.'[30]

The *Whig* continued to present the viewpoint that Belfast, the industrial capital of Ireland, could not be susceptible to famine, in spite of evidence to the contrary in the columns of its rivals. Indeed, in the subsequent months, the *Whig* emerged as the sole organ in support of government policy amongst the Belfast press. Moreover, unlike the majority of British and Irish newspapers, the *Whig* was sympathetic to Irish landlords. Responding to a number of criticisms of the landlords of County Antrim which appeared both in the Ulster press and the London *Times*, the *Whig* countered by stating unequivocally: 'It is really sickening to read the trash with which those vehicles endeavour to debauch the public mind.'[31]

The fact that the viewpoint of the *Whig* was representative of a minority was illustrated by a further town meeting on 26 December 1846. As in 1845, the assembly was convened to memorialize the government on its policy in relation to the distilleries. Arguing that they were now driven by 'dire necessity', many at the meeting noted how in earlier periods, when distress

had been less severe, the government had intervened to stop
distilling and so save grain. This point was disputed by others, who
believed that the shutting of distilleries would only result in more
redundancies and thus actually increase pauperism. In reply, it
was suggested that much of the projected loss could be offset by
higher duty being obtained from wine and other beverages. To
emphasize the amount of grain used in distilleries, a member of
the local chamber of commerce estimated that a sufficient quantity
was consumed to provide 1 lb of bread a day for the support of
almost 4,500,000 people. Three of the key speakers at the meeting
were Andrew Mulholland, merchant and philanthropist, Dr
Edgar, Presbyterian minister and founder of the Temperance
Society in Ulster, and William Sharman Crawford, the radical
landlord. As in 1845, Sharman Crawford delivered a passionate
speech arguing that, in the present situation, 'individual interests
must give way to public good'. He continued:

> Is it right that because there are those who are able to buy it,
> that so much of the food of the great majority of our poor
> famishing people should be so wasted? No. It is necessary that
> the higher classes of the community who can afford to buy
> luxuries should commiserate their condition and set an example
> of economy to the poor and prove that they themselves are ready
> to make sacrifices.[32]

The meeting appointed a deputation to wait on the government
to urge the necessity of suspending distillation. The *Northern Whig*
remained critical of such decisions. They styled the meeting as
having been held with 'less of knowledge than goodness of spirit'
and regarded the decision as 'wrong in general principle and
wrong in practical application'. The *Whig* argued that Dr Edgar
was 'innocent of any knowledge of the principles of trade and the
tendency of demand and supply' and accused Sharman Crawford
of 'running away with his judgment'.[33] Nevertheless, and possibly
bolstered by a similar memorial from Glasgow Town Council, a
deputation consisting of Edgar, Sharman Crawford and
Mulholland, met Chief Secretary Labouchere in Dublin Castle.[34]
Although stating that the government respected the views of the
deputation and would treat their proposals with courtesy,
Labouchere was unable to inform them of any decision on the
matter.[35] Despite similar requests from other towns in Ireland, no
action was taken on the question of the distilleries.[36] A criticism
of the government's inaction was voiced by one speaker at the
Town Hall meeting, when he stated that 'As long as England is
unvisited by the appalling distress that unhappily exists in this
country, it will never consent to the proposal of prohibiting the
use of grain in distilleries and breweries.'[37]

'Gnawing and Deadly Hunger'

The ideological and commercial concerns of the administration in
Dublin Castle and Westminster were increasingly divergent from
the needs of the poorer classes in Ireland. Belfast was no
exception. In October 1846 there was a sudden upsurge in
demand for relief in the town. Within a few weeks, the two soup
kitchens were distributing a weekly average of 1,500 quarts of soup
and 22 cwt of bread to 1,200 families. The fact that 80 per cent
of such aid was given gratuitously emphasized how widespread
destitution had become. Throughout the town, there was a variety
of other schemes to combat the lack of food and provisions. For
example, in an attempt to generate employment in the town, men
were put to work at breaking stones. The Police Committee agreed
to accept 500 tons at 3 shillings per ton. The extreme cold of the
winter weather prompted the relief committee to distribute both
coal – at the rate of 8d per cwt – and straw to the needy.[38] A depot
for the latter was obtained with the support of the town fire service,
which allowed the local relief committee to use their engine-house
loft in William Street.[39]

The distress also spread to previously unaffected districts within
Belfast. John Rowan, writing from Merville on 19 January 1847,
informed the Relief Commissioners in Dublin that because of the
destitution prevailing among the aged and infirm, a local
committee had initiated a subscription and established a soup shop
for the Whitehouse district.[40] The following day a meeting took
place in Dundonald, where a relief committee was established and
a sum of more than £100 was raised to support a relief station.[41]
One local man described how people in the area 'were so hard
pushed' that turnips, usually used as animal fodder, were boiled
and mashed for food. On production of a letter from their
clergyman or a local magistrate, they could go to the Macdowell
Mill behind Tullycarnet and receive seven pounds of meal.[42]

Holywood had also established a committee which, within a few
weeks, had raised subscriptions of almost £100.[43] In addition to
the main committee, an independent Ladies' Committee was
formed. On 1 December 1846, the chairman of the main
committee, Robert Kennedy, issued regulations governing the
distribution of food in their soup kitchen to 'the Working Classes
and industrious poor'. Following the model of the Belfast soup
kitchen, the premises were opened every Tuesday, Thursday and
Saturday between noon and 6 o'clock in the evening. The soup
was sold at 1d per quart and a halfpenny's worth of bread was
allowed. The committee estimated that approximately 100 families
would require free rations. An unspecified number would also
need to purchase food at a reduced rate.[44] The opening of the

soup kitchen did not end the problems facing the local poor. The Holywood Dispensary Committee attributed the increase in fever and influenza to the insufficient nourishment provided by a soup diet. They also recommended that some provision be made for fuel. Both recommendations were made on the plea of protecting 'public safety'.[45] The Holywood committee was helped by the donation of £100 in April 1846, from Dorothea Kennedy, the widow of a former local landlord, who now resided in England.[46] However, as summer approached, Henry Henderson, the secretary of the committee, warned that greater distress was inevitable because '[t]he small farmers have been reduced to beggars in consequence of the total failure of the potato crop. As yet, they have not much sought our aid, but they will soon be compelled to do so.'[47]

The largest proprietor in Knockbreda was William Keown of Ballyduggan House, Downpatrick. On hearing of the distress among his tenants he agreed to match any subscription raised by his tenantry. The latter, in turn, agreed to a tax of 1d per acre per month on their land. Thus Keown contributed £1 13s on a monthly basis to the local fund.[48] Only one townland in the area, Ballydolaghan, remained unaided, its owner, the Earl of Ranfurly, being absent. On being informed of the measures being adopted elsewhere, he instructed his agent, R.T. Gordon, to 'apply a sufficient sum to meet the wants of the deserving poor of the townland'.[49] Another absentee landlord, the Marquis of Downshire, contributed £20 each month for the use of eight townlands in the parish of Knockbreda. Given that the same areas returned a total rent of some £4,000 per annum, his effort was derided in the local press as 'really insignificant under the circumstances'.[50]

In the industrial suburb of Ballymacarrett, relief provision was most fully developed, although local need also appeared to be most acute. Despite being part of the Belfast Poor Law Union and an important industrial centre, for the duration of the crisis Ballymacarrett was treated as a separate district. An attempt by the Ballymacarrett committee to amalgamate with the Belfast Relief Committee had been rebuffed, leaving the district to fend for itself. A relief committee had been reconstituted in Ballymacarrett in December 1846, but because it had not been convened by the Lieutenant of the county, it was not eligible to receive any government grants. From its inception, food and coal were provided on a daily basis to more than 1,000 people who – due to a year of deprivation – were described as having become a 'half naked population'. In an effort to direct aid to the most distressed areas and to reduce any possibility of fraud, the committee divided the parish into seven manageable districts, each of which was supervised by a resident or somebody well acquainted with it. These persons had the sole responsibility for distributing tickets for the soup kitchens. The tickets contained the date of issue, the name of the person being relieved and the quantity of food to be given. This level of scrutiny was believed to be necessary as the funds of the committee were limited.[51]

The sense of aggravation felt at the apparent indifference of Belfast to the poor of Ballymacarrett was evident in an attack on the various relief bodies in the town proper made by John Boyd, secretary of the Ballymacarrett Committee. Claiming that the district could 'only look forward with anxious foreboding' he published an appeal in which he stated that 'it is a possible thing to have the scenes of Skibbereen and Bantry experienced at our own doors'. He continued:

It has been rumoured that the [Belfast] General Fund is to be allocated exclusively for the relief of the starving poor of Cork, Dingle, Donegal and the other far-off places and that those at our own doors are to be left to famish upon the gleanings of local charity, after its full crop has been gifted away to others who, although more talked about, cannot possibly be more necessitous. Surely hunger must be as gnawing and, if not relieved, as deadly in Ballymacarrett as in Skibbereen.[52]

Boyd concluded with an admonition to the wealthy merchants of Belfast, saying that if they continued to disregard the suffering in Ballymacarrett, the fever which was spreading throughout the parish 'may cross into the town, and produce equally, in its lanes and terraces, consequences the most deadly and disastrous'.[53]

The widespread suffering in Ballymacarrett was regarded with sympathy by the *Banner of Ulster,* which claimed that 'the people of Belfast have been benevolent at a distance and heedless of distress at their own doors'.[54] None the less, the newspaper, which was itself a Presbyterian journal, referred to the fact that in the past the weavers in Ballymacarrett had declared that they would welcome cheap food only if it came to them 'through a Protestant channel'. Whilst the paper still upheld Protestantism as the true faith, it urged: 'We would buy good potatoes, and be thankful for them, from the dominions of the Pope at this present moment.'[55]

In April 1847, the Ballymacarrett Relief Committee again applied to the government for a grant of money equal to that already subscribed. The application was refused on the grounds that the committee had not been constituted in accordance with government regulations. In desperation, they applied to the central board of the Society of Friends in Dublin, for support. The Quakers were sympathetic to the request, praising the Bally-macarrett Committee for having 'laboured unremittingly since its

DISTRESS IN IRELAND.

TO HIS WORSHIPFUL THE MAYOR OF BELFAST.

WE, the undersigned, beg respectfully to state, that a sum of about Two Thousand Seven Hundred Pounds has been subscribed in Belfast and its vicinity, as a com-mencement of a Fund for relieving Distress in Ireland, on the following terms :—

First—That relief be afforded to alleviate the present distress in Ireland without restriction to any locality.

Secondly—That the sum raised be entrusted to a Committee, to be elected from the subscribers, and by them.

Thirdly—That this sum be expended solely in supplying food.

We also beg to state that, at a meeting of subscribers and others, held this day, in the Town Hall, it was unanimously resolved—

"That a requisition should be respectfully presented to the Mayor of Belfast, to call a Public Meeting, for carrying into effect more fully the principles and objects above stated ; and that the Nobility and Gentry of this and the neighbouring counties be requested to co-operate with the inhabitants of Belfast and its vicinity."

We, accordingly, taking into consideration the great and increasing distress of many parts of Ireland, and anxious that an effort, on a large scale, should be made, in which all persons, able and willing to contribute, in connexion with the principles above stated, should be invited to unite, respectfully solicit you to convene a MEETING of the inhabitants of Belfast and its vicinity, to take measures for promoting this most desirable object.

Signed,
S. S. THOMSON, M.D., Chairman.
THOMAS M'CLURE, Secretary.
SAMUEL FENTON & CO.
JOHN EDGAR.
JOHN F. FERGUSON & CO.
W. FORSYTHE.
JOHN DUNVILLE & CO.
C. DENVIR, D.D.
THOS. CORBITT.
THOS. DREW, D.D.
JOHN BOYD.
WM. BRUCE.
THOMAS ANDREWS.
EDWARD COEY.
A. J. MACRORY.
J. & D. LINDSAY & CO.
EDWARD TUCKER.
CHARLES & WM. FINLAY.
JOHN HERDMAN.
C. B. GRIMSHAW.

In compliance with the above Requisition, I hereby convene a Meeting of the Inhabitants of Belfast and its vicinity, to be held at the Court-house, on THURSDAY, the 14th inst., at ONE o'clock.

JOHN HARRISON, Mayor.

Belfast, 6th January, 1847.   (57

Figure 1 *Belfast News-Letter*, 8 January 1847

Belfast, 6th Jan., 1847.

Fund for the Temporal Relief of the Suffering Poor of Ireland.

THROUGH THE INSTRUMENTALITY OF THE CLERGY OF THE ESTABLISHED CHURCH.

AT a MEETING of MEMBERS of the ESTABLISHED CHURCH, held in Belfast, on Monday, January 4th, 1847 (after several preliminary conferences on the present alarming state of distress in Ireland),

J. B. SHANNON, Esq., in the Chair,

After prayer for the Divine guidance, and lengthened consideration, it was unanimously resolved:—

"That the present awful state of destitution in which so many millions of our countrymen are involved, through the providential dispensation of God, and the consequent incessant demands upon the Clergy of the Established Church, especially in the South and West of Ireland, urgently call upon us to take prompt and vigorous measures for their relief; and that a fund be forthwith commenced for that purpose, to be called, ' Fund for the Temporal Relief of the Suffering Poor of Ireland, through the Instrumentality of the Clergy of the Established Church.' "

Resolved—" That all money entrusted to the care of this Committee shall be expended in the purchase of food."

Resolved—" That the following gentlemen be appointed a Committee, to carry out the objects of the preceding resolutions, with power to add to their number:—

The Rev. T. Drew, D.D.,	The Rev. E. J. Hartrick,
.. R. W. Bland,	J. B. Shannon, Esq.,
.. R. Oulton,	S. G. Fenton, Esq.,
.. A. Oulton,	James Crawford, Esq.,
.. C. Allen,	Dr. C. Purdon.

Treasurer—Dr. Purdon.

Hon. Secretaries—Rev. W. M'Ilwaine; Rev. T. Campbell."

Resolved—" That an address, embodying the substance of the foregoing resolutions, be drawn up, and extensively circulated."

Signed, J. B. SHANNON, Chairman.

Several Contributions to the Fund have been already received, which will be duly acknowledged. Further Donations will be thankfully received by any member of the Committee; or, by

71) WM. M'ILWAINE, }
THEOPH. CAMPBELL, } Secretaries.

DISTRESS IN IRELAND

Figure 2 *Belfast News-Letter*, 8 January 1847

formation in relieving the prevailing distress'. They agreed to release immediately from their Belfast depot 2 tons of Indian meal to the local committee. They suggested that it should be mixed with rice and distributed in cooked form. The Society of Friends also recommended that the Ballymacarrett committee should consider establishing a government soup kitchen in the district.[56] This option was not possible, as the Belfast Board of Guardians had decided that no part of the Union should impose this additional burden on local ratepayers.[57]

Desolation and Distress Unparalleled

At the beginning of 1847, the government acknowledged that the public works system was no longer able to cope with the demands placed on its resources. In Belfast, the various charitable and public institutions were also feeling the strain of having to provide for both indigenous and imported destitution. The local press carried detailed daily reports of the deteriorating situation in the town. The *News-Letter* offered the following synopsis:

> Notwithstanding the existence of a Union workhouse, a charitable society, soup kitchens and munificent private sub-scriptions, there is in the town a greater number of beggars and of really destitute people than, we are certain, ever crowded it at any former period. The streets are thronged with them, the houses of the better class of operatives are literally besieged with them and every humane institution is filled to inconvenience.[58]

Indicative of the latter point was the condition of the Night Asylum. Originally instituted as a temporary refuge for strangers and passing travellers, its numbers had been increasing rapidly since the end of 1846. The building itself was capable of accommodating a maximum of 70 persons. Between 1844 and 1846, the average number of occupants was 42; in December 1846, the number totalled 85, and by the following month had increased to 110.[59]

In a further attempt to reduce the number of dependent individuals, the Belfast Relief Committee decided to make conditions for obtaining relief more stringent by extending its labour tests. The Police Committee agreed to purchase a further 1,000 tons of broken stones, which allowed stone-breaking to be used as a test of destitution for men, while women were forced to pick oakum. A new branch of the relief committee, the employment committee, also procured work for more than 150 men in the cleansing of lanes and alleyways and the whitewashing of dwellings in the poor districts.[60] Again, the Police Committee facilitated such endeavours by supplying the necessary carts, buckets and brushes, while the work was overseen by two people appointed by the police.[61]

Despite such widespread efforts, in February a meeting of subscribers to the General Dispensary was told that 'at no period within our memory has such an amount of destitution prevailed in this town'. A representative of the Dispensary said:

> At every corner of our streets, faces, that bear the strongest impression of bodily suffering, meet us; the features of pinching poverty and distress are the too familiar objects that we encounter everywhere and may we not fear that cold, misery and every possible privation will be followed by pestilence.[62]

Such palpable evidence of suffering resulted in the formation of a number of charitable bodies in Belfast at the beginning of 1847. Many of them provided relief to suffering in all parts of the country, an exception being the Ladies' Society for the Relief of Belfast Destitution, which confined its work to Belfast.[63] The Society was founded on 15 February 1847. It paralleled the work of the Belfast Ladies Association for the Relief of Irish Destitution which had been formed in January, except that the earlier association provided relief to all parts of Ireland. Requesting the assistance of 'sisters of all creeds', the new group intended to establish a fund to 'relieve the wretchedness now prevailing in the town'. Hence their efforts were directed entirely to the area in and around Belfast.[64] In addition to distributing food, they were also to provide clothing and blankets to the needy, and created sub-committees for this purpose. In order to ascertain accurately the level of destitution, they requested that each of the local medical attendants furnish them with a report on the condition of their localities. Their comments emphasized how extensive suffering was in the back lanes and alleys of the poorer quarters, although it frequently remained unreported. Christopher Black, from the Dock Dispensary, remarked that he had never seen so many cases of destitution as during the present crisis. James Moore, representing the Shankhill District, acknowledged that the amount of distress and misery was 'very much greater and more extended than what is generally conceived'. Remarking on how whole families were huddled together on damp straw, he commented: 'Those most destitute are confined to their houses, unseen, unpitied, unrelieved – unable to apply to soup kitchens or go begging, from hunger, cold, weakness, sickness and even from want of proper covering.' Samuel Brown believed that the College District presented 'a picture of desolation and distress that I have never seen equalled in any part of the world; an amount of misery, indeed, even here, that the experience of our worst by-gone years could not possibly have led us to expect'. Echoing the comments

of Dr Moore, both John Clarke of the Cromac Dispensary and
A.E. Lamont of the Hospital District remarked on how 'a sense
of pride and shame prevented many from applying for relief'.
Lamont went on to say:

> Many families and individuals bear in silence and almost with
> resignation, hardships which are scarcely credible – many desire
> not to be classed under the heading of paupers for they shrink
> from being a burden on the public charities.[65]

Despite palpable evidence of suffering from a variety of diverse
sources, the *Northern Whig* continued to appear more concerned
with Belfast's pride than with its suffering. Commenting on the
prospect of the town relief committee applying for state aid, it
asserted:

> We almost dread that in a short time we shall see even the
> people of Belfast degrading themselves by going before the
> government to implore some crumbs of charity – that whereas
> at present there is a pride, and a not unnatural pride too, in
> sending driblets to Cork and Kerry, and we know not where
> besides, we shall have to witness the humiliation of external alms
> among ourselves.[66]

This viewpoint was widely rejected, as Dr Lamont's riposte
demonstrated:

> Let those who doubt the reality of such distress visit ... the
> wretched dwellings in some of the lanes and alleys off Carrick-
> Hill, North Queen Street, Lancaster Street and New Lodge
> Road, and they will see sufficient to blanch the cheek with horror
> or moisten it with the tear of pity – at least they will see enough
> to disabuse their minds of the erroneous impression that there
> is but a trifling amount of poverty and destitution in Belfast.[67]

Despite the increase in destitution, the Belfast Relief Committee
decided to postpone any application for government aid on the
grounds that they wanted to respect 'the honourable position
which this town has always maintained'.[68] Nevertheless, the *Whig*
continued to criticize the efforts of the various relief bodies, even
publishing the following extract from the *Glasgow Citizen*. The
paper explained how this article, coming as it did from an outside
source, justified Belfast's need to make a stand on independence
and pride, saying:

> In some few places, there is both gratitude to England and local
> effort among themselves on the part of our Irish brethren. Belfast,
> in particular, has maintained a position of proud independence
> and manly self-reliance during the whole of the present crisis.

The proposal of certain members of the soup kitchen committee of that town to go a-begging to England, having, by a large majority, been finally and indignantly rejected.[69]

Notwithstanding the stringent scrutiny of all applications for assistance, the demands of the various relief organizations continued to increase rather than diminish. By the end of February, the soup kitchens in town were distributing a weekly total of 20,000 quarts of soup and 42 cwt of bread.[70] This quantity represented a massive increase in food donations within the preceding five weeks, rations of bread having doubled whilst the quantity of soup distributed had risen from 1,500 to 20,000 quarts. The kitchen in Ballymacarrett, its funds augmented by a subscription of £100 from the major proprietor, Lord Templemore, was supplying 800 quarts of free soup per day and 5 tons of coal each week to almost 300 families.[71] This high level of dependency was comparable to the situation in some of the poorest Unions along the west coast. One of the relief committee members, Edward Clarke, estimated that such aid would be required for at least a further three months and he stated that without it, many of the 'lower orders' would have been starving.[72]

By the beginning of March, the Belfast Ladies' Clothing Society had provided blankets and clothes to almost 1,000 families in the areas of Ballymacarrett, Ballyhackamore and Ballynafeigh.[73] At the same time, the Society for the Relief of Local Destitution opened a school for girls, together with a workroom for women in the House of Correction.[74] On 23 March, they obtained use of the Lancastrian school building, thus enabling them to expand their female industrial school in which they taught knitting, sewing and needlework.[75] A similar institution was established at Strandtown by the Ballyhackamore Relief Committee.[76] As a consequence of the ever-growing demands placed on the charities, novel means were used to obtain funding. An evening of Shakespearean readings by a Mr Vandenhoff, 'unquestionably one of the most eminent tragedians of the day', raised £76 from one of the largest audiences ever seen in the Music Hall. Although organized under the auspices of the Ladies' Committee for the Relief of Irish Destitution, the actor expressed the hope that the proceeds would be applied exclusively 'to the relief of the suffering poor of the city'.[77] Similarly, an amateur theatre group performed a series of plays at the Theatre Royal on behalf of the destitute in the town.[78] The local relief society received a donation of £20 from the Belfast Chess Club in York Street.[79] Hughes' Bakery in Donegall Street sent a barrel of flour to the committee of St Patrick's Orphan Society, where approximately 200 young girls received lodgings, clothing, food and education, under the auspices of a committee remain till the 25th inst. in Belfast.   (430

THEATRE-ROYAL, BELFAST.

AMATEUR PERFORMANCE,
FOR THE RELIEF OF THE POOR OF BELFAST.

Under the Patronage of the Gentry and Merchants of Belfast.

W. DUNVILLE, Esq., Treasurer;
E. O'RORKE, Esq., Secretary.

On FRIDAY Next will be represented Knowles's Play of
WILLIAM TELL;
After which,
ROB ROY!

By the kind permission of the Hon. Colonel Spencer,
THE BAND
Of the 44th Regiment will perform several admired Overtures.
Performance to commence at Half-past Seven.

Prices :—Dress Circle, 3s.; Upper Boxes, 2s.; Pit, 1s.;
Gallery, 6d.   (445

Sales by Auction.

Figure 3 *Belfast News-Letter,* 30 March 1847

of Catholic women.[80] One of the Belfast markets took a halfpenny
from the purchaser following the sale of every pig. In this way, a
sum of £150 was raised for the Dock Ward Soup Kitchen.[81] A
generous gesture to the Belfast Ladies' Committee emerged from
amongst the men working in Coates and Young in Lagan Village,
who made a weekly contribution totalling £1. This aid was to
continue for 'as long as necessary'.[82]

'The Glorious Principle of Self-Reliance'

In the spring of 1847, soup kitchens began to replace public works
as the main form of government relief in Ireland. The soup
kitchens were organized through the administrative structures of
the Poor Law Unions and were to be financed through Poor Law
taxation, although in the first instance a government loan was
available. The Belfast Union was one of the three Unions which
chose not to take up the new relief measure – a decision lauded by

the local newspapers.[83] The *Banner of Ulster*, which had been critical of the town's refusal to support the Relief Committee in Ballymacarrett, now declared:

> We should endeavour to cultivate the glorious principle of self-reliance. Belfast has outstripped every town in Ireland in the munificence of its contributions. The fund raised here is a noble exemplification of our power as well as our will to aid our distressed fellow creatures.[84]

Regardless of the wealth of Belfast, the various relief bodies in the town were finding it increasingly difficult to meet the demands placed on them. In the soup kitchens, steam apparatus had been introduced in order to expedite the preparation of soup, but output was still unable to keep up with demand. Between 12 December 1846 and 20 March 1847, 278,671 quarts of soup and 775 cwt of bread were distributed in the two Belfast soup kitchens. By the last week of March, over 1,000 'wretched-looking beings' each day were receiving free rations of bread and soup at the old House of Correction, and the demand was expected to rise.[85] At this stage, the number of families on the books of the two soup kitchens was 3,008 which, estimating that each family contained five members, meant that over 15,000 people were relying on soup rations for subsistence, out of a population which in 1841 had totalled 100,992.[86]

The provision of food alone, however, was increasingly inadequate as the impact of one year of shortages took its toll on clothing, bedding and shelter. The Belfast Relief Committee acknowledged the changing nature of need when they commented:

> It will scarcely be credited that in a town like Belfast, the seat and centre of wealth and manufactures, there are to be found a vast number of families, probably not over-rated at 1,000, who have neither bed nor bedding of any description – whose only couch is a heap of filthy straw, in the corner of a wretched apartment, in most cases without any article of furniture whatever – a fact scarcely to be credited did it not come from an authority which is unimpeachable.[87]

The committee attempted to alleviate the situation by whitewashing some of the poorest dwellings and removing the dirty straw. They also opened a depot from which fresh straw could be obtained upon the recommendation of the inspectors of the committee. Within a few weeks, they had provided 1,342 rations of straw, weighing a total of 210 cwt. Despite this additional provision, the Belfast Committee shared the pessimistic view that destitution and disease were increasing.[88] The deterioration in the living conditions of the poor in the town was

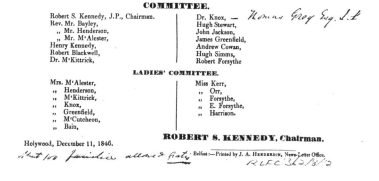

Figure 4 Soup kitchen poster, 1846

confirmed by a report in the *Belfast News-Letter* at the beginning
of May. It related that the poorest people were sleeping in the same
rooms as horses and dogs. Housing conditions in the Turf Lodge
area were described as 'filthy'.[89]

Poverty on the Streets

A major source of concern to the principal charities was the huge
influx of paupers from outside the town, especially the increase
in vagrants. Local medical opinion argued that a period of

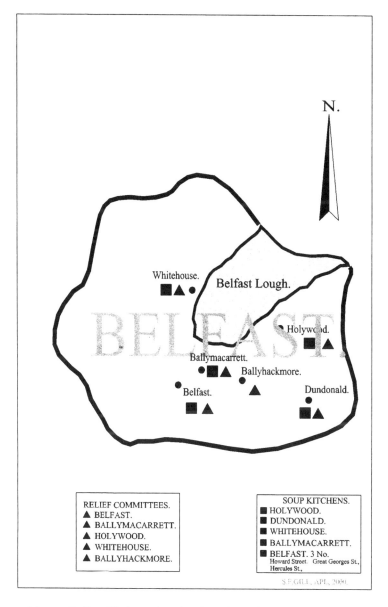

Map 2 Belfast Union, showing location of soup kitchens and relief committees

privation would inevitably be followed by one of disease, and it was feared that such large numbers on the streets of Belfast would not only burden the various charitable organizations, but would act as a catalyst to the spread of contagious diseases. On 20 February 1847, a meeting was held in the Town Hall to discuss the possibilities regarding the suppression of mendicancy. The debate was long and heated, with many opinions being proffered. One speaker estimated that between 120 and 150 beggars, most of whom were 'strangers', had come to town during each of the previous nine weeks. Dr Drew, the Anglican minister of Christ Church, took an unsympathetic approach to the problems caused by migrant paupers, despite the fact that he was involved in a number of charities which were providing relief in the west of the country. He argued that the only practicable way to safeguard the citizens of Belfast was by driving the beggars out and adopting measures to prevent any further incursions. Dr Edgar countered that 'the cry of wretchedness could not be satisfied by compulsory measures' and he advocated means to relieve and not suppress street mendicancy. Some of those attending the meeting were also critical of the actions of their fellow townsmen during the crisis. Mr Dargan, the building contractor, for example, was castigated for having brought 'hundreds of labourers from a distance to be employed in this neighbourhood while the poor of this town were neglected'. The meeting eventually voted to establish a Day Asylum where the poor could receive food and industrial training.[90]

The committee obtained a disused weaving factory at May's Dock near Queen's Bridge which was made available by the donation of a local textile merchant, Andrew Mulholland.[91] Before the building could be used, alterations had to be made. Consequently, it was not available until 12 April, when it admitted over 100 men, women and children.[92] The regime they encountered was to become a familiar experience for thousands of paupers in the coming months: the doors opened at 7 o'clock in the morning, with each person being initially sent to the wash-house and, after thorough cleansing, the males and females were separated and moved to the workrooms – the men and boys to pick oakum and clean grain, the females to make and repair clothes. Breakfast – bread and milk – was served at 9.30 in the morning and dinner at 2.30 in the afternoon. The building then closed at 7.30 in the evening and the paupers proceeded either to the Night Asylum or to 'any other place where they may find refuge'. In order to avoid the establishment becoming a haven for 'outsiders', the governors of the asylum stipulated that strangers would be allowed to stay for only one week, after which time they would have to obtain alternative shelter.[93]

The local newspapers heralded the asylum as a significant step in tackling the problem of growing distress in the town, one enthusiastically remarking that 'Those refusing to avail of the asylum and continuing their mendicancy will cease to be fit objects of charitable consideration.'[94] Although the new institution removed many paupers from the streets during the day, they simply returned to them at night and, if unable to procure shelter, were forced to sleep in the open. At this stage, cases of death occurring both on the streets of the town and in fields in the adjoining countryside were being reported. The following example, reported by the *Banner of Ulster*, where a mother and her three sons were refused entrance to the Night Asylum, was not uncommon:

> After making ineffectual applications at several places for lodgings, she was unfortunately obliged to make the open field – adjoining Mr Ritchie's felt-works in Ballymacarrett – her bed, where, in the morning, she awoke to find at her feet the lifeless body of her eldest son.[95]

The refusal to allow the family to enter the Night Asylum was due to the enormous pressure on the establishment. In the period 5 March to 5 April 1846, the nightly average was 49 people; for the same period in 1847 it had risen to 210, and occasionally 230 paupers had been 'crowded into the same limited space'.[96] On 14 April, even this number was surpassed when 263 paupers were admitted, the asylum committee pointing out that 'without such accommodation, multitudes must have perished in our streets'.[97] An attempt to obtain temporary premises on a rent-free basis had proved unsuccessful, consequently, the original building was extended in an attempt to provide additional room. The extensions accommodated an extra 180 people, but even this proved to be insufficient.[98] A number of paupers who did not gain admittance resorted to applying to the local police stations and the cells of the House of Correction for shelter.[99]

Even though it had only recently opened, the Day Asylum soon faced similar problems. On 15 April – three days after opening – there were more than 650 inmates, three-quarters of whom were said to be from 'the south' and fewer than 100 from Belfast. The following figures in the table overleaf illustrate the huge numbers repairing to the asylum.

The pressure on the Day Asylum reflected the vast numbers of people moving to Belfast from the surrounding countryside. Many of the inmates were unwitting carriers of disease, which was exacerbated by close confinement in rudimentary accommodation. Relief in the Day Asylum was also restricted to one week, following which some people were compelled to return to the streets. By the beginning of summer 1847, the town's various relief and medical institutions were full and, in many cases, exceeded capacity. The measures adopted by the local relief committees and the board of the Day Asylum to restrict access to relief represented little more than forlorn attempts to stem the tide of pauperism.

Numbers Entering the Day Asylum, April and May 1847[100]

Date	No. of Inmates
26 April	864
27 April	902
28 April	871
29 April	825
30 April	875
1 May	791
2 May	841

With the town's institutions crowded to such an extent, it was inevitable that disease would spread throughout the locality. Increasingly, hunger and disease became indistinguishable as causes of destitution. Moreover, the increase in mortality that followed in their wake created fresh problems for the relief authorities in Belfast.

CHAPTER 4

An Droch-Shaol. Disease and Death in Black '47

The second potato harvest failure, in 1846, coincided with a poor grain harvest, an industrial recession and a bleak winter. Inevitably, pressure on each of the various relief and medical institutions within the town increased dramatically. In response to the poor harvest the government had provided for the establishment of public works programmes but these schemes were quickly over-subscribed in many parts of Ireland. Yet, the relief works were little used in the northeast corner of Ireland. In Belfast, the public works scheme did not operate at all and in the county of Antrim, only 333 people (0.09 per cent of the population) were employed on the works.[1] The reluctance of landlords and other relief officials in east Ulster to use the relief schemes meant that the local workhouses became the main providers of official relief. The Belfast workhouse proved unable to cope with the demands placed on it. Consequently, the Guardians were forced to seek buildings which could be easily converted into accommodation.

In addition to the sharp rise in applications to the workhouse, the relief authorities had to cope with an increasing number of sick and debilitated paupers. Smallpox, diarrhoea and dysentery were particularly common, but the main disease associated with hunger and famine was fever. The spread of disease was exacerbated by the poor quality housing, overcrowding and lack of public health services within the poorer areas of Belfast. In this regard, Belfast was similar to other towns where fever was endemic and the living conditions of the poor 'enabled the disease to go smouldering so that it needed only the application of a suitable stimuli to cause it to burst forth in epidemic form'.[2] In 1847, the food shortages and the influx of paupers into the poorest districts of Belfast, provided this stimuli.

The problems caused by the migration of paupers into Belfast were also experienced by other towns and cities. In Cork, for example, the spread of diseases in 1847 was explained thus:

> Poor wretches come from the country in multitudes, and it is said that they linger about the suburbs until the evening and then carry in their famine and disease under the cover of dark … many cases lay themselves down and die … but though they

thus pass away, they leave behind them the pestilential influences under which they last sank.[3]

To prevent the influx of disease-ridden paupers into Cork, the Mayor issued a proclamation banning such people from entering the city, and employed men to patrol the city gates for this purpose.[4] In Dublin, even as late as 1850, external paupers were blamed for the persistence of disease in the capital. One newspaper reported that the Liberties area was full of fever-ridden *'strangers* from different parts of the country, especially Mayo, Galway, and other western counties ... all presented the same listless, stupid, care-worn aspect, and the same miserable squalid appearance'.[5] Famine-related diseases were also carried with those who moved overseas, contributing to the hostility and fear manifested against Irish emigrants. In Liverpool, the main port of entry for immigrants, the fever epidemic of 1847 started in the Irish quarters of the town and then spread to the areas inhabited by the indigenous population. The majority who died from typhus fever within the town were Irish. Other towns throughout Britain, especially port towns such as Glasgow, Newport and Bristol, suffered a typhus epidemic in 1847, which was blamed on 'the influx of Irish vagrants and the influx of fever'. Increasingly, the disease was referred to as 'Irish fever'.[6]

Institutional Responses to Disease

The institutions which provided relief to the poor were frequently unwitting incubators of disease. Increasingly, they were unable to respond to the demands placed on them, especially as medical assistance was far more costly than other forms of relief. One of the main killers of the poor was typhus fever, which was transmitted by body lice. In the overcrowded, insanitary conditions which existed in all the main relief institutions, the disease spread quickly. The rigid precepts upon which the administration of the Belfast workhouse was based also proved to be inappropriate to meet the needs of a hungry and diseased population. Ideology and humanity were frequently in conflict, especially in the boardroom of the Belfast workhouse. Increased mortality also added to the problems being faced by an already underfunded and over-stretched relief administration. Burial grounds in Belfast were unable to cope with the sudden increase in mortality. In 1847, therefore, Belfast – the most industrially advanced town in Ireland – was facing all the horrors of famine and suffering that were more usually associated with the west of the country.

By October 1846, there was general concern amongst the Belfast medical establishment about the spread of epidemic diseases, particularly typhus. The resources of the medical institutions were already stretched and disease was still advancing. Following consultation with its doctors, the committee of the town Fever Hospital announced that, due to overcrowding, it had to refuse any further admissions.[7] In a subsequent meeting at the workhouse, it urged the Board of Guardians to admit all new and convalescent patients to the Fever Hospital attached to the workhouse. Although the Guardians agreed, they were apprehensive that the workhouse was also feeling the mounting pressure created by the second failure of the potato crop and the attendant increase in related diseases.[8]

The Belfast workhouse had originally been built to accommodate 1,000 paupers but by October 1846 this number had been passed and by November, it was housing 1,103 inmates.[9] As was occurring in many other Poor Law Unions, desperate measures were adopted to increase capacity, including the conversion of the coal store and other outbuildings into temporary convalescent wards and the erection of canvas tents in the workhouse grounds.[10] Despite giving sanction to such emergency measures, the central Commissioners warned the Guardians that continued overcrowding would increase the risk of disease.[11] Nevertheless, the Assistant Poor Law Commissioner, Edward Senior, assured the Guardians that, while the workhouse and its auxiliary buildings were overcrowded, they posed no additional threat to the health of the inmates.[12]

The winter of 1846–47 was one of the coldest on record, with heavy snowfalls. The unusually harsh weather resulted in large numbers applying for relief. Many of the applicants were already sick, and this sharply increased the number of deaths in the workhouse. The Guardians sought an explanation from the medical officer regarding the sudden increase in mortality. In his defence, he pointed to the inadequacy of workhouse facilities to deal with outbreaks of disease. The majority of workhouse deaths had occurred amongst young children who had been accommodated in cold and damp nursery wards. Also, because of overcrowding in the workhouse Fever Hospital, a number of fever victims had been placed in temporary sheds, which had few facilities and no heating. In the workhouse Fever Hospital also, inadequate facilities exacerbated high levels of disease. Moreover, due to poor construction, the wash-house did not operate efficiently which meant that the inmates' clothes could be neither washed, fumigated nor dried adequately.[13] In the opinion of the medical officer, the spread of disease could be contained if these problems were addressed and if the floors of the sleeping areas – which were bare earth – could be boarded over and fireplaces provided.[14]

The pressure on the workhouse and its Fever Hospital continued in the new year. On 12 January 1847, a deputation from the Belfast Relief Committee asked the Guardians to increase the capacity of the workhouse hospital by renting more accommodation. The Guardians rejected this request, stating that under the provisions of the 1838 Poor Law Act, relief could only be provided to destitute paupers suffering from disease, and not to any other category of sick persons.[15] Yet, following Senior's recommendation that rented accommodation was preferable to temporary structures, the Guardians began to seek more permanent accommodation for the use of sick inmates.[16]

Suitable buildings proved to be difficult to procure. The Guardians' attempt to rent the old House of Correction, for example, was unsuccessful as the soup kitchen committee was already using it as a distribution centre.[17] Consequently, they were forced to continue to adapt the facilities already available to them. At the beginning of 1847, the piggery, stable and strawhouse were converted into wards for the accommodation of 600 paupers. In addition, galleries were erected in the girls' upper dormitory, while training rooms were converted into sleeping areas. These changes meant that a further 200 people could be accommodated. The Guardians urged the builders to progress with 'as little delay as possible' due to the 'great increase of disease in the Union'.[18]

By the end of January 1847, the number of workhouse inmates exceeded 1,500. Continuing problems with the wash-house led the master to admit that, as a result of this 'enormous evil', he could not ensure the maintenance of health within the workhouse buildings.[19] His fears were borne out by the rapid spread of disease amongst both the inmates and staff. Both the training master and mistress contracted typhus fever, and the medical attendant, Dr Coffey, died from the disease.[20] By February 1847, there were 110 patients in the fever wards, compared with only 30 in the previous November. Other diseases were also increasing. The medical staff made an urgent request for more accommodation for the infirm, explaining that 'the nature of the diseases, many most offensive in smell, and so many patients huddled together, renders any attempt to supply the necessary comforts and proper treatment, utterly fruitless'.[21]

The influx of sick paupers necessitated an increase in the number of medical staff and it increased administrative expenses. The Guardians had not anticipated the fever epidemic when negotiating their contracts in September 1846, hence the master was forced to buy an additional 10 tons of oatmeal in the market in February 1847. The medical attendants had also suggested that an improvement in diet was essential to the health of the inmates, amongst whom food-deficient related diseases such as diarrhoea and dysentery were 'frequent'. Consequently, the adult breakfast and supper meals were changed from stirabout to milk with bread or rice. Also, as more than half of the deaths were occurring amongst children under the age of seven, they were provided with a more substantial diet. Instead of stirabout for breakfast and supper, young children received bread and soup four days a week and rice and milk on the other weekdays.[22] This measure necessitated the employment of an additional cook. The Commissioners disapproved of this extra expenditure, which they described as being 'wholly without precedent'. They reluctantly agreed to sanction it, however, 'given the conditions of the House'.[23]

By the beginning of March, numbers in the Union Fever Hospital had reached 158, with 18 of its beds containing two patients each. The inability to isolate fever patients from other sick inmates resulted in outbreaks of diarrhoea, dropsy, measles, scrofula and smallpox.[24] In a measure described by Dr Reid as 'the means of saving many lives', the Guardians approached the committee of the Belfast General Hospital, a surgical institution which had been the town's main fever hospital until the opening of the workhouse infirmary, and asked them to accept all cases of smallpox and dysentery until the crisis had passed. The committee agreed to accept a limited number of patients at a cost of 1 shilling a patient a day. Additionally, the cost of burying workhouse paupers who died in the General Hospital – 1s 6d per burial – would be charged to the Union.[25] The Guardians immediately removed 49 cases of dysentery and 19 smallpox cases to the General Hospital.[26] The workhouse infirmary was then able to concentrate on cases of fever, which continued to escalate. On 9 March, there were over 200 fever cases in the workhouse and no sign of abatement.[27]

At this stage, the Guardians sought the assent of the central Commissioners to build a larger, better-equipped Fever Hospital. The Commissioners agreed, but stipulated that the cost was not to exceed £3,500. As was the case with all workhouse accommodation, the money would be provided from the Exchequer initially but was to be repaid over 20 years.[28] None the less, the Guardians believed that they could obtain better terms if they were allowed to make use of a loan scheme established by the government as part of its relief measures. It was the first time that the Belfast Board had attempted to obtain relief funding from the government. The Commissioners disapproved of this, arguing that 'The Belfast Guardians should set an example of reliance on their own resources and should not apply for a loan to ... government.'[29] The Commissioners added that if a loan was made available to Belfast, one of the richest Unions in the country, they would be unable to refuse similar requests from other Unions. The application for a loan was dropped.[30]

In addition to wrangles with the Commissioners, the Guardians were also facing problems with the General Hospital, as the number of removals from the workhouse exceeded the number agreed. The hospital authorities pointed out that workhouse inmates could only be accommodated by 'shutting out patients for whom the establishment was specially intended'. They suggested that the Guardians seek alternative accommodation.[31] This communication precipitated a desperate move by the Guardians. On 23 March – with 253 patients in the Fever Hospital and demand increasing – they announced their determination to 'refuse admission into the workhouse of all cases of dysentery, under any circumstances'.[32] This decision caused consternation amongst the medical officers within the town. The doctors in the General Hospital demanded that extra accommodation be provided by those authorities who were 'armed with the power of the law'. They warned that unless the decision was overturned immediately 'awful mortality will take place'.[33] Similar sentiments were expressed by the six district medical attendants who, in urging the Guardians to obtain additional facilities, counselled that 'vast numbers affected are in such abject poverty that it is perfectly impossible to treat them with any prospect of success'.[34] Taking cognizance of such warnings, the committee of the General Hospital agreed to limit admissions of surgical patients to 'extraordinary cases only', thereby allowing for increased numbers of dysentery patients in the establishment.[35] Despite the gravity of the situation, most of the diseases within the town were confined largely to the workhouse and the various medical institutions. But the situation was deteriorating rapidly. In the spring and summer of 1847, with disease continuing to spread, the epidemic began to spill out onto the streets of Belfast.

Fever Follows Famine

To those in the medical profession who had witnessed periods of food shortages in the past, it was inevitable that disease would follow. Dr S.S. Thomson warned how the impact of the insufficient harvest in 1816 was exacerbated by the spread of fever in Belfast in the following year. Given the consecutive failures of the potato crop in 1845 and 1846, he predicted that 1847 would see 'infectious distemper increase by degrees and ravage every class in the community'.[36] Nevertheless, although reports of fever were noted in particular areas, the feeling was that they were localized and posed no threat to the general health of the town. The resultant lack of preparation caused much anxiety to those who believed that an outbreak was imminent. John Boyd of the Bally-macarrett Relief Committee warned the town authorities in Belfast that if they did not address the spread of 'pestilential fever' on his side of the river, it would soon cross into the town and 'produce equally in its lanes and terraces, consequences the most deadly and disastrous'.[37]

Nevertheless, it took an unusual occurrence to alert the citizens of Belfast to the threat of fever. On 17 March 1847, an emigrant ship, the *Swatara*, was forced into port due to bad weather. It was on its way from Liverpool to Philadelphia and carried 296 passengers, most of whom were from Connacht. The ship had been damaged and required repairs which were estimated to take up to four weeks. Within days of its arrival, reports were circulating that the ship had been visited 'to an extraordinary extent' by typhus fever which, in the words of the *News-Letter*, caused 'a great sensation in the town'.[38] The local medical establishments moved quickly to provide aid. At a specially convened meeting on 2 April, the committee of the General Hospital agreed to admit as many fever cases as possible from the ship. Within three days 35 had been admitted.[39] None the less, the involvement of the medical authorities was short-lived. Four days after the meeting, the Board of Guardians received a deputation from the hospital informing them that their funds were exhausted and that the Guardians would have to meet the expense of any further patients from the *Swatara*. They also exhorted the Guardians to make swift provision for the remaining passengers. The Guardians responded by pointing out that they were legally responsible for supporting paupers who were inmates of the workhouse only. In answer to the suggestion that they 'waive the strict letter of the law', the Board agreed to meet such expenses if the Relief Commissioners in Dublin allowed them to do so.[40]

Whilst detained in Belfast, the *Swatara* was visited by several medical men who found it 'exceedingly ill-ventilated' and reported that the passenger quarters were so dark that they had to borrow a lantern to ascertain their state. The passengers had few resources and had been subsisting on a government allowance of 1lb of bread a day. The doctors recommended their immediate removal to a suitable location in the town and the fumigation of the vessel.[41] The passengers from the *Swatara* were provided with accommodation in Waring Street and they received £30 from the Belfast General Relief Fund for the purchase of food.[42]

By 20 April, two passengers from the *Swatara* had died. As the disease was making 'rapid progress' in the town and general neigh-bourhood, further mortalities were expected.[43] Both the General Hospital in Frederick Street and the Union Fever Hospital were 'crowded to over-flowing', a situation which prompted the following comment in the *News-Letter*:

> There are many poor creatures in the back lanes of this town suffering from the dreadful disease, for whom there is no room in the hospitals. This is a dreadful calamity inasmuch as the contagion will, in consequence, spread, and perhaps infect the higher classes of society.[44]

Whilst the prospect of disease amongst the higher classes appeared to be a real threat, the epidemic continued to be most virulent in the poorest districts. A reporter from the *Vindicator* described graphically a visit to Meek's Court, off Barrack Street, where the fever had been devastating the poorer classes for weeks. Its impact was heightened by overcrowding, lack of employment and inadequate relief. He cited a number of examples of such poverty thus:

> Bernard Brennan, cobbler, with a wife and three young children, has been idle for five weeks; gets but two quarts of soup with bread. John Thompson, with an unhealthy wife and four young children, earned during the week, but 3s. 6d. at breaking stones; gets two quarts of soup. Widow Mahoney, with three young children, one of which is very ill, gets but two quarts of soup with bread. John Smyth, confined to bed, has three young children, two of them apparently dying; gets three quarts of soup with bread.[45]

As fever spread in the town, the local institutions were unable to cope with the demands made on their limited resources (see Appendix V). By the end of April, the General Hospital contained only 45 medical patients; the other 160 inmates were suffering from fever, dysentery or smallpox.[46] In the same period, numbers in the workhouse hospital doubled from 254 (on 25 March) to 503, one month later. In many cases, up to four shared a bed, the healthy being forced to lie with the diseased.[47] The pressure on the General Hospital was even greater. In May, the institution contained 710 fever patients, in June, 1,106, and by July, the number had reached 1,242, after which it began slowly to decrease. All other surgical cases and other patients were removed temporarily to the Charitable Society. The fever epidemic of 1847 was the worst that the General Hospital had dealt with since its opening in 1817.[48]

Despite palpable evidence of virulent disease amongst the poorest sections of society, there was concern about the legality of some admissions to the Union Fever Hospital. The Guardians had adopted a policy of admitting not only the destitute who were suffering from disease, as stipulated by the Poor Law, but every applicant suffering from fever.[49] Included amongst the latter were members of the local constabulary who were vulnerable to infection due to their contact with people in all areas of the town. In June 1847, the number of day and night constables afflicted by disease had risen to ten which necessitated their temporary replacement by retired policemen.[50] None the less, the Guardians rejected the claim that the Union Hospital had now become 'a general hospital for fever for the town'. They believed that their liberal admission policies were justified on the grounds that 'many persons who, under ordinary circumstances are not destitute, are rendered so from attacks of fever and other contagious diseases'. They argued further that a 'strict legal interpretation' would lead to a spread of contagion.[51] Such manoeuvring with the precepts of the Poor Law was most unusual and indicated the extent to which the fear of widespread disease enveloped all relief authorities in the town. The controversy over the admission of policemen to the Union Hospital was only resolved when the committee on police affairs agreed, on 11 May, to move their men from the workhouse hospital to the town Fever Hospital.[52]

Great and Peculiar Urgency

Given the number of sick patients in the workhouse, it was not surprising that many workhouse staff became ill. During April alone, the schoolmistress, her replacement, the cook, two wardmasters, a nurse and the assistant master, all suffered from fever, while the disease afflicted both the orderly and the house surgeon, Dr Anderson, of the General Hospital.[53] With numbers rapidly increasing, extra accommodation was urgently sought. An early attempt by the local Board of Guardians to obtain the Lancastrian school as an auxiliary fever hospital was rejected by the Ladies' Relief Committee.[54] The Guardians also experienced difficulties in their attempts to construct a permanent fever building. The Relief Commissioners refused to provide the Union with a loan for this purpose. The Belfast Guardians felt that they were not being treated as sympathetically as other Unions. They cited the precedent of the nearby Lurgan Union, which received a government grant to construct a fever hospital. They also remarked: 'It is hoped that the wealth and liberality of Belfast will not be again given as a reason for refusing the requisite aid.' Their opinions were dismissed by the Commissioners who stated that the Lurgan situation had represented one of 'great and peculiar urgency'. The request by the Belfast Guardians for external financial aid was again refused.[55] Further discord with the Poor Law authorities was caused when Edward Senior criticized the Guardians for their liberal policy of admitting fever patients to the workhouse. He commented that the Belfast workhouse had, in effect, become a fever hospital and he insisted that either it close or that all fever admissions be halted at once.[56] The Guardians opted for the latter action and were soon followed by the General Hospital, which stopped admitting fever patients when the official number of admissions had been reached.[57]

The consequence of such drastic action was to multiply fever in the poorest districts. Dr Anderson observed that as a result of this edict, hundreds of fever victims remained in their 'miserable dwellings' with little hope of recovery. He also described how '[s]everal of these unfortunate creatures actually lay down before the Hospital in Frederick Street, hoping to be admitted into that asylum'. Anderson warned that unless some means were instantly adopted, Belfast would become 'a charnel-house, with infection in every corner and death in every street'.[58] His concern resulted in the committee of the General Hospital requesting the Mayor to hold a town meeting to 'take into consideration the alarming progress of typhus fever'.[59] Ironically, the *News-Letter,* which only six months earlier had discounted the seriousness of the crisis, now campaigned vigorously for increased institutional responses within the town. Its primary objects of concern were the wealthier rather than the poorer classes. One of its key suggestions was for the immediate establishment of a Board of Health, as had been done in previous crises. The paper issued the following warning to those who doubted the severity of the crisis:

> The calamity up to a very recent date has hitherto reached only the purses of the middle and wealthier classes; but the case is different now. The breath of pestilence is beginning to invade the houses of comfort and plenty and peace. Something of the misery which haunts the cottage of the poor is forcing its way into the castle of the rich.[60]

A town meeting held in the Commercial Buildings on 1 May heard many grim details of the widespread suffering. The Catholic Bishop, Dr Denvir, remarked that the extent of disease was 'hardly credible', while Dr McGee reported that deaths in the Union Fever Hospital had exceeded 600 in the first four months of the year. The Rev. William Johnston, a representative of the town soup kitchen committee, alleged that some landlords were more concerned with expense than with health, and a number of them had prevented the whitewashing of houses and lanes in the mistaken belief that they would incur some of the cost. In one case, the men employed by the soup committee to sanitize a court had been commanded to leave by order of the landlord. On visiting the area, Mr Johnston gave a brief account of some houses which required whitewashing:

> In one house there were lying ill of contagious diseases, four persons in one small room. The poor afflicted people had no straw to lie down upon, only a piece of dirty sackcloth. On this miserable bed nine persons, including the fever patients, were obliged to sleep every night ... In another part of the same room resided another family consisting of seven people, who also slept in the apartment – not near nine foot wide – four of whom were afflicted with a dangerous fever.

Various suggestions for increasing the hospital capacity were put forward at the meeting. Dr Marshall proposed that a number of houses be hired in and around town, while Dr Stevilly favoured the erection of sheds on the grounds of the Frederick Street Hospital. The meeting concluded by agreeing to obtain further accommodation as a matter of urgency and to request that the government establish a local Board of Health. The latter application received immediate sanction.[61]

Alternative and more radical proposals were voiced in a letter to the *Banner of Ulster*. The writer suggested that fever cases should be confined to one of the islands, such as Copeland, at the entrance of the Lough. Whilst there, the patients could be attended by volunteer, resident medical staff and, upon recovery, could be removed to another island or peninsula where they would undergo a 'rigid quarantine for a period prior to their final discharge'. The idea of establishing a quarantine island received little support.[62] The newly established Board of Health introduced a number of measures which helped to ease the situation.[63] The Charitable Society agreed to provide accommodation for medical and surgical cases which were to be removed from the General Hospital. Their consent was given reluctantly as their accommodation was 'very limited'. Moreover, the hospital was made responsible for all expenses incurred.[64] The General Hospital in turn agreed to erect sheds within its grounds, while Dr Anderson gave up his quarters to provide extra accommodation.[65] Having finally received the assent of Lord Donegall and the Ladies' Committee to use the Lancastrian school, steps were taken to convert it to a Fever Hospital. A further temporary hospital was provided in the old military quarters in Barrack Street, which were described as 'well-ventilated and clean'.[66]

Workhouse pressure was eased with the announcement that the central Board of Health in Dublin would pay for the treatment of all fever patients. The Guardians announced also that smallpox and dysentery cases would be confined to the Union hospital while the other institutions in the town would concentrate on people suffering from fever.[67] Furthermore, 'overseers of the town' were made responsible for the cleansing of lanes and alleys throughout the district.[68] From 1 May, the Charitable Society prohibited any inmates from leaving their premises.[69] A few weeks later, the Night Asylum was temporarily closed to allow fumigation to take place. Its nightly average of occupants had risen to 280. On one night, 25 May, 57 fever patients had to lie on bare boards without any treatment and in what were described as 'deplorable conditions'. The asylum had, in effect, become an auxiliary Fever Hospital. Its inability to meet the demands placed on it led a correspondent of the *Northern Whig* to describe it as 'a hotbed of infection'. These conditions resulted in its closure.[70]

By the spring of 1847, there were more than 1,300 fever patients in the various medical establishments. However, other diseases were also raging in the town. A sense of morbidity enveloped Belfast and was expressed by a short entry in the diary of James McAdam, a Belfast merchant: 'Fever here is unabated. Everything is in the most depressed state – all seems wrong.'[71] From each medical district came the same melancholy reports: Dock District – fever prevails to an unparalleled extent together with numerous cases of dysentery and diarrhoea; Shankhill District – fever, dysentery and smallpox prevail to an alarming extent; Hospital and Cromac Districts – fever, dysentery, smallpox and measles prevalent. Reports from the College District verified what had been predicted by doctors some months earlier 'Famine has been followed, and is now attended by, the usual result – a rapid spread of those diseases that ensue from insufficient nutrition.'[72] McAdam noted the change in one area as a result of the epidemic:

> I have recorded frequent visits to Woodburn in 1845 – then the neighbourhood had all the marks of prosperity. Now it has changed much for the worse. The engines of the mills there have stopped working and many of the workers' houses are closed up. [73]

Under such circumstances death became commonplace and visible. From the beginning of 1847, newspapers were carrying frequent reports of famine-related deaths occurring in the streets and even in the town centre. The following recorded examples which occurred in May and June 1847 demonstrated the high level of mortality outside the main relief institutions:

> Yesterday, a poor woman from Lisburn laid herself down on the footway in Chichester Street near Great Edward Street and died beside her husband and child. The latter were removed to the hospital.[74]

On Wednesday the 26th, a male and female were observed supporting one another in York Street. The woman sat down and the male stretched her on the footpath – she died in a few minutes. A poor woman had the same sad duty to do for her child on the same evening in May Street.[75]

At noon in High Street, a mother with an emaciated child slumped down under a shop window on the south side of the street. The child died in her arms five minutes later. Her son had died in similar circumstances three weeks ago.[76]

Yesterday at three o'clock, a beggarman was found dead at the corner of Matier Street, Shankhill Road – his name is unknown. At the same hour, a two year old child died in its mother's arms at May's Bridge. The cause of death is given as destitution.[77]

Similar public deaths were reported in other major thoroughfares in the town.[78] In August 1847, a newspaper reported: 'It is now a thing of daily occurrence to see haggard, sallow and emaciated beings stricken down by fever or debility from actual want, stretched prostrate upon the footways of our streets and bridges.'[79] Death on the streets was also occurring in the suburbs of Belfast, as the various relief institutions were unable to cope with the demands placed on them. One report from Ballymacarrett described how '[a] poor boy, aged ten years old, was found lying dead between his two brothers in a field' because he and his family had been unable to gain admission to the Night Asylum.[80]

Rising Mortality and Multiple Burials

During the summer months the sanitary condition of the town deteriorated, exacerbated by the unhygienic condition of many areas. Despite limited resources, the newly established Board of Health had been endeavouring to have the streets cleansed of manure heaps, but many remained. The *Banner of Ulster* noted a 'quantity of unwholesome and pestiferous water in the neighbourhood of Sandy Row, especially from the turnpike to the railway station'.[81] The lack of coordination between those responsible for the sanitary state of the town served to intensify further an already dangerous position.

In an attempt to isolate convalescent patients, the Board of Health purchased a field close to the workhouse on which they erected eleven tents each measuring 80 by 16 feet.[82] Throughout June, all medical establishments in the town were filled to capacity. There was also a concurrent increase in the numbers succumbing to disease.

Patients under the Care of the Board of Health in June 1847[83]

Date	Number of Patients
8	1,249
12	1,494
18	1,554
22	1,709
25	1,843
29	1,975

In the summer of 1847, deaths in the various public institutions were averaging between 70 and 80 per week. Many more perished in their own houses, their deaths going unrecorded.[84] Mortality was most prevalent amongst the poorest classes although it did affect all levels of society. The *News-Letter* remarked: 'We do not remember a period when there were as many respectable persons cut down by any disease as there are at present by this pestilential scourge.'[85] One such middle-class casualty was William Mulholland of Duncairn, a wealthy Belfast merchant and philanthropist. He had been responsible for opening the Day Asylum and was prominent in other fund-raising activities for the poor.[86] Yet for every affluent person who died, there were many hundreds for whom even a decent burial could no longer be provided. On 18 June, the *News-Letter* reported on the overcrowded condition of the town's public graveyards, claiming they were filled with putrefying bodies in a half-exposed state. Further, 'The dead bodies are in numerous instances buried little more than two feet below the ground and the graves being literally riddled with rat holes, the stench thus created is sufficient to create pestilential disease.'[87]

Although difficulties with burials only manifested themselves in the press in June, they had been evident to relief officials for some time. As early as 5 January, the Board of Guardians had acceded to an application from local magistrates to allow the burial in the workhouse grounds of unclaimed pauper bodies dying in and around the town.[88] The Guardians were severely rebuffed by the Poor Law Commissioners for this decision. Moreover, the Commissioners refused to sanction such an initiative, pointing out that it was open to abuse and 'contrary to the spirit and intention of the Irish Poor Relief Act'. Unable to challenge this assertion, the Guardians reversed their decision. To explain their action, they forwarded a copy of the Commissioners' order to the magistrates as well as to the trustees of the three graveyards in the town – Friar's Bush (the Catholic burial ground), Shankhill (for

Protestant interments) and Clifton Street New Burial Ground (the property of the Charitable Society).[89]

'Skibbereen Brought to our Doors'

Within weeks of refusing to allow non-residents of the workhouse to be buried in the grounds, the Guardians found themselves unable to cope with the demands being placed on them by the workhouse dead. Multiple burials were becoming commonplace in the Union graveyard with the master instructing that 'graves be not less than eight feet deep and a cover of not less than two feet be placed over the upper coffin'.[90] This order was opposed by Edward Senior, who stated that coffins should be covered with at least six feet of earth as well as bodies being placed in individual graves. Unusually, the Guardians did not accede to this request. They argued that 'however desirable separate interments may be' they were not practicable under the present circumstances.[91] They did, nevertheless, agree with Senior that in light of the 'crowded state and objectionable site of the ground' a new workhouse burial ground was a pressing necessity.[92] By this stage, weekly deaths in the workhouse were averaging 40. As the following table illustrates, the Belfast Union returned the highest mortality rates in Ulster throughout April 1847, with the exception of only one week.

Deaths in the Belfast Workhouse[93]

Week ending	No. in Belfast	Next Highest Union
3 April 1847	51	Downpatrick 40
10 April	48	Enniskillen 42
17 April	37	Enniskillen 47
24 April	47	Enniskillen 46
1 May	42	Enniskillen 38

Under the provisions of the new Poor Relief Act the Guardians could purchase 3 acres of land for burials. The committee appointed to obtain a new burial site was told to ensure that land for this purpose was situated away from the main building and the Fever Hospital.[94] The huge increase in mortality ensured that the Guardians were not alone in seeking new grounds. However, the various charitable bodies had no legal right to purchase ground and an Act of Parliament was required for a cemetery to be established by public subscription. On 27 March, the committee of the General Hospital sent a 'strong memorial' to the Town Council urging the necessity of a suitable burial ground for the poor of the town.[95] On 10 April, the General Hospital requested that the Charitable Society arrange for the burial of smallpox and dysentery sufferers in their cemetery. The Society had previously 'reluctantly' resolved to limit interments to those who died in the poorhouse, as their burial ground was almost full. Notwithstanding this resolution, the Society acceded to the request of the Hospital on condition that it would only be until 1 June 1847.[96] The Poor Law Guardians were also experiencing difficulties in acquiring a suitable site. In July, they accepted a tender for a site of 3 acres at the Blackstaff New Road, the cost of which was £300. Expressing regret at the high price, the Guardians argued that the expenditure was unavoidable 'as the pressure is very urgent and it will become incumbent on the board to make a selection without further delay'.[97]

Under these difficult circumstances the Board of Health urged the Guardians to allow general burials in the new Union ground. Given that no other public body was able either to purchase or to appropriate a burial site, the onus was on the Guardians to accede. Again, the Guardians were bound by the strict limitations placed on them by Poor Law legislation and the ever-vigilant central Commissioners. Although the Guardians acknowledged the 'calamitous consequences' of a lack of burial space, they pointed out that, even though they wished to open the new site to all, they had to adhere to the stipulations of the Poor Law Commissioners.[98]

On 2 July it was reported that Friar's Bush was 'so much choked with the dead' that the sextons were obliged to dig deep square pits capable of holding 40 coffins.[99] One week later, at the behest of the Board of Health, the Charitable Society resorted to the desperate measure of obtaining certificates from 'many of the most respectable medical practitioners' stating that it would be safe to open the graves of those who had died in the cholera epidemic of 1832–33.[100] This extraordinary development offered only a brief respite and, at a town meeting to discuss the issue, many harrowing details emerged as to how Belfast was burying its dead. The Rev. Richard Oultan gave the following description of the Shankhill graveyard: 'Coffins are heaped upon coffins until the last one often is not more than two inches under ground and in finding room for others, bodies that have not been long buried are often exhumed.' He added that if the matter was neglected any further, the population would have 'such scenes as are witnessed at Skibbereen brought home to their own doors'.[101]

The meeting was also informed that the Charitable Society had purchased another ten lots of ground, which would ensure proper burials for another fortnight only. It was decided to maintain pressure on the Guardians and a memorial was sent pleading that all those dying in destitute circumstances be permitted to be buried in their new ground, irrespective of whether or not they were inmates of the workhouse.[102] The Poor Law Commissioners responded to this request by reiterating that only those dying within the workhouse and Union Fever Hospital could be interred in the new graveyard.[103]

'*An Increasing Scarcity of Money*'

In addition to the difficulties attached to the burial of the poor, the general situation continued to deteriorate. Public concern was once more being voiced about the level of mendicancy in the town. The Day Asylum, originally established to combat the problem, was filled to capacity and numbers were continuing to arrive from the impoverished country areas. In March 1847, James McAdam remarked that the town was 'swarming with beggars from all parts of the country'.[104] Yet, whilst a number of those who came to Belfast were in a state of impoverishment, many were passing through the town on their way to a new life outside Ireland – on 12 April alone almost 1,000 passengers boarded vessels to travel to Quebec.[105]

The resurgent numbers caused renewed consternation amongst Poor Law officials, leading Edward Senior to suggest that the Guardians should prevail on the local authorities to clear the streets of the 'immense floating mendicant population which now infect the town to the extent of thousands'. He asserted that they had been attracted to the town by the various charities therein. He also accused them of being a 'source of contamination' and held them responsible for causing the recent epidemic.[106] The absence of a Law of Settlement in the Irish Poor Law meant that admission to a workhouse could not be refused to paupers from outside the Union. However, the Guardians restricted entry to the workhouse to those who were weakened and debilitated.[107] Similarly, the committee of the Day Asylum stipulated that admission to their premises was limited to those who could prove a long period of residence in Belfast.[108]

Further to these initiatives was the appointment of constables by the Charitable Society to apprehend vagrants and to have them immediately put to work or removed from the town. They were aided by the police committee, which agreed to allow the use of male and female cells in the old Court House and House of Correction for confinement of vagrants.[109] This new coordinated policy had immediate effects and it was lauded by the local press. The *Banner of Ulster* described the consequences thus:

It is scarcely necessary to inform our readers in Belfast of the very happy change in the matter of street-begging which has been effected during the past few weeks. The drab-coated servants of the Charitable Society have done more to produce a healthy reaction in our own social condition than could be well credited. Hundreds of wretched beings who have left their still more wretched dwellings to spread contagion during the day throughout town have been picked up and carefully tended to by the Board of Health, while the sturdy vagrant and the insolent juvenile impostor have been shipped or sent by railroad or coach to the various places to which they allegedly belong.[110]

The deepening of a trade depression added to the existing poverty, especially amongst residents of the town. On 30 April, James McAdam noted:

Trade was good until last year since when it has been gradually getting worse and is now in a wretched state over the country. Everything combines to cast a gloom – the scarcity of food, the destitution of the poor, the consequent increase of disease, which is now spreading among the better classes, the business of trade and latterly an increasing scarcity of money ... It is fearful to contemplate the prospect of the present summer.[111]

In May, four mills laid off 1,200 operatives, whilst two other mills dismissed almost 600 workers on a temporary basis.[112] Innovative means were introduced to cope with the situation. Some of the new mills, erected in the previous year, attached machinery to their engines to grind Indian corn, the substitute for potatoes, as a way of keeping their workers employed.[113] The local distress also led the Belfast General Relief Fund to restrict the remainder of its finances for use in the town alone rather than other parts of the country.[114]

For some paupers, charitable handouts were both demeaning and inadequate and the poor devised their own strategies for survival. The local press reported nightly raids on kitchen gardens in the vicinity of the old Ballynafeigh and Newtownbreda roads. The *Banner of Ulster* noted how 'bands of desperate looking characters have been busily at work in cutting down cabbage, rooting up turnips and securing everything worth laying hands on'.[115] Appeals were made to the police to apprehend those responsible.

The reduction in the numbers on the streets resulting from the stricter treatment of vagrants paralleled a gradual diminution in fever levels. In July, there had been 2,200 fever patients in the various hospitals; by the end of August this figure had fallen to 1,400.[116] However, mortality levels were still high, averaging 70 deaths per week. The shortage of burial sites continued to be a serious problem, leading the Board of Health to renew its attempts to obtain alternative locations. The Board convened a town meeting to discuss the matter on 23 August.[117] The gathering was highly critical of the workings of the Poor Law, especially what they regarded as a high-handed approach on the part of the Poor Law Commissioners in regard to burials. The meeting was informed that the Guardians had appealed to the Commissioners to allow their new ground to be made available for all burials but had been refused, despite the fact that the workhouse graveyard was the only one in the town which still had vacant burial plots. The Commissioners also threatened to prosecute anyone attempting to bury people who were not inmates of the workhouse when they died.

Although the meeting attempted to find alternative ways of dealing with the town's dead, the scale of the problem hampered their efforts. Dr Stevilly estimated that since June approximately 2,000 had been interred, and there was no sign of abatement. The Catholic Bishop, Dr Denvir, made the point that potential space in the existing graveyards was lost due to perpetuities for the families of 'the wealthy portion of the community'. Dr McGee observed that corpses had been left to lie in houses without coffins until the Board of Health paid for their burial. This practice had added to the general level of disease. Leading Anglican clergyman, Dr Drew, claimed that the town's graveyards were 'shameful to any Christian community'. He related gruesome details of a very recent interment in the Shankhill cemetery thus:

> A few days since I turned away in disgust when I observed the manner in which bones and skulls were thrown up and about and in which the spade was stuck into the coffins and dead bodies which had seemingly been but a very short time deposited.[118]

The debate about lack of burial space was also carried on in the local press. The *Northern Whig* reported how a huge pit had been dug in the same graveyard, into which 40 coffins were placed over a number of days. The situation was not resolved until the following year when, with far less mortality, an extension to the Shankhill graveyard was purchased, increasing its size by half.[119]

The Amended Poor Law

In August 1847, new relief measures were introduced, based on an extension of the existing Poor Law. Unlike earlier famine relief policies, the new measures were intended to be permanent rather than temporary. As a consequence of the Amended Poor Law Act, responsibility for all relief fell to the Guardians and hence to the local ratepayers. Significantly also, for the first time outdoor relief was now permitted under the Irish Poor Law. The new legislation was welcomed by the Belfast press, which argued that rural districts would now have to support their own poor, allowing the various town institutions to cater for local poverty.[120] The new law also stipulated that outdoor relief had to be provided through the medium of specially appointed 'relieving officers' who would supervise the distribution of rations. The Belfast Guardians viewed this requirement with hostility, believing that it would inevitably lead to a huge financial outlay, in terms of salaries and the increased demand for provisions. They were also opposed to the provision of outdoor relief on ideological and financial grounds; they believed that any liberalization in the provision of relief would create the impression among those in need that they somehow had a right to relief. There was also a widespread belief that outdoor relief would involve the individual electoral divisions within the Union in heavy administrative expenses. At a public meeting on 22 May in Holywood, it was claimed that if this electoral division decided to implement the new measure, they would have to face the expense of a government commissioner at £600 per annum, together with his secretary, whose salary would be another £100.[121] In general, the provision of outdoor relief proved to be the most contentious component of the amended Poor Law and it was debated for months within Belfast.

Although advertisements appeared in the local papers on 23 July seeking four relieving officers at a salary of £50 each per annum, the Guardians had already determined to offer little, if any, outdoor relief.[122] From the outset also, the Guardians were determined to make eligibility for outdoor relief stringent. Paupers who wished to apply for this form of relief would have to prove residence within the Union for a period of at least three years. Outdoor relief was also to be limited to those who were permanently disabled by age or infirmity. Furthermore, if such was granted, it was to be provided in the form of cooked food only.[123] The transfer of responsibility for all relief entailed by the new legislation signalled the closure of the soup kitchens throughout the Union. The Howard Street kitchen ceased operations in July, while the Great George's Street kitchen, although still feeding 1,300 families, terminated on 27 August.[124] Consequently, all future applicants for relief were, in the words of the *Banner of Ulster*, to be 'thrown on the resources of the national treasury and the care and attention of the Poor Law Guardians'.[125]

The following weeks saw a gradual fall in the number of fever patients in hospitals. At the beginning of September, the figure was 1,287 with 63 fatalities; by October, it was 977 and 42 respectively.[126] Although deaths were now mainly confined to those suffering 'severe dysentery', fever could still be fatal.[127] On 5 October, the death from typhus fever of Dr Anderson, House Surgeon of the General Hospital, was announced. The Rev. Richard Oultan was also reported as suffering from a 'dangerous attack' of fever, although he did subsequently recover.[128]

In early November, the convalescent camp hospital was closed, the tents having been purchased by the Guardians for future emergencies.[129] The Girls' Industrial School, established by the Ladies' Relief Association, moved to Frederick Street in August. It taught sewing, knitting and reading to between 50 and 100 girls, and supported an infant school of 120 children.[130] The Day Asylum continued to operate, the only alteration in its status being that both it and the old House of Correction were placed under the control of the Belfast Guardians.[131] Many of the inmates of the Asylum were children and this solution was seen as the best means of preventing their exposure to 'every species of physical and moral degradation'. The change in the nature of the establishment was noted by the *Banner of Ulster,* which declared: 'How pitiful was it a few months ago to enter the Asylum and contemplate the huddled mass of humanity and rags which presented itself and how pleasant the contrast now!'[132]

Following the dissolution of the Board of Health on 30 November, the Guardians assumed the main responsibility for public health in the town.[133] The various acquisitions by the Guardians had increased workhouse capacity by 400, which did not include the extensions still being completed. By being able to provide such extended indoor accommodation, they were spared the necessity of having to offer outdoor relief, notwithstanding the continuing influx of paupers from neighbouring areas. At the end of 1847, the Guardians pointed out that the 'great majority' of those seeking relief in the preceding months had come from distant parishes such as Toome, Drumall and Larne where 'the whole population had been drafted by some means into Belfast'.[134] Regardless of such pressure on their resources, the Belfast Guardians continued to eschew the introduction of outdoor relief into the Union. They thus earned the praise of various relief officials, for not giving outdoor relief came to be regarded as a benchmark of efficient administration and financial rectitude.[135]

The association of the Belfast workhouse and its environs with disease and death ensured that some people preferred to risk survival outside the confines of the institution. In December 1847, the local press reported the need for police protection in Bally-macarrett, Dundonald and Holywood where 'there was scarcely a night when farmyards were not plundered of fowl, turnips or potatoes'.[136]

The prospects for the harvest in 1848 were good and it appeared that Belfast had passed through the worst of the Famine. Nevertheless, there were still many people in need in the town. Dr A.G. Malcolm, in a lengthy letter to the *Northern Whig*, warned that other diseases would follow the fever epidemic and he urged the establishment of a permanent sanitary association. In his view, no long-term benefits could be gained from initiating a Board of Health in times of severe distress only. He argued that those in positions of responsibility should ensure that the health of the Union would become a priority in the months ahead. He further observed, that whilst the worst of the Famine appeared to be over, its legacy would continue to create difficulties for Belfast in subsequent years.[137]

Judgment upon Our Land

Against the backdrop of distress, disease and death, religious conflicts continued in Belfast. In 1847, the Orange Order was divided over the issue of holding a twelfth of July procession, despite the success of the commemorations in 1845 and 1846. There were concerns that the marches would inflame existing sectarian tensions, especially amongst supporters of repeal. Moreover, the effects of the crop failures and the industrial recession were having a serious impact on Belfast's population, including traditional supporters of Orangeism. The Presbyterian newspaper, the *Belfast News-Letter*, was one of the most vociferous opponents of a march during a period of suffering – suffering which they viewed in providentialist terms. At the end of June, the paper declared:

> Let it be remembered that this season, at least, is not a fitting one for any display of a triumphant character. While the afflicting dispensations of Providence are thickening about us like a cloud, through which we are only beginning to perceive a glimpse of the forgiving mercy of God, it is surely no time to further promote His wrath by thoughtless displays of party feeling.[138]

A few days later, the paper issued a more robust condemnation of the proposed march, saying that it was 'ill-advised, injudicious and absolutely indefensible, taking the melancholy condition of the country into account'. It added, 'every true rational man, here, as in the other principal Protestant districts of Ulster, condemn it; good sense is utterly opposed to it'.[139]

The *News-Letter* also published an appeal from the Rev. Hartley Hodson, the Deputy Grand Chaplain of the Grand Orange Lodge.

He had been invited to address the Belfast and Lisburn Orangemen on the approaching anniversary. He declined to do so on the grounds that:

> I consider the present condition of this country in general, and of Belfast and Lisburn in particular, imperatively calls upon you to refrain from your usual public rejoicings. Famine, pestilence and death are fast coming from Almighty God in judgment upon our land. Almost a million of our fellow-countrymen have, within a few short months, been swept away into eternity by hunger and disease, and thousands more are likely to follow them ... How many, alas, of your flags have but too recently enwrapped the dead? Suffer, then, the days of their mourning to be ended before you drag them forth to help in an untimely mirth. What one of your lodges is unbroken by death, unstricken by disease, unreached by affliction? Nay, where is the house that has escaped?[140]

In the previous year, the Belfast procession had cost £13,000, and Hodson urged that this money should be used to assist 'your famishing neighbours'. In his opinion, the revival of the marches in the previous two years had been necessary 'to restore your drooping spirits, to restore your strong confidence, to resuscitate your loyal institution' but now that these aims had been achieved, large public demonstrations were no longer necessary. Hodson's message was fully endorsed by the *News-Letter*. The paper believed that the Orange lodges were becoming subverted increasingly to the demands of a rabble element rather than those of respectable members of the Order. However, the paper was anxious that its motives should not be misunderstood – especially by Catholics – and explained:

> We are among the last who would counsel any real concession to the advancing spirit of disloyalty ... It is not because we are the less impressed with the serious difficulties which, as loyalists and Protestants we may be shortly called on to contend against, that we recommend an avoidance of any external manifestation of our principles ... It is not because the principles of Protestantism and Romanism – of loyalty and disaffection – are less widely separated now than they were in the days of our fathers ... it is because we have, or ought to have, other and nobler methods of displaying our reverences for the true religion and our fealty to the throne.

The paper pointed to the violent clashes that had occurred on the last twelfth of July and urged that Orangemen should show more restraint, especially in view of the distress of the people during the previous year.[141]

A ballot by the Belfast Orange lodges on whether or not to march was passed by only two votes. On 7 July, the Grand Master of the County met the various Orange lodges in Belfast and tried to dissuade them again from marching in the following week but he was unsuccessful.[142] Nevertheless, the Belfast lodges did agree that the procession should take place in complete silence with no banners being waved, as a mark of respect to 'the afflicted of the town'. Also, a collection was to be made on behalf of the distressed poor, which the masters of the Belfast district decided to give to the local Fever Hospital. On the morning of the twelfth, 27 Orange lodges from the town met at the Linen Hall. Despite the distress of the previous twelve months, the participants were described as being well dressed and respectable. Although the band led the procession, no music was played until they were out of the town when they struck up 'Protestant Boys'. The lodges proceeded to Purdystown where, on the estate of R. Ball, they were joined by lodges from Derriaghy and Saintfield, making a total of 40,000 Orangemen. A number of the speeches referred to the 'mighty calamity' which had affected the country in the previous year.[143]

On their return to town, the Belfast lodges stopped playing music to show that they 'deeply sympathized with their distressed brethren'.[144] They also halted at King William's Field where they formed into columns to prepare themselves for an attack. Rumours had spread that 15,000 of the workers on the nearby railway and new channel – who were almost exclusively Catholic and from the south of Ireland – were intending to oppose the procession. In anticipation of a clash, the town authorities deployed additional troops and extra constabulary to a number of well-known flashpoints. The fact that little trouble occurred was attributed to the heavy military and police presence in these places.[145]

The newspaper reportage of the day varied considerably. The News-Letter recorded a low attendance of only 3,500 people, which was about half the usual number.[146] The Banner of Ulster described the parades as consisting mostly of 'a few boys who, in the year 1847, with all of the suffering going on around them, would have been more fitly employed in studying and digesting the wise advice of that estimable man, the Reverend Hartley Hodson'.[147]

In contrast, the Belfast Protestant Journal asserted that 'peace, harmony and brotherly love characterized the celebration of the twelfth of July in Belfast in 1847'. The newspaper saved its anger for the millowners in Belfast – many of whom, as in the previous year, refused to allow their employees the day off. A number of employers also threatened that any worker who attended the Orange processions would be dismissed 'without the possibility of getting future employment'. The Journal described this order as 'despotic' and cited the case of two members of the district band who had asked for the day off, but had been refused. The paper asked: 'shall the individuals who amass capital by their industry and by their labours be denied the pleasure of one day's gratification?' And added: 'There are men who bear the Protestant name, and are members of Protestant churches, who think it no crime to subscribe funds for Popish mass-houses – who think it no shame to forge fetters for their own slavery.'[148]

The debate over the twelfth of July anniversary in 1847 demonstrated that divisions existed within the Protestant community in Belfast. The decision by many Orangemen to commemorate the anniversary in spite of the economic situation highlighted the importance that such displays of Protestant solidarity had acquired. In 1848, when militant nationalists attempted to bring about a repeal of the Union, this determination was put into practical use when the Orange Order offered to play the role of a counter-insurgency force. The crisis facing the poor of Belfast became secondary to the political challenge facing members of the Orange Order in the town.

PART III

A Divided Town

CHAPTER 5

Public and Private Responses

In 1847 – 'Black '47' – disease, mortality, evictions and emigration increased throughout Ireland. The increase was due to a combination of potato blight, a poor corn harvest, industrial recession and inappropriate or inadequate relief provision. At the beginning of the year the government acknowledged that the public works scheme, introduced only a few months earlier, had failed. It was replaced in the spring of 1847 by the Temporary Relief Act, more commonly known as the Soup Kitchen Act, which provided for the establishment of government food depots throughout Ireland. This legislation marked a departure from earlier relief policies by allowing for the provision of gratuitous food. Despite the success of this relief measure, it was of limited duration, being viewed as a short-term expedient. In the longer term, the government sought to introduce permanent changes to the Poor Law, enabling it to deal both with ordinary and famine relief.

At the beginning of the harvest period in 1847, the soup kitchens were closed and the amended Poor Law became responsible for all relief. To make this possible, relief outside the confines of the workhouses was permitted for the first time.[1] The change of policy marked an attempt by the British government to compel Irish taxpayers to be financially responsible for supporting their own poor. It also marked a change of attitude towards the victims of the Famine. Those groups depending on government relief were now officially categorized as paupers and subject to the stringent regulations of the Poor Law.

Tensions were also apparent between the Belfast authorities and the British government over the issue of removal, that is, the expulsion of Irish paupers from Britain. The British Laws of Removal, which were an integral part of the Poor Law legislation, stipulated that only Irish people who had resided in one parish for a period of five years were entitled to receive poor relief. Those who did not qualify could be returned to Ireland. The resultant abandonment of Irish paupers in ports such as Belfast created conflict with the Poor Law authorities in England and Scotland and with the British government. The dispute remained unresolved and was a source of grievance in the post-Famine decades.

A further feature of relief in 1847 was the emergence of a number of private charitable organizations which coexisted alongside government provision. In Belfast, they played a significant part in the provision of relief. Although individually their intervention rarely lasted for more than a few months, it often provided an important supplement to government relief. The enhanced role of Belfast's charitable societies created a number of problems, the legacy of which continued beyond the crisis year of 1847. The involvement of private charity in famine relief intensified the argument about which groups were most deserving of their benevolence – the indigenous poor of Belfast or the suffering in other parts of the country. These debates served to widen the gap between Belfast and the rest of Ireland. More significantly, the attempts by some of the charitable organizations to use the hunger of the poor as an opportunity to proselytize left a legacy of mistrust between Catholics and Protestants both in Belfast and elsewhere. Overall, the role of the charities proved to be controversial, reflecting existing religious divisions and ideological conflicts within the town.[2]

Government Relief. The Amended Poor Law

In the summer of 1847, soup kitchens were providing gratuitous relief to over 3 million people. The success of this scheme demonstrated the logistic ability of the government to provide large-scale relief to the Irish poor. The soup kitchens were financed through Poor Law taxation, although a government loan was initially available. Their establishment was not compulsory but it was left to individual Poor Law Guardians to choose to introduce them into a Union. Out of the 130 Poor Law Unions in Ireland, only the Antrim, Belfast and Newtownards Unions did not implement this legislation. The Belfast Guardians refused to open government soup kitchens on the grounds that in doing so, they would incur unnecessary expense.[3] Instead, they preferred to leave relief provision to the private soup kitchens already operating within the town and to the existing institutions. The demands made on the various relief establishments during the summer continued to increase. In June the workhouse was so overcrowded that the Guardians decided to admit only 'old and debilitated persons who cannot work for a livelihood'.[4] In August 1847, the Amended Poor Law Act was introduced. The new legislation ended all special famine relief schemes and made the Poor Law responsible for both ordinary and famine distress. This meant that the Guardians were responsible for all relief within their Union, including that of groups which previously had been outside their jurisdiction. Although outdoor relief was permitted for the first time under the new Act, the Belfast Guardians were determined not to avail themselves of this provision but to continue to offer indoor relief only. The decision was based on both ideological opposition to the granting of relief outside the workhouse and fears that if relief was made more attractive the costs would increase substantially. To cope with the increased demands on the workhouse, the Guardians decided to extend indoor accommodation. Until this could be done, paupers seeking access to the workhouse were refused admission, forcing them to seek relief from one of the private charities in the town.[5]

In December 1847, Edward Senior visited the Belfast workhouse. While commending the Guardians and their officers for the healthy condition of the institution, he was critical of the congested nature of the workhouse, saying that it was more overcrowded than any other he had visited. He warned the Guardians that if they did not acquire additional accommodation immediately, they would have to provide outdoor relief.[6] The Guardians moved quickly to obtain further accommodation. By the end of the month, they had leased the Day Asylum, with a capacity for 400, at the cost of £400 per year.[7] Shortly afterwards, they acquired the College Hospital, in Barrack Street. However, it could not be converted into an auxiliary workhouse until its final inmates were discharged during the last week of February 1848. As a consequence of its austere design and small yards, the College Hospital was deemed to be 'a good place for discipline'. Hence it was reserved for the use of able-bodied women who were deemed to require extensive supervision and regulation. The old House of Correction was rented for use as an auxiliary workhouse for aged and infirm paupers of both sexes.[8] In addition, a contract was concluded to build a new permanent addition to the workhouse which could accommodate up to 1,000 children. The building was to contain a school and training rooms.[9]

At the same time, the Guardians continued to extend available accommodation within the original workhouse. The old quarantine sheds belonging to the workhouse were set aside for paupers known as the 'casual poor'. There had been a rapid increase in casual paupers as poor people from the surrounding countryside travelled to Belfast in the hope of finding either relief or employment. Paupers who fell into this category were allowed to remain in the workhouse for only two or three nights. In keeping with the stringency of the Poor Law, they had to work during their stay – the men breaking stones and the women pounding freestone. Those who refused to comply with this rule were sent before the courts as common vagrants. To ensure the separation of the casual poor from other paupers, the former were supplied with a special admission ticket stamped with 'Two Hours' Work'.[10] The Guardians complained that the growth in the number of casual poor had put so much pressure on the Union's resources that it was limiting the amount of relief available for the indigenous poor.[11]

The Belfast Guardians felt particularly aggrieved by the burden placed on them as a consequence of the British Laws of Removal. The Removal Laws in Scotland, England and Wales stipulated that Irish paupers were eligible to receive relief only if they had been resident in the same parish for over five years. During the Famine, this legislation was used as a mechanism for returning Irish paupers to Ireland. There were also instances of people being returned to Ireland even if they fulfilled the legal requirement for receiving relief in Britain.[12] As there was no corresponding Law of Removal in the Irish Poor Law, when a pauper was landed at a port in Ireland, it became the responsibility of the local Union to provide relief. Consequently, the Belfast Guardians were obliged to provide relief to people returned from Britain and left in their Union. They described the large influx of deported Irish paupers as being 'oppressive' and they repeatedly asked for the laws to be changed. To ease the pressure caused by non-residents seeking relief in the Union, in July 1847, the Charitable Society established a committee to oversee the return of paupers from Belfast to their original homes. Within the space of 18 months, they had returned more than 11,000 paupers from Belfast to other parts of Ireland. Whilst the majority came from counties surrounding Belfast, a number originated in western counties such as Galway and Kerry.[13]

The poor health of many of the poor seeking admission to the workhouse continued to place a burden on both medical facilities and burial sites which the Poor Law was ill-equipped to meet. By April 1848, the workhouse graveyard was full.[14] The master of the workhouse had been in negotiations to purchase a 3-acre site known as Harrison's land, but the sale was beset with legal difficulties. Until these could be resolved, the Board of Guardians decided to bury their dead at the nearby Catholic Friar's Bush cemetery, at a cost of 1s 6d per burial.[15] However, all burial sites in Belfast, including Friar's Bush, were suffering overcrowding. Consequently, the request to use Friar's Bush graveyard quickly ran into difficulties when the administrators advised that the graveyard could support no additional interments. The Guardians were thus forced to apply to the Church of Ireland authorities for permission to use the Shankhill cemetery, which recently had been extended.[16] The Board also completed the purchase of Harrison's land at a cost of £900. The first recorded workhouse burial took place in it on 14 June 1848.[17]

Other institutions in Belfast were also facing problems regarding burials. On 12 September 1848, the General Hospital asked the

Guardians if they could bury their dead in the new workhouse graveyard. The Guardians refused, pointing out that Poor Law regulations stipulated that their grounds could only be used for inmates of the Union.[18] The Town Council came to the rescue of the Hospital authorities by granting them permission to inter in the Shankhill graveyard at a cost of 2 shillings per burial.[19] None the less, the decision by the Guardians created tension between the two institutions, especially when only a few weeks later the Poor Law Commissioners in Dublin, believing that the exigency had passed, ordered the Guardians to fence in part of the graveyard and use it for growing crops for consumption in the workhouse.[20] The central Commissioners did not anticipate that a new epidemic was about to appear in the town which would place an additional burden on workhouse facilities.

As the Poor Law struggled to respond to the crisis in Belfast, the role of private charity in saving lives became increasingly important. Private charity was particularly important in areas where official relief had broken down, was inadequate, or lacked the resources to deal with the demands being made on it.

Private Philanthropy

In recognition of the severity of the crisis in Ireland following the second appearance of blight in 1846, a number of charitable agencies were formed to provide supplementary aid to existing government provision. The Society of Friends, or Quakers, became involved in philanthropic activities at the end of 1846. They established fund-raising committees in Dublin, London and New York. The Quakers provided assistance throughout Ireland including to Ballymacarrett. Although they usually worked through the medium of local ministers and priests, their involvement was not tainted by accusations of proselytism.[21] The largest private relief organization was the British Association for the Relief of Distress in the Highlands of Scotland and Ireland, which was established in London on 1 January 1847. One-sixth of its income was to be allocated to Scotland and the remainder to Ireland. The Association's first and largest single subscriber was Queen Victoria, who donated £2,000. Other charitable bodies included the Mansion House Committee, which was based in Dublin and associated with Daniel O'Connell, and the Irish Relief Association, whose members included the evangelical Ulster landowner, the Duke of Manchester.[22] The latter body made a public appeal in the Belfast newspapers saying that the present crisis provided an opportunity 'for conveying the light of the

Gospels to the darkened mind of the Roman Catholic peasantry', leading O'Connell to accuse it of being ultra-Protestant.[23]

In Belfast, a large number of charitable bodies were set up at the beginning of 1847. For the most part, they were competing for the same funds and many of them closed their operations a few months later as subscriptions dried up. Belfast played an unusual role in the provision of private philanthropy. Whilst it was a major source of assistance to other parts of Ireland, a substantial proportion of charitable funds raised were distributed within the town. A number of the Belfast committees also acted as a conduit for relief raised in Britain. Yet the question of how to balance the competing demands of the Belfast poor with those in other parts of the country in the allocation of funds proved to be a source of division within the town.

One of the largest charitable bodies in Belfast was the Belfast General Relief Fund, which was founded on 5 January 1847. Its declared purpose was to provide aid to the poor of the country, irrespective of locality. This decision to assist all parts of Ireland rather than just Belfast led to the committee of the Fund being publicly condemned.[24] From the outset also, it decided that relief was to be provided in the form of food only. The two leading members of the Fund were the Rev. Dr Thomas Drew and the Rev. Dr John Edgar, Protestant evangelists who had gained reputations for their outspoken views on religious matters. Drew was the Anglican minister of Christ Church. He was involved in evangelizing amongst the poorer inhabitants of the town. He was also a member of the Orange Order. Edgar, a Presbyterian minister, was the founder of the Temperance movement in Ulster.[25] He had also established a number of evangelical missions in the west of the country. As a result of this work, he became involved in famine relief, notably through his association with the Belfast Ladies' Society for the Relief of Distress in Connaught. The participation of these ministers linked the work of the Fund closely with the two main Protestant churches. Within a few weeks of its establishment, subscriptions to the Fund exceeded £4,000. To oversee the distribution of grants, a committee was elected from amongst the subscribers.[26] Almost immediately, consternation was expressed in the local press that the vast bulk of the money was to be sent to the west and south, to the detriment of the poor of Belfast. The *Banner of Ulster*, for example, warned:

> There is not merely reason to fear, but an absolute certainty that the people of Belfast have been benevolent at a distance and heedless of distress at their own doors. We trust that the claims of persons in this neighbourhood may not be forgotten ... because we fear that there are many classes of suffering in the

proof of his capabilities.   (455

☞ Terms may be known of Mr. COOPER, Vicar's-Hill, Armagh ; or, of Mr. COFFEY, Music Warehouse, Belfast.

Public Notices.

THE LADIES of the INDUSTRIAL RELIEF COM-MITTEE for Belfast beg leave to state, that they will be happy to receive Work of any kind, to be made up at their Sempstress' Room, House of Correction, at the following prices :—

Fine Linen Shirts, ..	..	1s.	6d.	to 2s.	0d.
Common do., ..	..	0s.	6d.	to 0s.	8d.
Boys' Shirts, ..	..	1s.	0d.	to 1s.	6d.
Handkerchiefs Hemmed, ..	..	0s.	1d.	to 0s.	0d.
Veined Cambric do.	..	0s.	6d.	to 0s.	0d.
Chemises, ...	..	0s.	8d.	to 1s.	6d.
Petticoats, ...	..	0s.	10d.	to 1s.	4d.
Collars, ...	..	0s.	2d.	to 0s.	3d.

Table-cloths, Sheets, &c., Hemmed, at 1d. per Yard. Children's Clothes, and articles for export, made on the most reasonable terms.

Orders addressed to the Committee, House of Correction, or to Mrs. DUNDAS, Matron of the Work-Room, shall meet with prompt attention.   (511

BELFAST BAZAAR FOR THE RELIEF OF IRISH DESTITUTION.

THIS BAZAAR will be held in the LARGE ROOM of the COMMERCIAL BUILDINGS, and will open on MONDAY, the 5th of April, at TWELVE o'clock. The Bazaar will remain open, each day, from TWELVE o'clock till FIVE o'clock, P.M., and from SEVEN in the Evening, till NINE.

The price of admission, on the first day of opening, will be One Shilling in the Morning, and Sixpence in the Evening. On the succeeding days, the charges will be reduced to Sixpence in the Morning, and Threepence in the Evening. Children will be admitted at half-price ; and any ladies or gentlemen, purchasing tickets on a particular day, shall, for that day, be free to visit the Bazaar as often as they please.

It is almost unnecessary to add, that, in this case, tickets are not transferrable.

There will be a refreshment room in connection with the

Figure 5 *Belfast News-Letter*, 19 March 1847

BAZAAR FOR CONNAUGHT.

A SALE of LADIES' WORK, for the Benefit of
the FAMISHING POOR in CONNAUGHT,
will be held in the MUSIC HALL, on TUESDAY, 22d,
and WEDNESDAY, 23d of December.

Hours of Sale, each day, from ELEVEN till FOUR,
and from SEVEN till NINE, Evening.

Tickets of Admission (to be had at the door), 6d;
Children, Half Price.   Evening Admission, 3d each.

PATRONESSES.

The Marchioness of LONDONDERRY.
The Countess of ANNESLEY.

VICE-PATRONESSES.

The Misses Sharman Craw- | Mrs. Halliday, Clifden.
ford, Crawfordsburn. | Mrs. Mulholland,   Mount
The Misses Montgomery, | Collyer.
Wellington Place.

COMMITTEE.

Miss Allen	Mrs Moore
Mrs Arrott	Mrs Morgan
Mrs Barlow	Miss Montgomery
Mrs Bellis	Mrs Murphy, *Glengall place*
Mrs Byrtt	Mrs J Murphy
Miss Campbell	Mrs William Murray
Mrs Edward H Clarke	Mrs J Murray
Miss Cochrane	Mrs M'Comb
Mrs Cooke	Mrs M'Clure
Mrs Crawford	Mrs M'Entire
The Misses Cullimore	Mrs M'Kenzie
Mrs Dr Dill	Mrs R Orr
Mrs Edgar	Mrs Owden, *Brooklands*
Mrs Gibson	Miss Pollock
Mrs Hanna	Mrs T Porter
Mrs D Hamilton	Mrs Henry Purdon
Mrs W Hamilton	Miss Rea
Miss E Hamilton	Mrs Doctor Read
Mrs Hart	Mrs Reid
Mrs Heron	Mrs J Grubb Richardson
Miss Heron	Mrs Shaw
Mrs J A Henderson	Mrs Sinclaire
Mrs Heyn	Mrs Robert Simms
Miss M Harper	Mrs Stewart
Miss Jamison	Mrs Sturrock
Miss M Jamison	Mrs Wm Suffern
Mrs P Johnston	Mrs Tomb
Mrs Killen	Mrs Toye
Mrs Kerr	Mrs Tucker
Mrs Lanyon	Mrs Wakefield
Miss Lunham	Mrs Weir
Mrs Macrory	Miss Wightman
Mrs Mackay	Mrs Alex Wilson, *Maryville*
Mrs Dr Marshall	Mrs Robert Wilson
Mrs Meneely	Mrs Wylie
Mrs Moon	

TREASURER.

Miss HAMILTON, Mount Vernon.

SECRETARIES.

Figure 6 *Belfast News-Letter*, 22 December 1846

neighbourhood of Belfast not less distressing than in any other part of Ireland.[27]

Aware of the potential damage to any future subscriptions, the committee issued a rejection of such claims. To reinforce its policy of providing aid to every necessitous area, £100 was allocated to the Ballymacarrett Relief Committee on 10 February, which was part of a total of £445 disbursed to 27 districts on that day.[28] A fortnight later, the Fund gave the Belfast Local Relief Committee £1,000 in support of the soup kitchens in the town.[29] As local distress became more evident, demands on the resources of the Belfast Relief Fund increased. On 22 February, the Belfast Ladies Society for the Relief of Local Distress announced its intention to apply to the Fund for a grant to supply food to children in its proposed industrial schools. Consideration of the application was postponed while the committee monitored the effects of the recently introduced Temporary Relief Act on the Belfast Union.[30]

The new legislation allowed for the provision of outdoor relief in the form of free food, generally soup, in each Poor Law Union. It was the most liberal relief measure introduced by the British government, although from the outset it was regarded as a short-term measure, until more permanent modifications could be made to the existing Poor Law. Its implementation, however, was not compulsory. Out of the 130 Poor Law Unions in Ireland, Belfast was one of three which chose not to implement the new legislation, thus avoiding the administrative expenses entailed.[31] In general, the measure was widely adopted and by July 1847, over 3 million people were receiving free rations of soup daily at government soup kitchens located throughout Ireland. The measure proved to be both effective and economical as a way of providing relief in the Unions where it was introduced.[32] The success of this relief measure led some of the subscribers to the Relief Fund to argue that there was now less need to support distant areas. Instead, they argued, the destitute of Belfast should become the main focus of the Fund's resources, especially as the Temporary Relief Act had not been introduced into the Union. This proposition was not unanimous, the objectors including the rector of Christ Church and one of the joint secretaries of the Fund, the Rev. Thomas Drew. In arguing that it would be wrong to withhold money from the poor of the west and south, Drew stated that the committee would be perpetrating 'a great injustice'. He argued that if the subscribers had been aware that only Belfast were to benefit 'the magnificent sum of £7,000 would never have been collected'.[33]

Drew's comments were criticized also, with the *Northern Whig* in particular defending the claims of Belfast's poor. In its edition of 23 March, it referred to 'the absurdity and mischievousness of

the Drew policy', adding that 'our own poor have the first claim'.
Moreover, the paper claimed that there was an 'anti-Belfast
principle' evident among 'a considerable number' of the
membership of the General Fund. It estimated that more than
one-third of all paupers in the Union workhouse and fever hospital
were from other counties. Consequently, such areas were already
receiving Belfast's hospitality and there was thus no need to send
any further aid to claimants outside the town.[34] As Edgar pointed
out, if distress in Belfast was increasing, conditions in the more
isolated parts of the country would be far worse.[35]

The ire of the *Whig* was increased by the decision of the
committee on 30 March to refuse funding to the Belfast Ladies'
Society. This decision led to a vitriolic personal attack on Drew,
with the *Whig* referring to him as 'contemptible' and alleging that
'as far as Belfast is concerned, the committee is an obstacle to
humane exertion'. The paper also described how:

> The widowed mother of five pale orphans who has still too
> much pride to beg for them, and is yet too weak to work, blesses
> the good and kind-hearted gentlemen who have shut their eyes
> to her misery but opened them wide to the hearsay desolation
> of a family in Bantry or in the Glenties![36]

Whether or not it was influenced by such adverse publicity, the
committee agreed after 'much discussion' to donate £100 to the
Ladies' Society in aid of their industrial schools.[37]

Despite such public criticisms, the General Fund continued to
provide extensive aid. By early April, every county with the
exception of Louth had applied for assistance, with each area
providing horrific details of desolation and hunger. Considerable
amounts of aid also continued to be distributed within Belfast.
The Fund donated £250 to the proposed Day Asylum and £50
to the Destitute Sick Society. It also supported the Belfast soup
kitchens with its single largest allocation of £1,000 when the
income of the kitchens was described as being 'exhausted'.[38]
Additionally, grants were given to relief committees in Ballyhackamore, Ballymacarrett and Ballynafeigh. Furthermore, immediate
funding had been supplied to aid emigrants aboard the *Swatara*.
A sum of £120 was granted for this purpose.[39]

The Fund also provided relief to paupers who had been
removed to the Belfast Union from England and Scotland.
Although these paupers were legally entitled to receive relief from
the workhouse, a number of charities used a portion of their funds
to provide them with assistance. In total, the committee granted
£900 in five grants. They did this in the belief that the alternative
was for these 'strange paupers' to become 'a burden on the
community'. The paupers were given food for a short time and

then they were forwarded to their native Unions. The Ulster Railway agreed to take them as far as the line extended for a reduced fare. As the following table demonstrates, the paupers who were left by the British Poor Law authorities in Belfast came from all parts of the country. Although the vast majority were of Ulster origin, a high percentage also came from western counties.

Removal of Paupers from Belfast Union[40]

Co. of Origin	Grants for Removal (£s)
Antrim	3,789
Armagh	145
Carlow	35
Cavan	30
Clare	70
Cork	385
Derry	80
Donegal	360
Down	285
Fermanagh	65
Galway	105
Kerry	230
King's County (Offaly)	20
Leitrim	40
Limerick	205
Longford	10
Mayo	245
Meath	20
Monaghan	35
Queen's County (Laois)	55
Roscommon	105
Sligo	95
Tipperary	90
Tyrone	145
Waterford	65
Wexford	15
Wicklow	10

On 12 May 1847, although fever and distress were increasing in and around Belfast, the committee of the General Fund held its final meeting and announced that its relief operations were to cease. At this stage, donations to the Fund had reached £7,165 17s 11d. Four closing grants were made to relief committees in counties Clare, Cork and Mayo. The residual capital was retained as a reserve fund, to be used in cases of emergency in Belfast. During its brief existence, the Belfast General Relief Fund had distributed 206 separate donations. Every county in Connacht, Munster and Ulster had received aid from it, as had six counties in Leinster. Outside Belfast, the greatest beneficiary was County Cork which had received 30 individual grants totalling £382.

Palpably, the town of Belfast had gained considerably from the Fund, obtaining over £3,000 in grants, contrary to the criticisms voiced by the *Northern Whig*.[41] The number of grants provided was an indication of the extraordinary demands being placed on the charitable organizations within Belfast which were unable to be met by traditional means.

Women and Philanthropy

The contribution of women to private philanthropy was widely commended. Although middle-class women were excluded from most positions of responsibility, charitable work was deemed to be fitting employment for them. In Belfast, women played a significant role in philanthropic relief. On 1 January 1847, the Belfast Ladies' Association for the Relief of Irish Destitution was founded by members of the Ladies of the First and Second Unitarian Congregations. They hoped 'to sink all doctrinal distinctions ... for the one benevolent purpose of alleviating distress and preventing starvation without considering the religious denomination of those who are to be relieved'.[42] The new committee was comprised of 115 women from various Belfast Churches. Many of its supporters were also connected with the Ladies' Anti-Slavery Society. One of the most esteemed members of the Association was Mary McCracken, who was aged 77. Her family history was distinguished; her grandfather had founded the *Belfast News-Letter* in 1737 and her brother, Henry Joy McCracken, had been hanged for his role in the 1798 uprising. Throughout her life, Mary had been involved in a range of social issues and she was an advocate of preserving the Irish language and Irish cultural traditions.[43]

The association was divided into a number of sub-committees, including the Corresponding Committee, whose role was publicity and appealing for donations; the Industrial Committee, which was to procure and distribute materials for employment; the Clothing Committee, which collected and gave out clothing and blankets; and the Collecting Committee, which was to seek subscriptions in and around Belfast.[44] The work of the Belfast Ladies' Association impressed Asenath Nicholson, an American evangelist who toured Ireland in 1847. She praised the women's philanthropic activities, saying that they were:

> Not in the least like the women of Dublin, who sheltered themselves behind their old societies – most of them excusing themselves from personal labour, feeling that a few visits to the abodes of the poor were too shocking for female delicacy to sustain ... Yet much was given in Dublin; for it is a city celebrated for its benevolence, and deservedly so, as far as giving

state, that as the remaining stock will then be unpacked, they will be happy to see any of their friends, who may be disposed to purchase, To-DAY and TO-MORROW (29th and 30th), at the LOWER SCHOOL-ROOM, FISHERWICK PLACE, from Twelve till Four o'clock.   (173

Entrance from Queen Street.

BELFAST LADIES' ASSOCIATION

FOR

THE RELIEF OF IRISH DESTITUTION.

IT is proposed to hold a BAZAAR of LADIES' WORK, in Belfast, at Easter, commencing on EASTER MONDAY, in aid of the funds of the above Association, and all who take an interest in the cause of the suffering poor of our land will, it is hoped, contribute, to the utmost of their ability, to this object. It is feared, that want and destitution will be felt in the Spring and Summer, even more than at present; and surely none will hold back in this good work, but all will encourage the Committee in their attempt to relieve, as far as possible, those who are bowed down by the heavy hand of famine.

Particulars, as to the place of holding the Bazaar, &c., will be given in a future advertisement; meantime, all contributions of work will be received by the Treasurers and Secretaries, to whom it is requested they will be forwarded, on or before SATURDAY, the 27th of March.

TREASURERS.—Mrs. J. Andrews, 60, Donegall-Street; Mrs. J. S. Porter, 16, College-Square; Mrs. J. T. Tennent, Hazelbank.

SECRETARIES.—Mrs. D. L. Boyd, 7, Chichester-Street; Miss Murney, 18, High-Street; Miss M'Dowell, 35, Arthur-Street.

25th Jan., 1847.   (171

CONCERT

IN AID OF THE FUNDS OF

THE BELFAST RELIEF COMMITTEE.

THE COMMITTEE of the BELFAST CHORAL SOCIETY, having taken into consideration the present distressed state of the poor, have decided on giving a

CONCERT OF SACRED MUSIC

Figure 7 *Belfast News-Letter*, 29 January 1847

goes. But giving and doing are antipodes in her who has never been trained to domestic duties.[45]

The Ladies' Association also provided meals to poor emigrants who passed through Belfast.[46] A number of the children who received their bounty were in such an advanced stage of hunger that the food led to 'sickness and loathing during several successive days'.[47] The Association did not restrict its charity to any particular locality and it received applications from as far away as Thurles in County Tipperary, and as close as Ballyhackamore in east Belfast. The majority of its work was directed towards areas along the western seaboards, particularly in County Donegal.[48] In recognition of the increasing levels of distress within Belfast, a separate Ladies' Committee was established in February 1847, which confined its charity to the destitute within the town.[49]

The Ladies' Association provided relief in money, food and clothing. As the following table demonstrates, the Association received considerable resources from England.

Donations of Clothing to The Ladies' Association[50]

Area	No. of garments
Darlington/Staindrop	544
Carlisle	1,372
Newcastle upon Tyne	718
Leicester	650
Birmingham	210
Worcester	40
Darlington	65
Walsall	134

The work of the Association was aided by a number of shipowners agreeing to transport goods to Ireland free of charge, while the owners of the Dublin and Derry steam packets and the Ulster Railway then redistributed them at no charge within Ireland.[51]

In addition to providing relief, the Association believed that they had a duty to promote industrial endeavour amongst the poor, most especially women. They supplied many of their beneficiaries with flax and coarse woollens which were made into garments for sale. As the following communication demonstrates, the demand for this form of relief amongst poor women was high:

The employment which we have been giving consisted of spinning and knitting woollen yarn. For single thread, to be woven into cloth, we give four pence per pound; for twined, suited for knitting, six pence; and for knitting a pair of socks, five pence. From the numbers applying we were seldom able to give more than two pounds of wool or two pairs of socks to each person weekly, so that from eight pence to one shilling is the largest sum any one can earn in that time.[52]

In Belfast they viewed their endeavours as being particularly important because, as a consequence of the trade depression:

Many respectable women and girls are rapidly sinking into destitution from low wages, want of employment and the high price of food; their decent raiment is passing to the pawn shops and, they themselves, daily adding to the squalid wretchedness of our streets.

They believed that the type of gratuitous relief available at the soup kitchens was ideologically flawed as it would reduce the women to hopeless idleness. Instead, the Association preferred to give relief which would 'improve them in habits of self-helpfulness and industry'.[53]

The aims of the Ladies' Association were assisted by the establishment of the Irish Work Society in England. This group, whose patrons included the Duchess of Gloucester and the Lord Lieutenant of Ireland, raised its funds amongst the aristocracy. Its first subscription amounted to £630. The Work Society also provided an outlet for the sale of the goods produced by the poor in Ireland. To this end, it obtained orders for work in England, sent patterns and instructions for such work to Ireland and, when the work was completed, arranged for its sale in London.[54] These activities complemented the work that was being undertaken by the Ladies' Association in Belfast. The centrepiece of the activities occurred in April 1847. On Easter Monday, the Ladies' Association organized a bazaar in the Commercial Buildings at which clothes were sold. All profits were ploughed back into further relief provision. The close ties between the Ladies' Association and the Anti-Slavery organization were emphasized by the advice of the former who urged the latter 'to forego their annual subscriptions and instead purchase work at the bazaar'. The event was successful and raised £883 for the Association which meant that, in total, the Ladies' Association raised over £2,000.[55] By autumn 1847, its funds were exhausted and much of the support for charitable bodies had evaporated. The reduction in subscriptions was linked to the government's declaration that the Famine was 'over', following the harvest of that year. Nevertheless, the committee of the Ladies' Association, convinced of the value of the relief which they had provided, appealed to the British Treasury for financial support in order to continue their activities. This request was refused on the grounds that such intervention was beyond the scope of the government. As a consequence, the Ladies' Association ended most of its activities.[56]

The Belfast Ladies' Society for the Relief of Local Distress was established in recognition of the necessity for private charity within the town. Like the larger Ladies' Association, the Belfast Society concentrated its efforts on women and tied relief in with the provision of education or employment. The committee was soon divided, however, over the involvement of the National Board of Education in the provision of non-denominational schooling. The Board of Education, which had been established in 1831, was a non-sectarian body. In April 1847, the Belfast Ladies' Society decided to place their industrial school under the charge of the Board, which meant that it would pay all teachers' salaries. This decision caused dissent within the Ladies' Society with 49 voting in favour and 14 against. The latter group was opposed to mixed education and in protest at the decision, all of the Anglican members of the committee resigned. As a consequence, the work of the group was much reduced.[57] The Belfast Ladies' Industrial Association for Connaught, which provided employment in Connaught, continued to operate beyond 1847. In May 1848, the body sought a grant from the Society of Friends to establish further industrial schools in Connaught. The Quakers agreed to issue a grant of £500 if this amount could be matched from other sources. The grant was released in December.[58] Overall, the contribution of the various Ladies' Associations, although short-lived, was valuable in providing not only food but also clothing to the poor. In keeping with prevailing attitudes towards the provision of charity, relief and self-improvement were closely linked.

'Thorough Evangelization'

The second, more devastating failure of the potato crop in 1846 presented an opportunity for renewed efforts to proselytize. The resultant hunger and starvation of thousands of Catholics in the west appeared to provide the means of winning more converts. The campaign was helped by the fact that the failure of the potato crop was viewed through a providentialist lens and was blamed on the false religion of the peasantry of Ireland.[59] This interpretation was supported in Britain where:

> [a] vast institutional and ideological machinery lay behind the drive to make Ireland a Protestant country. This included not only a massive system of private philanthropy which had been in operation since the early century, but, more importantly, a fully developed political doctrine rooted in the belief that the

source of Ireland's social and political problems was the Catholic religion, and that the country would never be prosperous and developed until Catholicism and all its influences were eradicated.[60]

It also found favour amongst leading officials within the British government – including Charles Wood, the Chancellor of the Exchequer, and the Secretary at the Treasury, Charles Trevelyan, who together controlled the release of government finances. These men were Protestant evangelicals who viewed the Famine as a providentialist judgment.[61] As a consequence, following the second potato blight, 'proselytizing efforts redoubled, for many evangelicals saw the catastrophe as a providential opportunity ... to rescue the people from the darkness of popery and priestcraft'.[62]

The fact that the impact of the Famine appeared to be less severe in parts of Ulster was also explained in religious terms. In July 1847, the General Assembly of the Presbyterian Church in Ireland wrote to their sister organization in the United States:

> We are grateful to Almighty God while we humbly regard it as an illustration of the industry and general comfort promoted by our beloved Church, that in Ulster, where our principles are most widely disseminated, the visitation has appeared in a much less aggravated form than in those provinces in which the Romish system still, unhappily, maintains its degrading and paralyzing ascendancy.[63]

Within Ireland, a number of Protestant ministers saw the distress in the west of the country as an opportunity to revitalize their earlier proselytizing campaign. Since the 1820s, there had been a growth in proselytizing activity within Ireland, largely in response to the threat posed by the increasing power of the Catholic middle classes and the Catholic Church. The resultant mass conversions peaked in 1826–27, thus earning the sobriquet the 'Second Reformation'.[64] Although the number of converts to Protestantism declined after 1827, the granting of Catholic Emancipation in 1829 provided the evangelical movement with a fresh intensity and purpose. The resultant period of renewed activity was followed by the establishment of a number of Protestant 'mission' stations throughout Ireland. The most famous ones were established in Dingle in 1831 and Achill in 1834, both by members of the evangelical section of the Church of Ireland.[65] In Ulster, a number of Protestant ministers viewed the religious crusade to win the souls of Catholics as an integral part of their duties. In this endeavour, they had the support of several influential evangelical lay preachers including Lord Roden from County Down, the Duke of Manchester, who owned estates in

Armagh, and Lord Farnham from County Cavan. Each of these men undertook evangelical tours of the west in support of the Protestant missions in the 1830s and 1840s.[66] The Presbyterian Church was particularly active in attempting to establish missions in the west of the country. The most active proselytizer from Belfast was the Rev. Edgar, a minister and Professor of Divinity in the Royal College in Belfast. Edgar had strong links with the Presbyterian Church in Scotland, which formed a number of 'Ladies' Associations on Behalf of the Presbyterian Church in Ireland' in 1841. The principal societies were in Glasgow, Edinburgh, Aberdeen and Dundee.[67] The Dundee Association stated that its objective was:

> To aid the Home Mission of the Presbyterian Church in the evangelization of Ireland. This is proposed to be done by diffusing information, endeavouring to excite sympathy and promoting a spirit of prayer, especially on behalf of the Roman Catholic population of Ireland.[68]

Despite external support, the Presbyterian Mission felt that it was not progressing as quickly as it had hoped. By the end of 1846, Edgar and his followers had organized 144 schools in counties Mayo and Sligo, but progress elsewhere had been slow. The reappearance of the potato blight in 1846, therefore, was regarded as a God-given opportunity to win converts in the west of the country. In order to maximize the activities of the Presbyterian missions during the period of food shortages, Edgar appealed to the Free Church in Scotland, requesting that they send some of their ministers to visit those districts 'which God, in his providence, had so wonderfully opened up to their Evangelistic labours'.[69] The Free Church in Scotland was also receptive to providing support in Ireland. At a meeting of the Scottish Synod in 1847, a report was read which stated:

> the God who brings order out of confusion and light out of darkness, has over-ruled the famine in Ireland to open up Ireland for Protestant missions. The Protestant scripture reader is everywhere welcome; the Protestant missionary is respected and loved ... the same Roman Catholic people who heard a Presbyterian Missionary denounced by the Priests on the Sabbath, carried him in triumph on their shoulders before the week had closed.[70]

The Synod in Perth also interpreted the crisis in Ireland through a providentialist prism. They reported that in Ireland 'the late famine and its attendant results' had created an opening for all Protestant Churches, adding:

The recent awful calamity and famine which has overtaken Ireland and more especially the fact that this calamity has fallen upon the poorest, appeared to be God's way for preparing the hearts for the reception of the truth. The people are now alive to the selfishness of their priests; and instead of looking upon Protestants as their enemies, they now regard them as their friends.[71]

Further support was also provided by the Scottish Association, which reported:

A door of entrance to the native Irish has been opened up, so wide and effectual that scarcely is there a cabin in the country districts or a town or a village, to which the pure waters of the river of life might not be freely carried – if only the means of doing so were provided.[72]

Similar sentiments were voiced publicly by other Presbyterian ministers. In May 1847, the *Belfast News-Letter* published a letter from Robert Gault, a Presbyterian minister based in Balderg in County Mayo. He appealed for support from Presbyterians in Ulster claiming that 'The whole land is opened before us, if we had only the courage to colonize and the heart to seek its thorough evangelicization'.[73]

Charity and Conversion

A charitable organization whose activities were overshadowed by accusations of covert proselytism was the Belfast Ladies' Relief Association for Connaught. The origins of this body lay in the publication of a letter entitled 'Famine in Connaught' in the *Banner of Ulster* on 18 September 1846. The letter was written by the Presbyterian minister, the Rev. Edgar, who was involved in attempting to establish missions in the west. Edgar detailed the deprivation resulting from the loss of the potato crop in the west. He also appealed for aid 'in the name of the famishing'.[74] Such was the impact of his correspondence that Edgar was asked to give an account of his experiences to the congregation at May Street Presbyterian Church. In the course of his lecture, he proclaimed: 'Our brother is starving and till we have satisfied his hunger, we have no time to enquire whether he is Protestant or Catholic.'[75]

The outcome of Edgar's appeal was that a number of females in the audience, who 'impressed by the terrible calamity of their country, and desirous of doing what they could for the perishing, resolved to work with their own hands, that they might be able to give to those in need'.[76] In order to achieve these aims, the women formed the Belfast Ladies' Relief Association for Connaught with

a committee of 72 women. The committee immediately started to
fund-raise and within a few weeks, it had received over £750.[77]
The majority of the subscriptions were donated in Belfast,
although a significant number came from other parts of Ulster and
from Presbyterians overseas. External subscriptions included one
from the Islington Presbyterian Church in Liverpool of £200 and
£340 from New York.[78]

To raise additional funds, the committee decided to hold a
bazaar on 21 December 1846. Its success was helped by the
contribution of paintings from an artist based in London.[79] The
event raised over £650 which, together with other subscriptions,
was used to purchase food. However, one of the stipulations of the
Association was that no aid was to be granted to relief committees
or soup kitchens which were based in towns, on the grounds that
'secluded rural districts are more likely to be neglected by public
charities'.[80] Accordingly, resources were distributed to remote
districts such as Mullaferry, Spiddal, the Arran islands, Erris and
Ballymote.[81]

Despite its religious origins, the Association claimed to have a
non-denominational approach to the provision of relief. The
committee made a number of public statements in which it
outlined its rules of operation:

> The principle which from the first has been strictly adhered to
> in distributing aid is that no distinction be made on the ground
> of religious creed or connection; but that to the hungry of every
> sect and every church, food should be freely given.[82]

However, a letter from an unnamed Catholic priest of Down
and Connor to Archbishop MacHale of Tuam, which was
published in the *Belfast Vindicator*, cast doubt on the non-sectarian
approach of the body. The writer alleged that Dr Edgar's interest
in Connacht was to 'spread the doctrine of Presbyterianism among
Catholics of this country'. He further claimed that while Edgar
appeared to be 'on a mission of purest charity', this assertion was
only true on the 'surface'. 'Whilst he [Edgar] pretended to busy
himself with the temporal wants of the Catholics of the west, he
was providing a rich spiritual riposte for the Presbyterians of the
North.' As evidence of Edgar's true purpose, the writer quoted
from *The Trials and Triumphs of the Home Mission*, a pamphlet
written by Edgar which had alleged:

> We can have, however, no proper idea of the hold which popery
> has on the Irish heart unless we understand how entirely it is
> enslaved by SUPERSTITION. What folly can a poor, super-
> stitious Papist not be made by his priest to believe? Some believe
> that the seals along the shore are animated by the spirits of their

ancestors; some, that when a man offers to become a convert, all the Roman Catholic blood is drained out of him and Protestant blood poured in; and some, that the priest can punish the disobedient by changing them into goats, hares or asses.[83]

The *Belfast Vindicator* entered the dispute by expressing the hope that no man, more especially 'a minister of religion ... [would] stoop to means so unworthy and dishonorable for destroying the character of his fellow-Christians and fellow-countrymen'.[84] The assertions against Edgar were based on the fact that in the autumn of 1846, he visited Connacht for the purpose of inspecting the Presbyterian Mission schools which had been established in an attempt to gain converts from Catholicism to Presbyterianism.[85] In their zeal to obtain converts, evangelical Presbyterians in Belfast, through the medium of the Ladies' Association, used charity to gain what had previously proved to be elusive.

The activities of Edgar and his followers were condemned by the Dublin newspaper, the *Freeman's Journal* in the autumn of 1847, following the closure of the soup kitchens. In a scathing editorial, they claimed that:

the stoppage of all government relief was the signal for a general attack on the consciences of the poor. The agents of the charitable associations, who hitherto appeared as angels of light, no sooner got the field of destitution to themselves than they opened a slave market of immortal souls and held up, to tempt the passions of ravening hunger, the mess of pottage, which was only to be obtained at the price of what the poor, sorely tried creatures believed to be truth, on the profession of which their eternal salvation depended. The guilty agents in this immoral traffic are ... emissaries from the Exeter Hall Society, the Orphan Association, and the Belfast Society for the Relief of Distress in Connaught.[86]

Much of the conversion work was provided under the guise of education. In the spring of 1847, the period when the government soup kitchens became operative, the Ladies' Association decided to stop issuing money for the purchase of food but to initiate a system of schooling in order to provide for the long-term welfare of Connacht. The Belfast Presbyterian churches, through the involvement of the Rev. Edgar, were closely involved with this scheme. In total, in their main year of activity, 1847, the Belfast Ladies' Society for the Relief of Distress in Connaught raised over £15,000. As a consequence, between 1847 and 1849, 32 schoolmistresses were dispatched to the province to establish industrial schools for women and girls. The setting-up of the schools was helped by the donation of grants from the Society of Friends in Dublin.[87]

The extent to which their funds enabled the churches to infiltrate Catholic strongholds in the west may be gauged by the anxiety of a priest from Ballycastle, in County Mayo. In a communication with Archbishop Murray of Dublin in June 1848, he pleaded for some assistance to enable him to 'counteract the efforts being made to proselytize my parishioners'. He continued:

> There were last year waste lands in my parish – the Presbyterian minister and many others connected with the Belfast societies have brought a great part of the said land and intend to form a colony here. They have money in abundance and many hearers on Sundays for the sake of getting meal and money.[88]

The centrepiece of the educational system established by the Ladies' Association was the use of the Bible. Many of the Bibles were supplied by the Hibernian Bible Society, an overtly proselytizing agency, which had been seeking converts in the west since the beginning of the century. As the Rev. Edgar remarked: 'The system aims to improve by industry the temporal condition of the poor females and similarly by the truth of the Bible, the spiritual condition.' Edgar also believed that much improvement was already evident through Bible education:

> Discipline has done much to effect the reform, example more, but most of all, the living truth of God. That truth, which was resisted by the pupils at first, is now, cheerfully committed to memory, deeply felt by some and highly prized.[89]

Edgar, however, believed that greater efforts were necessary and he exhorted his followers to make increased efforts at conversion on the grounds that:

> They are bigoted Romanists, you say, steeped in superstition, and the slaves of priestcraft. The more shame for us I reply, who have not exerted ourselves as we should to enlighten them and convert them to God; and the greater shame and the deeper disgrace will it be to us still if we do not embrace the opportunities which Connaught is offering now; for its people are as accessible as spiritual fields white to harvest.[90]

One of the major successes of Edgar's missionary activity was the enlistment of a former Catholic and native Irish speaker, Michael Brannigan, who was ordained by the Presbytery of Tyrone as a missionary. In 1845, when he travelled to the west, 'his addresses in the native tongue awakened much attention'.[91] Brannigan was put in charge of a number of mission schools in County Mayo, where each child was provided with half a pound of meal a day, supplied by the British Relief Association. The Bible was also read throughout the course of the day. Due to a lack of funds, the provision of free food was ended in August 1848. The consequence was an immediate reduction in the attendance at the schools. In December 1847, there were 1,000 pupils in the twelve schools under his care. A year later, although the number of schools had increased to 28, the number of pupils had only grown to 1,120. Brannigan explained this as being due to the fact that the lack of food had forced the children to seek relief in the workhouses. He was dismissive of the people who 'were so uncharitable as to conclude that it was the food, and not the Bible, that the children loved'.[92] Brannigan believed that although the workhouse gave the children refuge, it denied their spiritual needs.

> they are not happy in that place of confinement – they have no Bibles there – no catechism except the one belonging to the Church of Rome ... and instead of sitting under the joyful sound of the Gospel, they are obliged to kneel before a Popish altar, and listen to the mummeries of a Latin Mass.[93]

Brannigan's appeal for additional support was published in the Belfast press. He emphasized that support was necessary so that the children would not have to go into the workhouse where they would be 'trained up in degrading subjugation to the priest'.[94]

If Edgar and the Belfast Ladies' Relief Association for Connaught were accused of covertly using relief as a mechanism for winning converts to Protestantism, at the beginning of 1847 an organization was founded which did not attempt to disguise its proselytizing ambitions. 'The Fund for the Temporal Relief of the Suffering Poor of Ireland through the Instrumentality of the Clergy of the Established Church' was established in the first week of January 1847. The committee consisted of twelve men, including Thomas Drew, the evangelical preacher, the Rev. William M'Ilwaine, and the senior medical practitioner, Dr Purden. The committee declared that its origin lay in the fact that:

> Numerous and heartrending appeals for assistance have reached the clergy of the Established Church resident in Belfast and its neighbourhood, from the suffering brother ministers in the south and west whose houses are daily besieged by crowds of starving claimants for relief.[95]

The aim of the Temporal Fund was to obtain and distribute funds in order to feed the suffering poor. It also viewed its purpose as being to offer spiritual succour to the distressed people 'in order that advantage may be taken of these providential circumstances'.[96] The committee of the Fund explained:

in numerous cases an opening has been made for conveying the light of the Gospel into the darkened mind of the Roman Catholic peasantry thus severely suffering; they have listened with the deepest attention to the ministers of the church proclaiming the way of salvation while humanely engaged in efforts to rescue their bodies from famine and disease. A wide and effectual door is thus thrown open to our brethren in the hitherto benighted parts of Ireland.[97]

None the less, the religious objectives of the Temporal Fund were greeted by a barrage of criticism in the local press. The *Banner of Ulster* accused it of having introduced 'a spirit of sectarianism' into the provision of relief, adding:

At a time when such frightful destitution is prevalent, it is surely most unwise to put forth denominational peculiarities in such an offensive form and thus to give the impression that proselytism is to be the basis of charity. We regret this movement all the more as it is likely to interfere with the other efforts made in the cause and to add to the existing calamity, the element of religious animosity.[98]

The *Northern Whig* was also unequivocal in its condemnation, describing the Fund as 'the most revolting record we have yet met connected with the visitation'. The paper recommended that the citizens of Belfast would ensure its swift demise on the grounds that:

It will be a woeful thing if even the open and common field of charity, benevolence and love, be converted into an arena for sectarian conflict. But this will not be permitted in Belfast. People here are deeply impressed with the sacred duty of endeavouring to guard their unfortunate fellows from starvation, and they will, on such occasion, sink or put down party feeling, the operations of which, whether they proceeded from political difference or religious distinctions, would be alike misplaced and, as we believe, sinful.[99]

The most vigorous opposition to the Temporal Fund came from the Catholic community. The *Belfast Vindicator* castigated what it described as the 'tithe-fed soul hunters who throw the poison of their bigotry into the fountains of public charity'. The paper urged the clergy of the Established Church to disregard the Fund and to donate their income derived from the tithe to the poor, adding:

The reverend bigots of Belfast cannot direct the current stream into which the humane are pouring their directions; they resolve, therefore, to direct the fountains that feed it into other channels.

What the public of this town reach to the destitute without distinction of creed, the clergy would grasp at and withhold until the victim pledged his immortal soul for a morsel of bread.[100]

The conduct of the Temporal Fund also drew comment from newspapers in Dublin. The *Dublin Evening Packet*, for example, declared the fund to have been established by a 'knot of Belfast fanatics'.[101] More emphatically the Belfast Repeal Club declared the clergymen associated with the fund to be 'fiends of hell'.[102] Even the Anglican Archbishop of Dublin, Richard Whately, publicly denounced the Belfast clerics, proclaiming:

all the grace of charitable action is destroyed if we present ourselves as seeking to take an ungenerous advantage of misery and convert our benefactions into a bribe to induce men to do violence to their consciences.[103]

In spite of such opposition, on 2 February 1847, the Temporal Fund was able to report that it had extended relief to twelve parishes where 'in nine cases out of ten the sufferers are our poor Romanist fellow-countrymen'.[104] One correspondent stated that 'every door is now thrown open to us' and urged ever greater assistance: 'I do believe that if the north would only advise and send us aid, temporal and spiritual, popery would, in these quarters, be shattered to her very centre.' Similar sentiments were forthcoming from County Kerry, where one supporter, whilst displaying his joy at the success, explained:

In the midst of this temporal distress, God is preparing the hearts of the people to receive His precious word. There is a general desire on the part of the poor creatures to attend scriptural instruction ... so that while the poor body is hungering for the bread of life that perisheth, the soul is hungering for that bread which endureth everlasting life ... Persecution has ceased and priestly influence is scarcely felt. It is a wonderful change in three months and the Lord has done it'.[105]

Given their success, the committee of the Temporal Fund felt justified in rebuffing an appeal from the Belfast General Fund to combine resources and create one large fund for relief 'without distinction of sect or party'.[106] By 16 March, they had received subscriptions totalling almost £2,000, the majority of which originated in England, both from individuals and church congregations. Thus they were enabled to make 108 donations of which, as the following table demonstrates, almost half were given to Munster, although every county in Connacht and Ulster also received funding.[107]

Grants Provided by the Temporal Fund to 16 March 1847

Munster		Connacht	
Cork	30	Galway	5
Tipperary	7	Leitrim	2
Limerick	5	Mayo	8
Kerry	4	Roscommon	6
Waterford	3	Sligo	2
Clare	2		
Total	51		23
Leinster		**Ulster**	
Queens	5	Antrim	2
Longford	2	Armagh	1
		Cavan	1
		Derry	1
		Donegal	10
		Down	2
		Fermanagh	4
		Monaghan	1
		Tyrone	5
Total	7		27

Source: *Belfast News-Letter*, 16 March 1847.

The Bible and Protestant Dominion

The early association of private charity with proselytism cast a shadow over the efforts of other private charitable endeavours, especially organizations that originated in England or Belfast. It also provoked debate concerning the role of private charity, even about those bodies that did not engage in proselytizing. The proselytism set in motion in response to the hunger of the people did not disappear as the condition of the poor began to improve. A number of people who had been involved in the provision of Famine relief used their expertise in the cause of conversion. The anti-Catholic dimension of proselytism was further inflamed by the concurrent increase in Protestant anger at the growth of Catholic political power. Hence, in March 1848, the Grand Orange Lodge cautioned:

> The present disorganized and deplorable state of Ireland can only be attributed to the base policy of statesmen who have treacherously betrayed the trust confided to them by Protestants, in granting unjustifiable concessions to Popery, and that no attempt to remedy existing evils will be successful until the Romish Emancipation Bill, the Maynooth Endowment Bill,

and all such measures are entirely repealed, and the Constitution restored to its original integrity.[108]

The efforts of Irish proselytizers were helped in 1849 by the founding of the Society for Irish Church Missions to Roman Catholics. Although its headquarters were in London, it had branches in Ireland. Helped by large donations from England, the Society provided proselytizers with a more organized and formal network of administrative support. By 1854, 125 separate mission stations had been formed in Ireland, with the west and southwest being particularly targeted.[109] The Belfast Anglican minister, the Rev. M'Ilwaine, declared that the principal aim of the Belfast association was 'to communicate through the medium of the Irish language the saving truths of the Gospel to the Irish speaking population of the country'.[110]

In 1848 Edgar also had decided that although the worst of the Famine appeared to be over, he and some of his followers should continue the work of the body but limit it to the field of 'industry and general reformation'. The Society of Friends agreed to give financial support for this activity. With this purpose in mind, Edgar sent 30 young women to supervise the schools in 'wild Connaught'. The two spheres of activity in the schools were knitting and the sewing of muslin. Within less than a year, there were 12,000 pupils attending these schools.[111] The finished articles were sold in British markets. By 1849, the Belfast Ladies' Society for the Relief of Distress in Connaught had become primarily an organization for proselytizing, under the direction of Dr Edgar.

In a letter to a Belfast newspaper, explaining his activities and calling for further support, Edgar explained that despite the success of the schools, they had encountered many difficulties, including:

> utter ignorance of order, punctuality, manufacture, or manu-facturing implements ... lying, thievish habits, dark houses unfit for work, irregularity of means of conveyance, ignorance of the English language – but, over and above all, the opposition, with a few exceptions, of the Romish priests, of which I could tell strange tales.[112]

The opposition of the priests was largely due to the fact that one of the rules of the schools was that the Bible had to be read daily, combined with other religious instruction by the teachers. Edgar described this approach as being based on the fact that:

> We embrace the opportunity of their being under the charge of our mistresses, of affording them all the advantages of the precept and example of Christian schoolmistresses, associated

with the enlightened devotional reading daily of a portion of
the Bible.

The *Banner of Ulster,* praising the exertions of Dr Edgar,
suggested that as a consequence of his labours, 'the morals and
social conditions of a great number of our people have been raised
from the lowest depths of misery and degradation to a very high
standard of excellence. Who can now say that the Irish people are
not eminently susceptible of improvement?'[113] At a paper
delivered to British Presbyterians in 1852, however, Edgar warned
of the threat which Catholicism continued to pose, not merely in
Ireland but further afield. He described to his audience the impact
of the influx of 'increasing swarms of illiterate, profligate Irish
Romanists' and went on to say:

> We have no serpents in our land but our Romish population,
> like fiery flying serpents are spreading over the face of other
> lands. Here are the headquarters of infection from which goes
> forth disease more fatal than cholera or plague. Here, the
> reckless spirits are trained who destroy the peace of Scotland,
> England and America; yet Maynooth produces more priests
> than Ireland needs and thus the public funds of Britain are
> employed in training agents for ill, ring-leaders in rebellion and
> riot in lands across the sea.[114]

As the Famine receded from Ireland, it was clear that proselytism
had taken firm root in a number of areas. Moreover, it had become
inextricably linked with periods of food shortages. Those who
accepted the food – usually soup – became known as 'soupers'.
They were frequently ostracized by their own community, and
sometimes denounced from the pulpit, especially as the Catholic
Church began to regroup when conditions in Ireland improved. In
some cases, British soldiers were deployed to protect the soupers
from the wrath of their former co-religionists.[115]

Whilst proselytism was mostly associated with the west of the
country, Catholics within Ulster were also vulnerable. In Belfast,
Catholicism was frequently combined with poverty, political
alienation and social dislocation, which made the need for religious
conversion appear particularly compelling to middle-class
Protestant evangelicals. Accordingly, the Belfast Religious Tract
Society had been founded in 1816 and in 1827, the Belfast Town
Mission was established. These bodies were most active in the
poorest districts of the town – the Protestant poor also being
viewed as a worthy target for spiritual regeneration. During the
Famine years, Church Missionary Societies opened food kitchens
throughout the north, including Holywood in the Belfast Union.
In these kitchens, the soup was made from meat, and it was

reported to be deliberately given out on Fridays, when Catholics were forbidden to consume meat.[116]

By 1851, the various proselytizers claimed to have converted 35,000 Catholics throughout Ireland during the previous five years. The actions and apparent success of the proselytizers caused anxiety within the Catholic Church. The Catholic Bishop of Down and Connor, Cornelius Denvir, was condemned by other members of his Church for not being more forceful in opposing proselytism in Belfast.[117] Overall, the struggle to win converts to Protestantism contributed to a deterioration in relations between Catholics and Protestants in Ireland, divisions which were further emphasized by the uprising in 1848 and the sectarian clash at Dolly's Brae in 1849.[118] From each of these encounters, Protestantism appeared to emerge triumphant. Moreover, because the vast majority of dead had been members of the Catholic Church, the Famine was presented as the judgment of God on a false religion. Increasingly also, the rural migrants to Belfast (the majority of whom were poor Catholics) transferred the religious tensions of the countryside to the town. Hence, proselytism and sectarianism proved to be mutually reinforcing, whilst they had both served to polarize existing denominational differences in Belfast. As one contemporary noted: 'the Bible, without note or comment, is not less a means of Protestant dominion than the Orange Yeoman's military array'.[119]

The legacy of proselytism was to damage the reputation of all Protestant Churches rather than just the small number of advocates who had been involved in such activities.[120] One of the main concerns of the Catholic hierarchy in the 1850s was the threat of proselytism and the decade was dominated by the struggle between Protestants and Catholics for the souls of the Irish population.[121] A consequence of such aggressive evangelization was to increase community discord in Belfast. In the wake of the Famine, a more militant form of Protestantism, which was overtly anti-Catholic, emerged in the town. Throughout the 1850s, the Rev. Drew made frequent appeals for the need for Protestants to maintain their distinct religious identity. To achieve this aim, he believed it was necessary for all Protestants to unite politically. In 1854, Drew was instrumental in founding the Christ Church Protestant Association, its purpose being:

> to regain all the ground lost by Protestantism since Catholic Emancipation. The Association supported not only the repeal of this act, but the withdrawal of Maynooth's grants, the abolition of nunneries and the dissolution of the national education board.[122]

In the decades following the Famine, religious and political affiliation became more inextricably linked in Belfast. Despite the passage of a Party Processions Act in 1850, violent clashes did not end. The extent of the antagonism was evident during sectarian fighting following the twelfth of July 1857. The riots were sparked by an anti-Catholic sermon preached by Rev. Drew, who had risen to be Grand Chaplain of the Orange Order. Significantly, the Commissioners of Inquiry appointed to enquire into the conflict included the full text of Drew's sermon in their evidence, drawing the special attention of the Lord Lieutenant to his inflammatory comments.[123] Yet, following this riot, Protestantism underwent a resurgence, associated with the Ulster evangelical revival of 1859.

The involvement of the Belfast proselytizers in relief provision during the late 1840s extended far beyond the boundaries of the town. The attempt by some charitable organizations to link relief with religious conversion served to intensify existing tensions both within the town and with other parts of the country. In Belfast, the legacy of inter-religious tensions inflamed by the proselytizers was to stretch long beyond the Famine years. Consequently, the role of the various charitable bodies in providing much-needed relief was often overshadowed by controversy. Unfortunately, the work of charitable bodies which did not attempt to proselytize was also regarded with suspicion, whilst their valuable role in saving lives was diminished. The result was to create a legacy of bitterness and division rather than one of appreciation.

CHAPTER 6

Conflict and Rebellion

The 1847 potato harvest was small but relatively free from blight. The harvest coincided with a significant shift in relief provision as the Irish Poor Law was made the main agency for government assistance. Many of the charitable organizations which had been formed a few months earlier ended their activities which meant that the Poor Law became the main refuge for the poor. Yet, the short-term involvement of some religious bodies in providing aid was to have a long-term impact. During 1847, private philanthropy had become identified with proselytism and had set in train a reinvigorated Protestant crusade which continued even after the need for relief had disappeared.[1] One legacy of famine proselytism was increased mistrust between the Catholic and Protestant Churches.

An attempted nationalist uprising in 1848 reinforced religious divisions. Ironically, the actions of the Young Irelander insurgents, who had argued for a non-sectarian approach to politics, precipitated a polarization in Irish politics, which was increasingly defined along religious lines. In the wake of the 1848 uprising, Protestantism emerged even more unified and the Orange Order positioned itself in the vanguard of the defence of both the Constitution and the Protestant Churches in Ireland. The backdrop to the political struggle was continued destitution in Belfast. Although some signs of economic recovery were apparent in the town, the imprint of the suffering was still evident in the continuing demands being made on the relief organizations. The nature of deprivation changed though, as overcrowding, lack of sanitation and disease replaced unemployment and hunger as the main causes of destitution. A further burden was placed on the provision of relief in Belfast by the removal of Irish paupers from Scotland and England to the Union. Despite protests from the town's authorities, the British government refused to change the legislation. The introduction of the Rate-in-Aid tax in 1849, which transferred the financial responsibility for relief to Irish ratepayers, led to further discord between the Ulster Unions and the British government. Yet, by 1850, Ulster Protestants were more firmly attached to the Union with Britain than they had been five years earlier. In Belfast in particular, political alliances became increasingly based on religious affiliations rather than on economic factors. The divisions, which had intensified during the Famine, changed Belfast society even as the worst effects of the catastrophe were beginning to subside in the town.

Rising to the Challenge. The Role of the Belfast Workhouse

In the harvest of 1848 blight reappeared in some parts of the west as virulently as in 1846. For the most part, the northeast was blight-free. In Belfast and its vicinity, the corn and potato crops were small but generally healthy. The general improvement in agricultural output contributed to a more general recovery of the local economy. This progress was in stark contrast to the situation in the west of the country where distress and mortality were increasing.[2] Yet growth within local industry proved to be slow. One of the consequences of the recent industrial slump was that less flax had been sown in 1848 than in the previous year – 53,868 acres compared with 58,312 in 1847.[3] The economic depression had combined with widespread political unrest in Europe to deprive Belfast of some of her usual markets. At the same time, the burden of poor rates had become heavier. These circumstances had, according to one Belfast newspaper, exhausted the 'energies and reserves' of local industrialists.[4] Consequently, emigration from Ulster had remained high.[5] Whilst the overall food supply was showing some small signs of improvement, the legacy of the previous three years was evident in the unhealthiness of many paupers and poor people. Increasingly, the Belfast workhouse was taking on the role of hospital and burial ground for paupers. In addition to providing relief and medical support for the native poor of Belfast, the workhouse was also continuing to have to cope with a stream of poor people from the surrounding countryside. Moreover, a continuing source of grievance for the Guardians was that they had to provide assistance to people who had been removed from Britain because they had not resided there for long enough to be eligible for poor relief.

An indication of the small but healthy potato harvest in the Belfast area in 1848 was apparent when a limited quantity of potatoes was reintroduced into the workhouses diet. At the beginning of August, the Guardians decided that 'the original allowance of potatoes for dinner be procured for the officers in place of bread as requested by them'.[6] The optimism that the crisis had passed did not last for long. On 11 October, the Guardians were warned by the Sanitary Committee that an outbreak of cholera was imminent and that they should arrange for the cleansing and whitewashing of the poorest areas of the town.[7] Although concerned about the expense of such measures, two wards were set aside in the Fever Hospital for the treatment of cholera patients.[8] The authorities believed that if an epidemic occurred, it would do so in the overcrowded and poorest districts of the town. Yet, inadvertently, the Guardians were fostering the conditions for just such an outbreak in some of their auxiliary buildings. On 25 November, Edward Senior visited the College Hospital, which housed 450 boys. He commented on the 'oppressive' atmosphere in and around the building, with little or no room for the inmates to walk or exercise and the yards liable to flooding in wet weather. He concluded that the site was 'dangerously overcrowded' and was, consequently, 'a most improper place for young boys'. Moreover, he warned that 'To allow them to remain there during the winter would entail most serious risk of contagious disease breaking out which ... with the whole body of inmates predisposed to receive it, would be extremely formidable.'[9]

Within a few weeks the first cholera mortality occurred in Belfast. Its source was a man who, with his family, had been forcibly removed from Scotland to Belfast under the controversial Law of Settlement.[10] Upon landing in the Union, it became the responsibility of the local Poor Law authorities to provide the man and his dependants with relief. His death precipitated the speedy enactment of measures designed to counteract the spread of cholera throughout the Union.[11] The Guardians were pessimistic that these precautions would be undermined by the constant influx of returned paupers from Britain, mainly from the ports of Liverpool and Glasgow. The people deported from Glasgow, who were the most numerous category, were in particularly poor circumstances as frequently they had not been supplied with food or clothing prior to departure.[12] The number of removals also continued to be high, with as many as 40 such paupers each day seeking admission to the Belfast workhouse.[13] As the following table illustrates, the overwhelming majority of casual night lodgers were from Scotland:

Casual Night Lodgers, 1849[14]

Week Ending	Total No.	From Scotland
17 February	22	21
28 February	14	14
7 March	42	35
14 March	24	18
21 March	27	16
4 April	38	30
Total	167	134

In general, pressure on the resources of the Belfast Union remained high in 1849. At the beginning of 1849, workhouse relief was still double its pre-Famine level. On 10 February, there was a total of 2,857 inmates in the main workhouse and Fever Hospital wards. There were a further 155 inmates in the Barrack Street institution, 298 in the House of Correction, and 200 in the Francis Street building.[15] In keeping with their reluctance to provide outdoor relief, the Guardians continued to expand the provision of indoor relief. In January 1849, they negotiated with the trustees of the Magdalene Asylum to use the penitentiary for accommodating healthy inmates, but their bid was unsuccessful.[16] However, the Guardians obtained the use of a building in Francis Street owned by Mulhollands, which could accommodate up to 1,000 paupers. They leased the building until 1 July at a cost of £150. As a consequence, total workhouse accommodation increased to 4,073.[17] The Central Commissioners disapproved of the location, claiming that it was situated in 'the worst part of town' and stipulating that access should be strictly limited to able-bodied women.[18] Frustration at having constantly to confirm every detail of daily workhouse routine was evident in the Guardians' statement that they were 'of the opinion that the Commissioners interfere unnecessarily in the details of management'.[19]

In October 1849, a new building for the use of pauper children was completed. As a result, the auxiliary workhouses at the House of Correction in Victoria Street and the College Hospital in Barrack Street were closed.[20] By the end of the year, all temporary buildings erected on the site of the main workhouse had been removed. The demand for workhouse relief was also beginning a slow decline, helped by a good harvest and a revival in the local economy. The Guardians were thus able to face the new decade with the confidence that they had weathered the difficulties triggered by the potato failure of 1845.[21]

Emigration and Removal

In addition to people migrating to Belfast looking for either employment or relief, a large number also travelled to the town as it was a major port of embarkation for both Scotland and England. Emigration from Ireland during and in the immediate aftermath of the Famine was unprecedented. Overall, emigration was responsible for more population loss than mortality. Within Ulster, this was particularly true. In the critical period 1847–48, over 40 per cent of those leaving Ireland were from Ulster. Even before the Famine, emigration from Ulster had been high, which had resulted in the establishment of Irish networks overseas and awareness of job opportunities. Emigrants from Ulster tended to favour movement to Scotland rather than to England. The vast majority of famine emigrants, however, chose North America as their destination. Ulster Protestants – especially wealthy ones – preferred British North America (Canada) to the United States.[22] Liverpool was the cheapest port of departure for transatlantic ships, encouraging emigrants to travel to Britain first. The choice of North America was partly based on the fact that the distress in Ireland coincided with a trade depression in the British economy, which made traditional emigration routes less rewarding. Nevertheless, large numbers of emigrants continued to leave Belfast for Glasgow, leading a Glasgow newspaper to refer to 'The Irish Invasion'.[23] The recession in Britain meant that many emigrants were unwelcome, and contributed to some paupers being returned to Ireland under the Laws of Removal, especially from the beleaguered ports of Liverpool and Glasgow.[24]

The desire to flee from Ireland put pressure on ports such as Belfast, Dublin, Derry and Cork as they were major ports of embarkation. As early as December 1846, the *Belfast News-Letter* outlined the burden being placed on the port towns by people leaving the country.[25] The report also demonstrated that even at this early stage of the Famine, people were willing to risk a winter crossing in their desperation to leave Ireland. Continuing high levels of emigration in 1847 led one northern paper to warn that emigrants were drawn from the better-off classes which meant that they were losing 'the flower of our people'.[26] In 1848, Lady Dufferin, a respected poet and wife of a local landlord, felt sufficiently moved by the constant transit of people through Belfast to compose 'Lament of the Irish Emigrant'. Not all emigrants reached their destination. In July 1847, the *Banner of Ulster* published a list of Belfast emigrants who had died in the quarantine hospital in Grosse Isle, Canada. Between May and July of that year 41 emigrants had died in this single location. Fifteen of these deaths had been children aged five or under (see also Appendix IV). Additional lists of emigrant deaths were printed intermittently in the paper.[27]

Even though the local economy commenced a slow recovery after 1848, high emigration continued from the port of Belfast. Again, there was a general perception that it was the artisan classes who were emigrating from the north of the country. The *Downpatrick Recorder* warned that 'much of the wealth and comfort of this hitherto prosperous county is being transported to the shores of America, and other parts of the globe'. The paper blamed Poor Law taxation for the continued emigration of wealthier farmers.[28]

The fact that the majority of famine emigrants were Catholic worried some members of the Presbyterian Church. In July 1847, Dr Morgan, the Moderator of the Presbyterian General Assembly, believed that the Famine had led to an unforeseen danger, when he warned that:

> There is another aspect of this subject – disease and death – perhaps more serious still. With the removal of many of the people one consideration ought powerfully to affect us. These people are the blinded and bigoted children of a fallen church. They hold their error and they cleave to their superstitions with a tenacity almost remarkable. Wherever they go, they carry their principles and habits with them. They are filled with the spirit of proselytism. In Ulster, England, Scotland and America, they are the same as in Munster and Connacht. Whoever may change, Irish Roman Catholics never change, and wherever they have the power, they exercise it.[29]

A similar caution was repeated a few years later by the Rev. Edgar who warned British Presbyterians that:

> the towns of Scotland are oppressed and defiled by increasing swarms of illiterate, profligate Irish Romanists ... crime in Liverpool has tremendously increased on account of the huge portion of its people who are now Irish Romanists; Manchester groans under a similar bane; and London feels it necessary to devote a special agency in her City Mission to bring reforming influences to bear on the increased masses of Roman heathenism which are adding fearfully to the number and atrocity of her dangerous and perishing classes.[30]

The vast majority of famine emigration was self-financed. Following the first failure of the potato crop, however, an emigration committee had been established in the Ballymacarrett district of Belfast. A rare example of government intervention in emigration also took place in 1848 when a scheme was introduced for Irish female orphans to be sent from the workhouses to Australia.[31] Many of the initial cohort of girls were from the Belfast Union.[32] The scheme quickly became immersed in scandal leading to its demise in 1850. By 1847, both landlords and Poor Law authorities were viewing subsidized emigration as a way of removing a sustained financial burden for a one-off payment. The problem of long-term pauperism was partially addressed in the 1847 Poor Law Amendment Act, which facilitated the ability of Guardians to assist paupers to emigrate. The legislation proved to be cumbersome to administer and few boards of Guardians made use of it.[33] An Amendment Act in 1849 made the emigration of workhouse paupers easier to administer. In its wake, Poor Law emigration did increase.[34]

Overall, emigration during and after the Famine provided an important safety-valve, without which the level of excess mortality would have been higher. One enduring consequence was that political divisions evident in Ireland were transported overseas, resulting in the intensification of Orange and Green politics in places such as Liverpool, Glasgow and Canada.[35] Increasingly also, a view of emigration as banishment took hold, fulfilling the prophecy of the *Illustrated London News,* made in 1852, that the emigrants:

> are carrying with them, in too many instances, we are afraid, a feeling of bitter hatred to this country. They blame England for the evils that have befallen them in their own land, instead of blaming as they ought to do, their own landlords, their own indolence, their own religious and party feuds, and their own listless reliance upon the easily raised but miserable root, the potato.[36]

For the Belfast Guardians and other Unions on the east coast the continuation of the Laws of Removal in the English and Scottish Poor Laws, but not in the Irish legislation, proved to be an enduring source of discontent. Even as pauperism decreased within the Belfast Union, the number of removals from Britain remained high and they contributed to a further deterioration in the relationship between the Guardians and the central Poor Law Commissioners. In 1846, the English Settlement Laws were changed, giving an Irish person who had resided continuously in one parish for five years or more a legal settlement. This legislation meant that famine emigrants did not have a right to receive poor relief and thus that they could be removed back to Ireland. Furthermore, in June 1847, when Irish distress was at its height, the law was changed making removal from Britain easier and less bureaucratic.[37] The impact of this legislation was two-fold; it deterred Irish paupers from seeking relief in Britain, whilst facilitating the large-scale removal of those who did. Because there was no similar legislation within the Irish Poor Law, the paupers were left at the most convenient port to Britain. The Belfast Board of Guardians repeatedly registered their abhorrence at the continuance of the existing system in which the absence of a Law of Removal in Ireland meant that paupers could seek relief in any workhouse in Ireland. They deemed such a system to be illegal and asked the Commissioners for an alteration in the law. The latter were far from sympathetic, disclaiming that they had any authority to interfere with the legislation. They also pointed out that the large number of Irish paupers landing in Glasgow and Liverpool was proving to be a great burden on those local

authorities. In a remark which served only to heighten the
frustration of the Guardians, the Commissioners concluded that
the difficulties of Belfast 'necessarily attaches to those places
which, from their advantageous position as seaports, are channels
of intercourse between Ireland and Great Britain'.[38] This reply
engendered great anger among the members of the Board which
was reflected in a series of resolutions which attacked both the
Commissioners and the Poor Law. The Commissioners were
accused by the Belfast Guardians of being:

> armed with, and sometimes exercise, an arbitrary power in
> matters which would be much better kept in the hands of the
> Guardians ... who have more accurate means of judging on many
> points than a body who can only form its opinion upon reports.[39]

Although conditions had improved in the Belfast Union by
1849, paupers removed from Britain continued to put a burden
on the resources of the Union. Additionally, the conflict over the
proposed Rate-in-Aid tax reawakened the issue of a law of removal
in Ireland. The debate also extended beyond the confines of the
boardroom of the Union. In January 1849, the General Purposes
Committee of the Town Council discussed the issue of removal,
prefacing the debate with the declaration that they did not usually
interfere with poor relief matters. They felt justified in doing so
because 'there is one principle embodied in the existing law
bearing so heavily on seaport towns, and particularly Belfast, as to
warrant the council in entertaining the subject, namely, the power
given to justices in England and Scotland of conveying Irish
paupers to the nearest seaport in Ireland where they become the
responsibility of that authority'.[40]

Because the Irish Poor Law did not contain a Law of Settlement,
there was no legal provision for the Belfast Guardians to remove
paupers who claimed relief in their Union. Yet, the Guardians used
removal as a way of clearing the Union of claimants for relief. The
onward removal of paupers from Belfast to their Unions of origin
was facilitated by the financial support of the Belfast General Relief
Fund. Many of these paupers had been returned from Unions in
England and Scotland. By January 1849, the Relief Fund had
provided five grants of £9,000, which had allowed the removal of
11,608 of what they termed 'strange paupers' to their native places.
The majority of paupers were from the neighbouring counties of
Antrim and Down although a number also came from as far away
as counties Cork and Kerry. The cost of the removals was eased by
the Ulster Railway's offer of a reduced rate for transmitting the
paupers to the end of their line.[41]

In March 1849 a deputation from Belfast, which included the
Mayor, travelled to London where they met the Prime Minister,

Lord John Russell, in order to protest against the introduction of the Rate-In-Aid tax. The same deputation also met Sir George Grey concerning the removal of paupers from Britain. They informed him that between July 1847 and January 1849, 12,100 paupers had been landed in Belfast who were entitled to immediate relief within the Union. When Grey asked what they would like the government to do, the deputation asked that a Law of Settlement be introduced into Ireland. This was refused.[42]

The conflict over the removal of paupers from Britain extended beyond the Famine years and continued to be a source of grievance between Irish and British Poor Law Unions. The dispute demonstrated the unequal treatment of Irish paupers within the United Kingdom. During the Famine years especially, the paupers were the main losers in the struggles between the Belfast Poor Law authorities and the British government. Yet, despite frustration at the government's handling of the catastrophe, an attempted nationalist uprising in 1848 produced a new Protestant alliance in Belfast whose allegiance was clearly to the British state rather than to an independent Irish nation.

'Orange and Green Will Carry the Day'

In addition to the deepening economic depression between 1845 and 1847, these years also witnessed increased political tensions between those who wished to maintain the Act of Union and those who sought its repeal. Although repeal did have support amongst middle-class Protestants in Belfast, in general, allegiances were divided along religious lines. The Famine was increasingly regarded by supporters of repeal as a manifestation of the failure of the Act of Union. This belief was stated unequivocally in the *Belfast Vindicator* in January 1847 when it proclaimed that 'the real blight of this country has been the blight of a foreign legislation'. It continued with an appeal:

> Charitable, kind-hearted merchants of Belfast, you are paying the fine attached to the degradation of submitting to be inhabitants of a province – to be ruled, fleeced, taxed, neglected and despised by haughty Englishmen. Amiable, kind-hearted and virtuous ladies of Belfast – you, who with noble-minded devotion, cast aside all distinctions of creed and class and rush into the field of charity to save the hunger-stricken – you are the mothers, sisters, wives of men who are content to see their country a province. It is an alien legislation that has inflicted the hunger you would relieve.[43]

By 1847, the repeal movement had divided into those who continued to support moral force to achieve their ends and those

who argued that physical force was necessary – the 'Old' Ireland
and the Young Ireland movement respectively. The leaders of
Young Ireland realized that if the demand for repeal was to
succeed, they needed to win support in Ulster, especially in
Belfast. Under O'Connell's leadership, however, the repeal
movement was closely associated with Dublin and, due to the
involvement of both the parish priests and the Church hierarchy,
it was regarded as coterminous with Catholicism. O'Connell also
showed little interest in winning support in the north of the
country, visiting Belfast only once, in January 1841, when he
accepted an invitation from the Belfast Loyal National Repeal
Association to speak in the town. The outspoken Presbyterian
minister, Henry Cook, challenged O'Connell to a public debate,
but the latter refused, describing his protagonist as 'Bully Cooke,
the cock of the north'. The government anticipated trouble and
sent 2,000 additional troops. During O'Connell's stay, he was
mostly confined to his hotel room and when he did make a public
address from the balcony, he was drowned by cries of 'No Pope'
and 'No Surrender'. Although a few liberal Protestants attended
a repeal dinner in his honour, the vast majority of support came
from middle-class Catholics. O'Connell left the town escorted by
four carriages of police and a foot police patrol.[44]

The radical Young Ireland grouping within the repeal
movement argued for an inclusive, non-sectarian approach to
winning political independence. In 1845, they fell out with
O'Connell because of their support for the introduction of non-
denominational universities in Ireland, which O'Connell referred
to as 'Godless colleges'. In July 1846, the Young Irelanders left
the repeal movement as they refused to agree to O'Connell's
pledge that they would not resort to physical violence.[45] In January
1847, they reconstituted themselves as the Irish Confederation.
By this stage, O'Connell was 72 and the repeal movement
appeared to have lost much of its direction. O'Connell's death in
Italy in 1847, on his way to visit the Pope, left a vacuum in Irish
nationalist politics, which Young Ireland sought to fill.

The leaders of Young Ireland came from a diverse range of
backgrounds. Thomas Davis and the MP, William Smith O'Brien
were Protestants, Thomas Meagher was a Catholic from
Waterford, Charles Gavan Duffy was a Catholic from County
Monaghan, John Martin a northern Protestant, and John Mitchel,
who was born in County Derry, was the son of a Presbyterian
minister. The deepening crisis within Ireland was blamed by the
Young Irelanders on the British government whilst a national
government was presented as a solution. In April 1847, Smith
O'Brien withdrew from Westminster arguing that he could achieve
more benefit in Dublin than in London.[46] During the summer, a

number of confederate clubs were established, mostly in the towns, and they became the main agencies for planning an armed uprising.

Despite the non-sectarian approach of the Young Ireland leadership, the repeal movement continued to be associated with Catholicism. But like O'Connell, the leaders of Young Ireland recognized the importance of winning the support of Protestants in the north, especially in Belfast. In 1845, O'Brien, the leader of the group, produced 'An Address to the People of Down'. The address combined reassurances – that northern industry would not be damaged by an independent Irish legislature – with sentiment – invoking the spirit of the Volunteers of 1782, whose actions had led to the establishment of an independent Irish parliament.[47] Although a number of members of the repeal clubs in Belfast shifted their allegiance to the Young Irelanders, the majority remained faithful to Daniel O'Connell and, after his death in 1847, to his son, John.

In November 1847, a number of leading Young Irelanders, including O'Brien, Mitchel and Meagher, who were referred to collectively as 'the Dublin delegation', visited Belfast. They were hopeful of winning the support of northern Protestants, including Orangemen, and thus 'of adding a new province to Irish Ireland'. Sharman Crawford, the local landlord and MP, agreed to meet members of the delegation but also warned that local Orangemen might 'render the experiment dangerous'.[48] John Martin, who visited Belfast in advance, advised that despite local opposition, a successful meeting could be held. Robert Tennant, however, who subsequently became MP for the town, warned that such a meeting would inflame rather than reduce 'party bitterness'.[49] The meeting was advertised as being for 'the friends of Irish nationality'. It was held in Belfast's Music Hall and attendance, by ticket only, was 1 shilling. In advance, the audience was told that there were to be no interruptions at the meeting but that if 'opponents of sufficient eminence and ability will come forward' a second meeting would be held.[50] The meeting was a sell-out and the hall was filled one hour in advance of the speakers. Despite attempts to exclude them, a large portion of the audience were members of 'Old Ireland' who were accused of purchasing their tickets using bogus names. Even greater numbers of this association were outside the hall and were prevented from entering by a large contingent of constabulary with fixed bayonets and batons.

From the outset, the Old Ireland group disrupted the meeting by cheering for John O'Connell, whistling, shouting and letting off squibs and firecrackers. The first speakers were heckled so loudly that they could not be heard. When Meagher attempted to address the audience, a number of people mounted the platform and fighting started. Order was briefly restored but Meagher was interrupted by the windows of the hall being broken and a further attack made on the speakers, forcing them to leave the stage. When Meagher resumed, he referred to the actions of the Volunteers in 1782, describing the events as one of 'the proudest reminiscences of Ulster'. He admitted that until recently the repeal movement had 'worn the features of a Catholic movement' but that the Confederation wanted to appeal to all citizens of Ireland. Meagher also outlined the ways in which the Act of Union had failed all of the Irish people saying: 'The landlord was swamped, the tradesman was bankrupt, the farmer was in the poorhouse, and the famine was scourging the land.'[51] Yet Belfast, and a number of other industrial towns in Ireland, had prospered despite England and the injustice of her parliament. Despite the fact that few Protestants were present, Meagher attempted to calm Protestant fears. He argued that the Union had not safeguarded the interests of Irish Protestants. Moreover, if Ireland did achieve legislative independence, Irish Catholics would not allow themselves to be controlled by priests or by a new 'Catholic Ascendancy'. Meagher ended with a rousing appeal to Irish Protestants, asking them:

> Swear it, that the rule of England is unjust, illegal and a grievance. Swear it, that as you have been a garrison of England for years, from henceforth you will be a garrison of Ireland ... our fathers fought and conquered for a nation – be their memories pious, glorious and immortal.[52]

Mitchel, a northern Protestant himself, repeated many of Meagher's assurances, adding:

> I have joined with Catholics because I know they would cut off their right hands before they would hold them up to advocate any measure of intolerance ... I say then, that Catholic ascendancy is impossible in Ireland; and I am willing, and I hope there are others willing, to make a similar league with the Roman Catholics, and to pledge ourselves on our side, that every vestige of our old Protestant ascendancy shall be pulled down and trampled.

Smith O'Brien, the final speaker, appealed to 'the men of the North to assist your brethren in the South and West of the country'. He also assured the Protestants that, as a Protestant himself, he felt confident that the rights of Protestants would not suffer under an independent legislature.[53]

A full report of the meeting was sent to the Lord Lieutenant in Dublin. It was described as being attended by 'considerable riot and disorder', which was only contained by police intervention.[54] The local Protestant and Whig newspapers carried accounts of the meetings. The *Northern Whig* was dismissive of the fact that the Young Irelanders, who found it difficult to control a meeting of repealers in Belfast, desired to disrupt the British Empire. The paper warned that without the support of Ulster, Ireland could not survive economically.[55]

The second meeting of the Irish Confederation in Belfast was scheduled to be held four days later. It was cancelled due to the intervention of the Belfast magistrates who banned it. The audience, which had already gathered outside the theatre, appeared to be mostly supporters of Old Ireland as they were cheering for John O'Connell. The Dublin delegation were reported to be 'very much dissatisfied' with this decision.[56] O'Brien, Mitchel, Meagher and a number of the other speakers were prevented from entering the theatre by the police. O'Brien then endeavoured to address the crowd outside the theatre over the noise saying: 'Men of Belfast – I come here – in the performance of a sacred duty.' His attempted speech was stopped by the appearance of a number of 'ferocious' bulldogs, one of which was told to go for O'Brien's throat. Order was restored when the police attacked the dogs with bayonets. O'Brien accused the men of behaving illegally in banning the meeting and he again tried unsuccessfully to enter the building. Mitchel accused the magistrates of acting illegally and said that the meeting would be held on the following day. A third attempt to enter the theatre by O'Brien was equally unsuccessful. O'Brien then proceeded to Hercules Street, the heart of Catholic Belfast, where he appealed to the population to support the Irish Confederation. The crowd shouted for John O'Connell whilst accusing O'Brien of being a 'hangman' and 'murderer', blaming the death of O'Connell on his wrangles with Young Ireland.[57] A number of stones were thrown, one of which hit him in the face. He was prevented from travelling further down the street and instead returned to his hotel, escorted by policemen.[58]

The third meeting of the Irish Confederation was allowed to go ahead by the Belfast magistrates. Again, a large number of Old Irelanders attended the theatre with a view to disrupting the meeting. Many were prevented from going inside which meant that attendance was 'very thin'. A number of Old Irelanders were present and they repeatedly interrupted the speakers. O'Brien told the audience that he had expected to receive 'a tolerably rough reception in Belfast', but he did not know whether it would be initiated by Orangemen or by those 'who thought they were struggling for repeal upon erroneous principles'. He had come to the north to address those opposed to the repeal of the Union and he was aware that 'repeal had hitherto been looked upon almost exclusively as a Catholic movement' but he believed that Protestants as well as Catholics had a right to conduct their own affairs. Whilst O'Brien acknowledged that Belfast appeared to be the only part of the country that had prospered economically under the Union, he felt its prosperity had been exaggerated. The previous summer he had travelled through the northern counties and 'It was with the deepest concern he found that the misery so unhappily prevalent in the south of Ireland is also to be seen in the tracts of the North he visited.' O'Brien's speech was again disrupted by supporters of O'Connell who upset the meeting with rattles and gunpowder squibs. Meagher was able to take the stage for a few minutes during which he announced that although their reception had been bad, it would not prevent them from visiting the north again. The audience at that point became so unruly that the assembly had to be abandoned.[59] Following the meeting, O'Brien was escorted to the Royal Hotel by the police in order to protect him from the crowds who, according to a local magistrate, 'seemed inclined to offer violence to his person, accompanying him with groans and hisses and opprobrious epithets'.[60]

In the evening, members of the Dublin delegation and a number of their Belfast sympathizers dined in Kerns Royal Hotel and drank toasts to 'The Union of Irishmen'. Despite their public outings having met with sustained hostility, the Young Irelanders regarded their visit to Belfast as worthwhile.[61] They believed that a number of Orangemen were sympathetic to their demands and that a substantial number of Protestants had attended the first meeting. However, they had not attended subsequent ones because the first meeting had been 'turned into a bear-garden by a gang of Old Irelanders – butchers from Hercules Street, for the most part – who clamoured to be let loose at the murderers of the Liberator. They interrupted the speakers with incessant bellowing.'[62] The *Nation* newspaper supported this interpretation, stating in one of their editorials that 'Ulster is no longer unanimous for the Union'.[63] Ironically, members of the Dublin delegation had travelled to Belfast with the intention of reassuring and winning the support of Protestants, but their presence at the meetings had been overshadowed. Instead, it was Old Ireland who had opposed the Young Irelanders and who, despite being opposed to physical force, had demonstrated a willingness to deploy it against their former colleagues.

The War of the Placards and the 1848 Uprising

At the beginning of 1848, divisions within the Irish Confederation resulted in the departure of the increasingly radical John Mitchel.

The revolution in France in February made the threat of an uprising in Ireland change from rhetoric to a reality. On St Patrick's Day, Mitchel called for an uprising which led the *Belfast News-Letter* to respond with the warning that 'The Orangemen of the north too, have declared in an address to the Lord Lieutenant, their readiness to ... act as a native garrison of their country.' The paper also called on the government to 'crush the conspirators'.[64] In Belfast, the activities of the nationalists led to what was termed 'the war of placards'. Posters, half orange and half green, appeared throughout the town saying 'Orange and Green will carry the day' and invited all people to a meeting to offer their congratulations to the people of France and to demand a repeal of the Union. Local Protestants were annoyed that the placards implied the support of Orangemen and the following day fresh placards appeared saying 'Derry, Aughrim and the Boyne. Loyal Orangemen of the North, you have been insulted by a treasonable placard' and calling for a counter-meeting in which they could declare their support for Queen and Constitution. A third placard then appeared from the district secretary of the Belfast Orange Lodges saying that the second placard had been 'a ruse of the repealers' and warning them against popery 'with its Jesuitical cunning'. The notice told the Orangmen not to act unless they were told to do so by their district lodge. The Orange lodges in Belfast also sent a deputation to the Mayor saying that they had been 'insulted' by the appearance of the placards 'in which their own glorious colour is combined with that which ever has been associated with the purposes and practices of disloyalty and rebellion'. They also stated that they were in readiness to aid the authorities if called to do so. To defuse the situation, the Mayor issued a proclamation appealing to 'all well-disposed inhabitants' of Belfast not to attend either meeting. Provision was also made for special constables to enlist and for the military to be present.[65] Although meetings and processions did take place in Belfast on 17 March, they proved to be less confrontational than in previous years and the constabulary and military had nothing to do. The *Belfast News-Letter* described the day as a 'failure' for repealers. The local Orange lodges used the events surrounding the day to reaffirm their loyalty and to issue warnings that they were willing to intervene against the repealers.[66] The resulting declarations of loyalty from Orange lodges led the London-based *Morning Chronicle* to praise the 'Protestant peasantry of Ulster' for their loyalty in times of need.[67] As revolutionary tension increased in 1848, the repeal movement was being linked with Catholicism, whilst loyalty was associated with Protestantism, especially the Orange Order.

    In April, O'Brien and a number of other Young Irelanders visited France with the hope of winning support for an uprising.

O'Brien returned with an orange, white and green banner presented by the revolutionary government, but without any promise of military support. He continued to hope that Orangemen would unite with the Catholics to bring about an uprising. Although a Protestant Repeal Association was formed in Dublin with a branch in Belfast, few Orangemen supported the movement.[68] In April 1848 placards appeared in Belfast advertising a repeal meeting in the local theatre and calling for local Protestants to attend. When questioned by magistrates, the proprietor of the theatre denied that he had leased his theatre for this purpose. At the appointed time 'a very large excited crowd of persons' gathered, and when they were denied access to the theatre, they went to a club room. At the club, a speech was made from the window and the gathering dispersed at eleven in the evening. Although the army was in attendance, it was not required to intervene.[69]

The increased activities of nationalists worried a number of Protestants in the north. In the summer of 1847, the *Belfast Protestant Journal* called for Protestants to unite and use the forthcoming general election as an opportunity to destroy the 'enemy of Popery'.[70] These concerns were intensified following the revolution in France which led a number of northern Protestants to call on the government for firmer action against the confederate clubs. In April 1848, the Mayor of Belfast convened a meeting for the purpose of discussing the apparent revolutionary threat from the nationalists. He described it as 'the most influential, respectable and numerous ever held in Belfast'.[71] Following the meeting, a 'Loyal Address of the Inhabitants of Belfast' was sent to the Lord Lieutenant. In the communication, the writers declared their opposition to a repeal of the Union and offered their services in order to prevent it being brought about.[72] The Lord Lieutenant responded by saying: 'the opinions of a community so distinguished for energy, enterprise, intelligence and honourable industry as the inhabitants of Belfast must at all times command the most respectful consideration'.[73] The memorial was also forwarded to the Home Office in London and the Home Secretary presented it to the Queen. Sir George Grey, the Home Secretary, informed the Lord Lieutenant of 'the satisfaction with which Her Majesty's government has received this gratifying proof of loyalty and affection from so important and enlightened a portion of her people'.[74] A number of Orange Lodges, believing an uprising to be imminent, started to practise military manoeuvres. They also asked the government to supply them with additional ammunition and arms.[75] One correspondent from Belfast offered to raise a company of 100 men in order to 'defend their lives and properties'. He believed that the current

AN AGGREGATE
MEETING
OF THE
CITIZENS OF BELFAST
Favourable to the Right of the
IRISH NATION TO MAKE ITS OWN LAWS,
WILL BE HELD IN
THE THEATRE ROYAL,
AT SEVEN O'CLOCK ON FRIDAY EVENING,
The 7th of April, in the Year of Liberty and Revolutions.

The Committee of the Re-united Nationalists of Ulster will lay before the Meeting, for adoption, certain Resolutions and Documents calculated to be of service at the present time. Among them will be

A PETITION TO HER MAJESTY,
An ADDRESS to the FRENCH PEOPLE
A MEMORIAL TO THE TOWN COUNCIL.

To pay the expenses, the price of Tickets of Admission will be.

Boxes and Stage, Sixpence; Pit, Threepence; Gallery, 1d.
The LOWER BOXES will be reserved for Ladies.

To be had at OWEN KERR'S, Chapel-Lane; the Vindicator Office; the National Reading Room for George's Ward, No. 7, Arthur Place; and at HENDERSON'S, Castle Place.
AN EARLY APPLICATION FOR TICKETS WILL BE NECESSARY.

Ireland, rejoice! and England, deplore; Faction and feud are passing away; "Twas a low voice, but 'tis a loud roar,— "Orange and Green will carry the day." Landlords fooled us, Oligarchs ruled us, Hounding our passions to make us their prey;	But, in their spite, the Irish UNITE, And 'Orange and Green will carry the day.' Orange, Orange, Bless the Orange; Tories and Whigs grow pale with dismay, When, from the North, Bursts, the cry forth,—

"ORANGE & GREEN WILL CARRY THE DAY."

Figure 8 Poster advertising meeting for Irish independence, 1848

threat of treason had led 'the Protestants of the North to consolidate by all means in their power'.[76] Both the Prime Minister and the Lord Lieutenant, although reluctant to arm the Orangemen, believed that at some stage they might require their help. Lord Clarendon, therefore, advised that the Orangemen 'ought not to be too much snubbed'.[77] The nationalist *Nation* newspaper, in an editorial entitled 'Ulster Beware', warned that the 'foreign government' in Westminster was fostering Orange lodges whilst repressing repeal clubs. They appealed to the repeal Protestants and Catholics of Belfast to arm themselves.[78]

John Mitchel's arrest for sedition in May and sentencing to 14 years' transportation galvanized the leadership of the Young Ireland movement into action. In July, the Confederation reunited with some of the more radical O'Connellites and formed the Irish League. A secret War Council was appointed to plan an uprising. The government responded by suspending habeas corpus and banning the confederate clubs and radical press. Other leaders of Young Ireland were also arrested. In May 1848 a Protestant Repeal Association was formed in Dublin with a branch in Belfast.[79] Both groups drew their support from the urban middle classes but not from the Protestant landed classes. At the beginning of July, the Belfast Protestant Repeal Association issued an address to the Orangemen of Ulster asking them, on the anniversary of the Battle of the Boyne, to proclaim '[t]hat it is the opinion of the Orangemen of Ulster that the Act of Union ought to be repealed, and a domestic legislature re-established in Ireland'. The address continued that the leaders of the Orange Order had led the rank and file 'into the just contempt and execration of all men of independence, by making you exhibit yourselves before Europe in the ridiculous and humiliating positions of mercenaries, garrisoning your own country for the benefit of strangers'.[80] The local press and Orange lodges responded angrily to the statements. The Orange Order sent an address to the Queen in which they rejected repeal and stated 'emphatically the determination of these men to die rather than submit to a repeal of the Union'.[81] One Belfast lodge issued a public response to the repealers, saying:

> The Protestants of Ulster have everything to fear from an Irish legislature. In the first place they have to dread the ascendancy of a system the most intolerant that ever made its appearance on the face of the earth; secondly, they have to dread the influx of Jesuits; thirdly, they know well that they could not have a fair representation in the senate; and lastly, they believe that the liberty of conscience that they can now have under a British government would be taken from them.

The *Belfast News-Letter* congratulated the Orangemen for their declarations of loyalty, adding 'popery won't change its spots'. They also criticized the Protestant repealers for disgracing the name of Protestantism.[82]

The *Warder*, an avowedly Protestant newspaper, warned the repealers that despite attempts to entice them from 'Arch agitator to convicted felon' the loyalty of the Orangemen had not wavered, 'nor will they now, when most wanted, take to the bland nonsense of the Belfast Protestant Repealers'. The paper also portrayed the anticipated rebellion as being exclusively Catholic, warning that 'A vast and infernal conspiracy is gradually organizing the popery of Ireland for a savage revolution.' They called on 'our Protestant brethren' to stand together in the coming battle.[83] The twelfth of July commemorations in 1848 were viewed by the Orange Order as an opportunity to show that northern Protestants did not support repeal and were willing to fight to defend the Union with Britain.[84] The *Belfast News-Letter* was of the opinion that the repeal agitation had given Orangemen 'more ardour' and won them friends amongst the Protestant population.[85]

In Belfast, the town authorities prepared for an uprising to take place during the summer. The Police Committee asked the Lord Lieutenant if the force could be 'immediately armed and trained to military discipline'. Although it was agreed to give the police staves and other similar weapons, the Lord Lieutenant felt that they should not be given firearms.[86] The magistrates estimated that within Belfast there were four or five Confederation Clubs and that 'some hundreds of disaffected persons are actually in possession of Fire Arms or other weapons'. They asked for permission to start swearing in special constables.[87] Informants were also used by the magistrates. One informant took the magistrates to a house which contained 400 pikes and 100 firearms, and a delivery of more of the latter was expected.[88] A number of arrests were made, primarily of members of the confederate clubs. One man was arrested for saying 'To hell with the Queen' to a local constable.[89] One of the leading Belfast Young Irelanders, John Rea, a Presbyterian solicitor, was arrested and imprisoned in Kilmainham Jail in Dublin, but he was subsequently released without charge.[90] A Frenchman who was arrested en route to Belfast claimed to be one of eight members of the French National Guard on a special mission to assist an uprising in Ireland.[91]

On 29 July 1848, the *Nation* newspaper made an appeal for 'Catholics of Ulster and repeal Protestants' to arm themselves.[92] On the same day, a small uprising took place in County Tipperary, the leaders realizing their inability to mount a successful campaign in Dublin or Belfast. The easy defeat of Smith O'Brien and his 100 followers marked the collapse of the attempted insurrection. In the ensuing months, the uprising was used by Protestants in the north as an example of the disloyalty of people in the south of Ireland. At the beginning of 1849, during a dispute over new taxation, the *Banner of Ulster* reminded the government: 'It is notorious that Ulster has long been the stronghold of British connection; and that within the very last year she has rendered the most important services to the British Crown.'[93] The Orange

Order was also regarded as having played a significant part in the defeat of the repeal movement. On the twelfth of July anniversary in 1849, one Ulster newspaper gave its opinion that 'Ulster is still sound, despite the ingratitude of the government ... Twelve months ago, the red hand of republicanism was lifted against our venerable institutions ... We know how that appeal was met, the Twelfth of July 1848 gave the reply and marshalled thousands who stood forth that day.'[94] At the meeting of the Belfast lodges, they were reminded that 'this time last year the Orangemen were, under God, the means of rescuing this country from carnage and the dreadful effects of a bloody civil war'.[95] Again, the Protestants of Belfast placed themselves as defenders against the encroachment of Catholicism. Instead of the 1848 uprising uniting Protestants and Catholics in Ireland and allying Ulster more firmly with the rest of the country, it contributed to a widening gulf, with long-term political repercussions both for Belfast and the rest of Ireland. This political divide was reinforced by the actions of the Belfast proselytizers and meant that during the course of the Famine, Catholicism had become even more associated with laziness, poverty and political disloyalty.

The Rate-in-Aid Dispute

The economic improvements which were evident in the Belfast economy after 1848 did not extend to the whole of the country. In 1848, 1,500,000 people were still dependent on poor relief, and in some Unions in the west, disease and mortality were still increasing.[96] The ideological separation which existed between the British government's attitude to poor relief in Ireland and in Britain was further demonstrated in 1849 when, as a consequence of the introduction of the Rate-in-Aid tax, the financial burden of relief shifted from the United Kingdom to Ireland.

To deal with the demands of some areas, in February 1849, the government announced the introduction of new legislation which they hoped would finally end the need for Irish Poor Law Unions to seek financial assistance from the British Treasury. It was also intended to be the final special relief measure for Ireland and was to mark the end of famine-funding for the country. A closing grant of £50,000 was given for use of the poorest Unions but even the provision of this small amount met with opposition in parliament.[97] At the same time, up to 50 additional Poor Law Unions were to be created. Only one new Union was eventually formed in Ulster, in County Cavan.[98] As a result of the new measure, a national rate of 6d in the pound, known as the Rate-in-Aid was to be levied on all Irish Unions for two years. The money raised would then be reallocated to 23 Unions, which had been officially designated as 'distressed' in the south and west of the country. Only one of these districts, the Glenties Union in County Donegal, was situated in Ulster. The proposed tax demonstrated that, even in the midst of a national crisis, Ireland was to rely on her own resources rather than those of the United Kingdom as a whole.

The decision to make famine relief an Irish rather than a British responsibility was criticized by a number of senior government officials, including the Chief Poor Law Commissioner in Ireland, Edward Twistleton. Twistleton believed that the tax marked an abdication of the responsibilities of the British government resulting from the Act of Union of 1801. He resigned in protest at its introduction.[99] Sir Robert Peel also, who had remained silent on government policy since his downfall in 1846, condemned the proposed measure, arguing that the Irish Poor Law should be more aligned with practices in England.[100]

The proposed Rate-in-Aid was widely unpopular in Ireland although opposition was most vehement in the Poor Law Unions in eastern Ulster, where it was opposed by landlords, Poor Law Guardians and the local press. From the outset, the tax was portrayed as being a burden on Ulster rather than the whole of Ireland. Increasingly, the tax was portrayed as being a direct transfer of monies from Ulster to Connacht. In this regard, the propaganda of the Ulster Unions was successful in that the contributions of Munster and Leinster were generally ignored in debate. Ironically, the Rate-in-Aid fell more heavily on the province of Leinster than on Ulster. The administrators of the Ulster Unions were in the forefront of the protest, declaring that they were being penalized for having managed their finances, whereas their counterparts in the west had not done so. This argument was supported by the Poor Law Inspector, Edward Senior, who described the tax as a dividend for the 'indolence' of the west.[101] Moreover, in the light of the loyalty of the people of Ulster in the repeal crisis of the previous year, the proposed legislation was viewed as a particularly ungrateful action by the government.

In Westminster, the proposed Rate-in-Aid dominated parliamentary debate at the beginning of 1849, and the determined opposition of the northern Irish MPs led to it being referred to as 'the Ulster Question' in Westminster.[102] One Ulster MP, Sir William Verner, informed the House that the proposed rate was 'very poor return to the men of the north for the loyalty they had exhibited'.[103] A Repeal MP from Dublin, however, asserted that 'the loyalty of the people of Ulster was, after all, conditional loyalty. It was pounds, shillings and pence loyalty. It was sixpenny loyalty.'[104] An English MP took the northern Guardians to task for ignoring the role of 'provinces and counties in the south of Ireland, whose loyalty, religion and virtues were quite on a par with those of the north'.[105] The Ulster MPs were also accused of being unappreciative of the efforts which had been made on behalf of Ireland in Britain in the preceding years. The Home Secretary, George Grey, described their stance as 'unreasonable' in view of the fact that the province 'paid no income tax or assessed taxes because Ulster formed a part of Ireland and not of England'.[106]

Extra-parliamentary activity was also fiery and the Rate-in-Aid dispute dominated the Ulster press. The *Newry Telegraph* made an unequivocal declaration about the Rate-in-Aid which created an impression that Ulster was different from – and superior to – the rest of Ireland. The paper posed the question:

> It is true that the potato has failed in Connaught and Munster; but it has failed just as much in Ulster; therefore, if the potato has produced all the distress in the South and West, why has it not caused the same misery here. It is because we are a painstaking, industrious, laborious people, who desire to work and pay our just debts, and the blessing of the Almighty is upon our labour. If the people of the South had been equally industrious with those of the North, they would not have had so much misery among them.[107]

The *Northern Whig* referred to the proposed measure as an 'anti-Union scheme'.[108] The *Banner of Ulster* described the proposal as unreasonable and added: 'It is notorious that Ulster has long been the stronghold of the British connection, and that within the very last year she has rendered the most important services to the British crown.'[109] The paper repeated this theme over the following few months. In May, as the bill was about to be voted on in the House of Commons, the *Banner* warned that if the measure was passed, it would be used as 'an argument against the connection between the two countries and against the trust which ought to be placed in the impartiality and justice of the Imperial Legislature. It is, therefore, dangerous to the stability of that Union on which the stability of the British Empire depends.'[110] A number of Protestant newspapers viewed the conflict in terms of Catholics against Protestants. The *Warder*, which described its purpose as being 'to defend the Protestantism of Ireland', warned that 'Russell will find that the Protestant public opinion is a very different thing from the High and Mighty defiance of Mr O'Connell.'[111]

The Ulster Boards of Guardians were at the forefront of the protest, frequently allying in their opposition to the measure. In

February, the Belfast Board petitioned both houses in Westminster. A few weeks later, a deputation from the town, which included the Mayor, William Johnston, and the town's MPs, Lord John Chichester and Robert Tennant, met the Prime Minister. They reiterated the view that the Rate-in-Aid was being imposed exclusively on Ulster. The deputation said that they were opposed to the principle upon which the tax was based, believing that it ought to be levied on the whole of the United Kingdom. According to a report in various Belfast newspapers, Russell 'appeared disconcerted by the statement of the deputation and was extremely guarded in his observations'. He defended the Rate-in-Aid on the grounds that 'Ulster, which was the most prosperous part of the country, might feel called upon to contribute for this purpose, considering that great efforts had already been made by England.'[112] The London *Times,* which had been at the forefront of a campaign since 1847 not to give further aid to Ireland, described the interview with the Belfast delegation as an indication that 'Ulster is on fire ... a great battle is to be fought. The Union of the empire is to be imperilled; and all for what? That Ulster may not have to pay a sixpenny rate in aid.'[113] Russell's answer demonstrated the determination of the government to treat the Famine as an Irish rather than a British responsibility and not to give in to the demands of the Ulster Boards.

A series of public meetings were convened at which local notables spoke against the proposed tax. The opposition was increasingly expressed in divisive terms, based on supposed differences between the north and the south, Protestants and Catholics, and hard-working northerners versus indolent southerners. This rhetoric was evident at a large public meeting held in County Down at the beginning of March. The speakers included Lord Downshire and Lord Roden, County Master of the Orange Order. Downshire informed the meeting that 'It is a shame to levy a tax on the industrious portion of one part of Ireland for the benefit of the less industrious – I might almost say, indolent portion of the inhabitants.'[114]

At the beginning of May, a mass rally was attended by representatives from the Belfast, Armagh, Cookstown, Derry, Downpatrick, Larne, Lisburn, Lurgan and Newtownards Unions. Whilst the Unions continued to oppose the measure, they agreed that they would not be willing to engage in 'active opposition' to the bill, preferring passive resistance.[115] The final public meeting against the Rate-in-Aid was held in Belfast on 23 May, when the bill was awaiting Royal Assent. The meeting was not well attended, and the speeches were dispirited and acknowledged that the campaign had failed. Fourteen Ulster Unions, including the Belfast Board, decided to accept the legislation.[116] A week later the bill became law and the rate was imposed in June. A number of Ulster Unions continued their opposition by delaying the payment of the new tax. At the end of 1851, however, the arrears of the Belfast Board amounted to less than £400 out of a Rate-in-Aid assessment of over £9,000.[117]

Despite the concerted opposition of local elites in Ulster, and the effective use of propaganda, they were unable to effect any change in government legislation. The Rate-in-Aid dispute showed that loyalty to the British government was conditional and had been weakened by what was perceived to be years of concessions to Catholics. At the same time, it demonstrated that the Act of Union was not a true financial Union as, even during a disaster such as the Famine, the British government was determined to place the responsibility for supporting Irish poverty on Irish property. Nevertheless, the warning that the tax would damage loyalty to the Union proved to be ephemeral. In the long term, the rhetoric in which the Rate-in-Aid dispute had been expressed contributed to an impression that there had been no famine in eastern Ulster. In the later years of the Famine, therefore, religious and political detachment combined with economic superiority to make Belfast appear separate and distinct from the rest of the country. In the post-Famine decades, as Belfast grew in economic prowess and in civic confidence, the catastrophe of the late 1840s and the town's conflicts with the British government were marginalized or forgotten.[118]

CHAPTER 7

'The Crisis is Passed'

Throughout much of 1847 and 1848, widespread destitution had coexisted in Belfast with nationalist agitation for repeal of the Union with Britain. Both circumstances were to have a significant impact on the subsequent development of Belfast. The nationalist uprising in the summer of 1848 led by the Young Ireland group, although small and unsuccessful, deepened existing political divides within Irish society. In response to the nationalist threat, Belfast and a number of other Ulster towns portrayed themselves as loyal Protestant garrisons surrounded by disaffected and disloyal Catholics. The resulting sectarian violence in 1849 led to legislation banning 'party' processions.

The loyalty of the people of Ulster was felt also to have been betrayed by the introduction of the Rate-in-Aid Act in 1849, which forced solvent Unions to subsidize destitute Unions in other parts of Ireland. Guardians in Belfast and other Unions in Ulster viewed this transfer of funds as unjust and its recipients as undeserving. The Rate-in-Aid controversy, therefore, deepened the debate about the respective claims of Belfast's poor and those from other areas. By 1849, society in Belfast was more divided that it had been three years earlier. At the same time, the Famine was viewed as being associated with the west and south of Ireland, whilst a myth was being created that – as a result of their own efforts – the north of Ireland had suffered less intensely than elsewhere. All of these conflicts shaped post-Famine Belfast which, in turn, affected its relationship with the rest of the country.

The Path to Recovery

By the summer of 1849, the prospects for the Belfast poor appeared to be auspicious. The corn and potato harvests were healthy. The mills were once again working full time and employment was readily available. In describing the linen trade, 'our staple article of manufacture', one local newspaper reported that 'every mill and hand is being fully employed'.[1] Exports from the port were buoyant, in particular those of butter and linen. The signs of stabilization which had been evident within the Belfast economy in the previous year appeared to be giving rise to a renewed confidence which, in turn, resulted in further industrial and commercial growth. At the same time, the threat of a nationalist uprising had disappeared, contributing to a more secure political and economic climate. The Rate-in-Aid crisis appeared also to have peaked and the veiled threats against the British connection evaporated. The predictions of the imminent collapse of the Poor Law system had proved also to be hollow.

Despite the economic disruption of the late 1840s, economic progress was evident within Belfast. One reflection of progress was in the development of a transport infrastructure, linked by a network of new bridges, roads and railway lines. In November 1845, work commenced on the Belfast to Ballymena railway which was completed in April 1848. Three months later, Holywood was reached as part of the Belfast and County Down Railway project.[2] The main line from Belfast to Newtownards was opened in May 1850.[3] The opening of these routes helped to integrate the markets in the northeast of the country. At the same time, they served to increase the pivotal role played by Belfast in relation to the surrounding towns. Their completion also demonstrated that, in the midst of crop failures and economic recession, large amounts of capital were available for investment in a variety of commercial projects.

A major achievement in Belfast's economic progress was the opening of a new channel from Garmoyle Pool to Belfast Lough on 10 July 1849. Its opening meant that large vessels could traverse the River Lagan regardless of the condition of the tide. The opening of the channel was carried out with due pomp and ceremony – champagne being poured into the river and a band playing 'Rule Britannia'. Initially, the channel was called Dargan's Channel, after the engineer who designed it, but in deference to the visit of the Queen to the town a few weeks later, it was renamed the Victoria Channel.[4] The opening of the new channel was symbolic of the commercial progress of Belfast in the midst of widespread economic devastation. At the same time, in conjunction with the development of railways, it marked an important step in the industrial development of Belfast by facilitating access to the town's harbour from other markets in Ulster. Ulster's markets, in turn, benefited from Belfast's links not only with Britain but with the rest of the Empire. These developments demonstrated that despite a depression within the agricultural and textile sectors, the Belfast economy possessed an underlying resilience. Moreover, the economic changes made in the 1840s contributed significantly to Belfast's commercial growth and industrial dominance in the second half of the nineteenth century. They also reaffirmed Belfast's economic supremacy not only within Ulster, but within the whole of Ireland.

Civic pride was also evident in the building of a university college and a new court house in the town in the late 1840s.[5] The confidence of Belfast manifested itself in a number of other ways. In 1849, the Town Council invited the British Association for the Advancement of Science to hold their next meeting in Belfast, to be organized by the Natural Historical and Philosophical Society of Belfast. In this way, the town would host 3,000 scientists from all over Europe. The Council had been reluctant to issue such invitations previously due to a lack of suitable accommodation and reception areas in the town. By 1849, however, they felt that Belfast possessed sufficient facilities and good enough transport links to host such an event. More importantly, the Council believed that 'Belfast has now arrived at such a position that, in considering her own feeling of self-respect, it could accommodate the Association with that public spirit in which she ought to do it.'[6] Overall, despite the devastation and deprivation of the previous years, Belfast entered the second half of the nineteenth century with renewed economic vigour and a firm confidence in its place amongst other European cities.

Yet, despite Belfast's economic improvement, poverty, hunger and disease remained evident within the town. The sufferings resulting from food shortages and unemployment had been replaced by problems caused by homelessness, disease and social dislocation. Consequently, a substantial number of Belfast's population were marginalized in the midst of a more general recovery. The influx of paupers from the surrounding countryside continued and contributed to the problem of impoverishment. They added both to Belfast's population growth and to the existing public health problems. The appearance of cholera in Belfast in December 1848 also contributed to a rise in mortality in the town. The fact that many of those affected were Catholic and possessed neither capital nor skills added to existing religious tensions within the town.

The summer of 1849 became notorious for a violent sectarian conflict which took place at a small mountain pass called Dolly's Brae, not far from Belfast. This confrontation became symbolic of deeper sectarian tensions existing within Ulster society. As a consequence, poverty and famine were replaced as the main problems in Belfast by divisions which followed religious rather than economic lines. Nevertheless, a month after the incident at Dolly's Brae, Queen Victoria visited Belfast and, temporarily, sectarian differences appeared to be forgotten. But the clash at Dolly's Brae had political implications which extended far beyond 1849 and which were to cast a shadow on the development of post-Famine Belfast. Increasingly, poverty and unemployment in Belfast became more closely associated with Catholicism.

Sectarianism both in the workplace and in gaining access to housing became more marked.

Throughout the summer months of 1849 local newspapers anxiously provided information on the state of the potato and corn crops. At the beginning of July, sightings of the blight were reported in County Limerick. By the end of the month, there was reported to be 'a great supply of potatoes' in the Belfast markets, which were blight-free and only 4d per stone.[7] Throughout August, as large supplies of potatoes continued to be available in the Belfast markets, further cautious optimism was apparent.[8] If the spell of dry weather continued, it was hoped that there would be no blight in Ulster.[9] By September it was evident that there was very little potato disease in the vicinity of Belfast. Moreover, the crop was reported to be a bumper one. The oat crop was considered to be healthy although small, whilst the wheat crop was good.[10] As a consequence of the anticipated abundant harvest, a spirit of optimism was evident. One newspaper stated:

> A feeling of hopefulness is beginning to spring up, while the sense of utter despondency which seemed to have overpowered all classes is giving way to a more healthy course of action in the belief that the crisis is passed.[11]

In addition to relieving poverty and disease, the Belfast Guardians were also involved in issues of a more political nature. At the end of 1848, a large number of Boards of Guardians in Ireland formed a national Poor Law Amendment Committee with the objective of bringing about changes in Poor Law legislation. The Belfast Guardians had attended some of the early meetings but withdrew on the grounds that they 'did not wish to mix themselves up in any agitation'. Instead, at the beginning of 1849, they formed their own committee for the purpose of modifying the Poor Law.[12] Apart from the unfairness of the Law of Removal, one of the main complaints concerned what they perceived to be the arbitrary powers of the central Commissioners. The Guardians sent a number of recommendations to the government for the reform of the Poor Law. When these met with a negative response, a deputation was sent to London, which met a similar reaction.[13]

In the spring of 1849, the Guardians became embroiled in a further dispute with the Poor Law Commissioners. The conflict was due to a new directive that required all Catholic inmates of Irish workhouses to be given nine days' holiday a year in recognition of their special religious feasts. The Guardians were outraged at this order, referring to the holy days as 'days of idleness'.[14] They also pointed out that Catholics 'in the north' (an area never clearly defined) had never had the same holidays as those in the south and had never complained about the situation.

The Guardians appointed a sub-committee which reported that the small number of holidays given to workers in Ulster had benefited manufacturers and had contributed to the commercial success and wealth of the area. If Catholic paupers were granted additional holidays, one result would be to 'create jealousy, dissatisfaction and disunion, and to draw a broader line of demarcation between the different religious denominations, instead of uniting them or fusing them into one'. The sub-committee also pointed out that many rich people and ordinary workers did not have nine days holiday in a year. They concluded that the regulation would place the destitute in a better position than people outside the workhouse. The Guardians asked the Commissioners to withdraw the regulation on the grounds that it was unwise to 'fling the element of religious discord, and in such an offensive form, into the administration of the system'.[15] The Commissioners' negative response widened even further the gulf between the Belfast Board and the central authorities.[16]

In the summer of 1849, the Belfast Union became implicated in a scandal which involved both the British and Australian governments. At the end of May, the Belfast Guardians were informed that a report about orphan emigrants recently sent to Australia from the workhouse was very critical of the training provision within the Union.[17] As a consequence, a formal enquiry was established, conducted by a Poor Law official, Caesar Otway.[18] The project which had led to the emigration of the orphans had been suggested by the Australian authorities at the beginning of 1847. One of the motives was that the Australian government was anxious to rectify the gender imbalance in the country by attracting more females to settle there.[19] The British government used the scheme as an opportunity to clear Irish workhouses of young orphaned females who, in the words of one Poor Law official, were in danger of becoming 'permanent deadwood' within the system.[20] Females aged between 14 and 18, therefore, were to be sent to Australia where, it was anticipated, they would become domestic servants. In the first instance, due to the intervention of Charles Trevelyan, the Permanent Secretary at the Treasury, females from northern workhouses were given preference over those from other Unions. Trevelyan – an evangelical moralist – believed that Protestant girls would be morally superior and more hard-working than their Catholic counterparts.[21] Accordingly, the first batch of orphan emigrants included a disproportionate number of inmates from northern workhouses, including the Belfast Union. On 6 October 1848, 183 inmates from workhouses in Ulster arrived in Sydney on board the *Earl Grey*.

The scheme was quickly beset with scandal. The girls were accused of behaving promiscuously during the long sea journey, swearing, mixing with the sailors and committing crimes of petty theft. More damagingly, following their arrival in Australia, they displayed little propensity for domestic work. The Belfast girls were singled out as particularly riotous, and were accused of being 'notoriously bad in every sense of the word ... for the most part addicted to stealing, and to using the most obscene and gross language, language that no person decently brought up could use'. A number of the Belfast girls were also charged as having been 'public girls', that is, prostitutes.[22] The Australian authorities complained to the British government who, in turn, directed the Poor Law Commissioners, to instigate an enquiry. The remit of the investigation was to discover if the selection procedures had been followed properly and if the good character of each of the 59 girls sent from the Belfast Union had been verified.

Following a searching enquiry, the Commissioners concluded that the Belfast Guardians had followed the selection process properly and that they had tried to ensure that suitable candidates were chosen. Consequently, girls with a 'suspicious moral character' or who used bad language were excluded from the selection. The Commissioners, therefore, exonerated the Guardians from the charges against them. At the same time, they acknowledged that the girls' behaviour had been improper. This omission was attributed to the fact that from an early age the girls had been sent to work in the mills. They regretted that the candidates had not 'undergone a greater amount of previous training and education in the workhouse', especially as a number had been inmates of the workhouse for over four years. Yet they did not believe that the girls were of 'depraved character'. Nor did the Commissioners agree with the Australian authorities that bad language was a sign of moral turpitude. The Commissioners also felt that the matron on board the ship had contributed to the girls' behaviour as she had failed to supervise them adequately. The conclusion of the report in regard to the Belfast Union emphasized:

> the peculiar circumstances of the town, wherein there is great and constant demand for the labour of young girls in factories, the effect of which may be to sometimes expose them at an early age to the contamination of evil example, and to familiarize them with the use of improper language.[23]

The Cholera Epidemic

In 1849, the Belfast Guardians had to confront a new disease which was especially prevalent amongst the poor of the town. The appearance of cholera in various ports and towns within Ireland had a short-term but devastating impact on mortality rates. The first cholera fatality in Ireland occurred in the Belfast workhouse in December 1848. The victim was an Irish pauper, Thomas Tiernan, who had been removed, with his family, from the Edinburgh Union.[24] Although Tiernan was blamed for introducing cholera into Belfast, the local Poor Law Inspector believed that the disease was already present in the town before his arrival.[25] Following Tiernan's death, the disease spread rapidly both in the workhouse and in the town, with doctors warning that it was a particularly virulent strain. In January 1849, because mortality had risen so sharply, the Guardians decided that they would no longer consult relatives of the dead about burial arrangements but inter them as quickly as possible.[26]

The cholera outbreak in the town had serious implications for the Poor Law Guardians who were responsible for providing treatment paid for from the local rates. To cope with the anticipated epidemic, Belfast was divided into a number of dispensary districts each of which was allocated medical attendants who were available both day and night.[27] The Guardians also paid for a covered car and pony to be supplied to medical staff so that newly reported cases could be dealt with quickly.[28] In January, an agreement was reached with the General Hospital whereby cholera patients could be removed from the workhouse at a cost of 2s 6d for the first day and 1s 3d thereafter.[29] Shortly afterwards, it was decided to divide the town into two large medical districts; those patients residing in the north and east to be sent to the General Hospital and those in the south and west, to the workhouse hospital.[30]

Within the workhouse itself, people were employed to sit up all night in the sleeping wards, in order that any cases of cholera could be reported immediately.[31] As a further preventative measure, the diet of the children was changed from stirabout and buttermilk to boiled bread and sweetmilk. They were also supplied with flannel belts, which were regarded as an effective palliative.[32] Regardless of these measures, disease within the workhouse spread rapidly, afflicting both inmates and staff.[33] By the beginning of February, the medical officers in the workhouse complained that they could no longer cope with the number of cholera patients. Due to a shortage of nurses, workhouse inmates were employed both to work in the hospital and to bury the dead. Those involved were confined to a sequestered ward but they were allowed the same rations as the workhouse porter.[34] By February, the disease had reached the outlying districts of Belfast, including Ligoniel and Dundonald.[35] To raise general awareness, the Guardians published instructions about what to do if a member of the public suspected a case of cholera.[36]

Other public bodies also took a variety of measures to prevent the spread of the disease. The military authorities in Belfast ordered the troops stationed in the town to stay in their barracks until the crisis had passed.[37] The committee of the Charitable Society prohibited inmates from leaving the Poorhouse and visitors from entering it for the duration of the epidemic. They also issued strict guidelines for those wishing to attend church; inmates being restricted to Trinity Church of Ireland, the Catholic Chapel in Donegall Street, or Rosemary Street Presbyterian Church. Whilst inside, inmates from the Poorhouse were to be seated separately from the rest of the congregation, a roll being taken on their entrance and prior to leaving.[38] It was not until December 1849 that the committee of the Charitable Society allowed the inmates to attend their usual places of worship without restriction.[39]

By the end of February, of the 515 cases reported in the Belfast Union, 179 had died.[40] Whilst cholera affected all classes, its impact was heaviest on the poorest sections of society, exacerbated by overcrowded and unhygienic accommodation.[41] Local medical officers attributed its rapid spread to the reluctance of some of the poor people who contracted the disease to attend a hospital, preferring to stay in their homes, for fear of inevitable death in such institutions.[42] Due to what was termed 'the great objection' of people in Ballymacarrett to attend the workhouse hospital, a temporary cholera ward was fitted out in a local store.[43] The medical officers were also instructed to inter immediately corpses of people who had died from the disease.[44]

In March, cholera was reported to be 'subsiding rapidly' in the town.[45] At the beginning of April, the workhouse master confirmed that no new cases had been reported in the institution. It had also disappeared from Dundonald and Ligoniel, where it had been particularly virulent.[46] Yet, hopes that the contagion had passed proved to be premature as it reappeared in May and within a few weeks was present in all parts of the town.[47] It was also reported to be attacking 'the better classes' rather than just the poor.[48] At this stage, 2,835 people had been treated for cholera within the Belfast Union and the death toll had risen to 871. By the end of July, the number of new cholera cases began to decline sharply. The decrease in both cholera and fever led the Board of Guardians to reduce medical provision. The Guardians also accepted the resignation of Dr Browne from 1 August as his services were no longer required in treating fever patients.[49] Following this date, the number of new cases declined rapidly. In the middle of August the total number of reported cases had reached 3,269.[50] By October, the authorities reported that the disease seemed to have disappeared with no new cases being reported in the town.[51] In the ten months since the first case appeared, the number of cholera victims in the town had reached 3,448, with 1,126 deaths.[52] However, the disease had not terminated. Almost 200 more cases appeared in the town, the final two occurring in December. Since its first appearance, the rate of mortality due to cholera in Belfast had been 36 per cent. Belfast's mortality rate compared favourably with that of other large towns such as Dublin and Galway, which experienced 44 per cent and 47 per cent mortality respectively (see Appendix VII).[53] Due to the reluctance in admitting to having the disease, however, the official mortality figures underestimated the impact of the epidemic.

Orange against Green

In 1848 political life in Belfast was dominated by fears of repeal of the Union and revolution. The Orangemen increasingly identified themselves with the forces of law and order against the perceived threat of rebellion. Various lodges responded to the situation by offering to arm themselves in defence of the country and of Protestant principles.[54] Orange lodges throughout Ulster declared their willingness to act in defence of the government as 'the native garrison of their country once again should their assistance be required'.[55] They informed the government that if they were provided with arms they would be able to defeat any uprising without the intervention of the military.[56] The Orangemen of Belfast also issued a statement warning of the possibility of an attempted uprising in the town, asserting:

> We are not free from apprehension in Belfast ... thank Providence, the loyalty of Ulster is not a mere name ... we are prepared here to come forward in any way we are required, under the control of the authorities, to act our part in the repression of outrage.[57]

The twelfth of July commemorations in 1848 became a microcosm of the wider struggle between nationalism and loyalism. Many of the press which traditionally had opposed the anniversary activities, in the face of the threat of armed rebellion, now regarded them in a positive light. The *Warder,* commenting on the decision of the Orangemen to march, said: 'we rejoice heartily in their decision to do so'.[58] The *Northern Whig*, which in the preceding years had opposed the anniversary marches, viewed them in 1848 as being 'regrettable but necessary'. They blamed 'the rebellious set' for reviving old tensions, the consequence of which was that 'The Orangemen felt that they had to give an answer to the attempts to seduce them to the repeal ranks.'[59] The *Belfast News-Letter* was also full of praise for the behaviour and demeanour of the Belfast Orangemen, remarking that 'They walked with the proud step of men conscious of their moral and physical superiority.'[60] The nationalist press, on the other hand, was apprehensive that the government and the Orange Order were forging a new alliance. The *Nation*, in an article entitled 'Ulster beware', warned that the government was deliberately fostering Orange societies whilst suppressing repeal ones.[61]

In preparation for the anticipated trouble on the twelfth, a large force of police which included two officers, four head constables, ten constables and 238 rank and file were sent to Belfast from Dublin on 9 July.[62] On the day of the anniversary, 30 lodges from Belfast travelled to Carrickfergus, where they were joined by Orangemen from Larne. They convened at a meadow provided by Mr Robinson, who also supplied refreshments including whiskey. Many of the speakers referred to the repeal agitation. Dr Drew read a letter from the Belfast Repeal Association which asked the Orangemen to join them in their struggle. It was treated with derision. Another speaker, referring to the various encroachments made by Irish Catholics in the preceding years, said that Orangemen should not be content until they had brought about a repeal of the Emancipation Act of 1829.[63] Following their return home, an incident occurred in Sandy Row when a Catholic girl, carrying a green branch, was attacked by Orangewomen. The clothes were torn from the top part of her body and all of her hair pulled out. She was only saved by the intervention of some of the men. There were a few other skirmishes in the town, which included stones being thrown and windows broken in Durham Street, Brown Street and Pound Street. A number of firearms were also discharged.[64] This apart, the day passed peacefully in Belfast and the town was reported to be quiet by ten in the evening.[65]

As fears of a nationalist rebellion grew, the Protestant press warned increasingly against the encroachment of Catholicism, expressing themselves in ever more sectarian terms. Within Belfast this was particularly evident as the town had a flourishing Protestant/Orange newspaper tradition which included the *Courier*, the *Belfast Protestant Journal*, the *Orange Citadel* and the *Warder*. These fears were not dispelled even after the suppression of the rebellion. The *Warder*, for example, in January 1849 reminded its readers: 'Our position has been to guard the Protestantism of Ireland. We believe it to be worth preserving and every blow it receives inflicts a wound on the United Kingdom.' In addition, they warned against the current 'Papal project and Roman-led Jew plot'.[66] Increasingly, Catholicism became synonymous with Nationalism and disloyalty to the Union.

Throughout 1848 and the early months of 1849, newspapers were reporting an increase in malicious fires in the vicinity of Belfast. In general, Catholics were blamed.[67] These accusations led a number of the wealthier Catholics in Belfast, including merchants and members of the Catholic Church hierarchy, to send a memorial to the Lord Lieutenant denying the 'slanderous insinuations published in certain newspapers imputing said incendiary outrages to an organized conspiracy of Roman Catholics'. They concluded by pointing out that the accusations were 'injurious to the harmony which ought to exist in a community of mingled sects and parties'. The memorialists asked for the Lord Lieutenant to instigate an investigation into the matter. This request was refused.[68]

The St Patrick's Day commemoration in 1849 by a number of Catholics was inauspicious, although some sectarian clashes took place, the most serious one occurring at Crossgar where two Protestants were killed. The Belfast newspapers reported the incident in partisan ways – the *Warder*, laying all the blame on the Ribbonmen, claimed that the Orangemen had 'acted purely on the defensive'.[69] Although there were rumours that the government was going to renew the Party Processions Act, which had the support of many Protestant newspapers, they proved to be unfounded.[70]

Following the conflict at Crossgar, some of the nationalist press called for party processions to be banned. The *Belfast Vindicator* was cynical that the government would allow them to continue as Britain benefited from faction fighting in Ireland. The paper went on to say:

They tell us the Orangemen are loyal and peaceable and should, therefore, be indulged in their innocent exhibitions, because they have been accustomed to them. According to this argument, the duration of a wrong, so to speak, consecrates its justice ... The party riots that have so long disgraced our country must, by the power of good men, if not the strong hand of government, be put down.[71]

In such a highly charged atmosphere, the twelfth of July commemoration became a flashpoint for wider political tensions. A number of people in Ulster were aware of the potential conflict and urged restraint. The Bishop of Down and Connor wrote a letter, which was published in the local press, asking the Orangemen not to march. His letter initiated a debate in the newspapers. Lord Massareene responded to it by publicly criticizing the Bishop and explaining why he had invited the Belfast and vicinity Orangemen to gather on his estate.[72] The conflict surrounding the twelfth anniversary was also followed by some of the British press. *The Times* referred to the Orange Order as 'that rather impracticable body ... who are resolved upon celebrating the twelfth of July with all its ancient mummeries'.[73] The magistrates in Belfast and Antrim, although they did not anticipate any trouble, asked if constabulary from other parts of the country could be sent to Belfast and to the Antrim meeting.[74]

On the morning of the twelfth, the Belfast lodges assembled at the Linen Hall. Each section was accompanied by fife and drum and they were preceded by a brass band. Thirty-eight train carriages were required to carry the Orangemen to Lord Massareene's estate in Antrim. One of the dignitaries present was Viscount Dungannon. The speeches made the usual attacks on the Church of Rome and warned against its ascendancy. Another common theme was the system of national education and the new 'godless' university colleges. At the same time, the Orangemen congratulated themselves on their role in suppressing the rising of the previous year, Dr Mortimer O'Sullivan from Belfast reminding them that 'this time last year the Orangemen were, under God, the means of rescuing this country from carnage and the dreadful effects of bloody civil war'.[75] The meeting of the Belfast Orangemen was reported to be the largest ever. The magistrates had expected approximately 3,000 Orangemen and 10,000 spectators to attend the meeting, but as many as 20,000 people had been present, making it one of the largest ever held. Moreover, in the previous twelve months a large number of merchants and nobility had joined or rejoined the Order.[76]

The early reports on the twelfth were favourable, with the processions being described as peaceful and with larger attendances than ever. However, a conflict took place on the evening of the twelfth in Ballymacarrett when two men, driving through the village on horses decorated with orange lilies, were attacked by local railworkers. Local Orangemen came to the rescue of the men and a general fight took place in which a number of people were injured.[77] Later in the evening more fights occurred and shots were fired but the constabulary were able to restore order easily.[78] One of the men who had been attacked in Ballymacarrett, John Cleary, subsequently died.[79] The verdict of the inquest a few days later was 'manslaughter by some person unknown'. In expectation that Cleary's funeral would result in widespread rioting, extra troops were brought into the town but the day passed peacefully.[80] None the less, the incident had long-term repercussions as it was followed by sporadic rioting in Belfast, especially in the area around Barrack Street, leading one local paper to say that the locality 'had acquired a disgraceful notoriety since the last twelfth of July'.[81]

The events in Belfast on the twelfth of July were overshadowed by reports of a conflict at Dolly's Brae, a small mountain village which was occupied exclusively by Catholics. In 1849, the Rathfriland Orange lodge decided to march through the village to attend a rally at Castlewellan. The route chosen by the Orangemen was neither a traditional nor a direct one. One Protestant newspaper said that the decision to march through the village was due to the murder of two Orangemen around St Patrick's Day, incidents which had 'exasperated the feelings of both parties to the highest pitch'.[82] Dublin Castle, warned of a potential confrontation, dispatched extra magistrates, troops and constabulary to the village, but allowed the march to take place. Lord Roden, the Grand Orange Master of the County, permitted the Orangemen to congregate on his estate and provided them with alcohol. He also urged them to do their duty as loyal Protestants. Despite the military presence, a collision did take place in the evening in which five Catholics and one Orangeman were killed. The dead Catholics included a ten-year-old boy who was shot through the abdomen and a woman of 85 who was stabbed with a bayonet.[83] A large number of Catholic homes were burnt down, including the priest's house and the church. One Belfast newspaper justified the event by saying that the Orangemen had been 'roused beyond endurance' and commended them for 'displaying very considerable skill and the greatest bravery'.[84]

The incident received widespread coverage in both the British and the Irish press throughout July, only being supplanted by preparations for the visit of Queen Victoria at the beginning of August. The confrontation at Dolly's Brae was debated in the House of Commons and resulted in the appointment of an official enquiry. During the heated parliamentary debate, John Bright, the radical MP for Birmingham, said that Dolly's Brae had occurred because both the police and the Orangemen viewed Catholic people as their enemies but, in his opinion, 'the only crime of the people in the north' was to have been born Catholic. Bright demanded that the subsequent investigation should be 'searching and impartial'.[85] Following the completion of the official enquiry, the magistrates present at Dolly's Brae were reprimanded for allowing the incident to get out of hand. More significantly, Lord Roden was removed from his position on the judiciary as a magistrate, despite some protests in the House of Commons.[86] A further consequence of the conflict at Dolly's Brae was that the following year the government introduced the Party Processions Act which banned all political and party demonstrations. Lord Clarendon predicted that the outcome of the conflict would be positive and would lead to 'the extinction of Orangeism'.[87] Regardless of his optimism, in the short term, the conflict at Dolly's Brae exacerbated existing sectarian tensions in Belfast at a time when the increasing Catholic population was regarded by its Protestant neighbours as both a threat and a burden. In the long term, the conflict at Dolly's Brae became embedded in Orange folklore as a significant victory of Protestantism over Catholicism.[88]

A Royal Visit

For a few days in August 1849, class divisions, political factions and sectarian differences were set aside when Queen Victoria visited the island. Hitherto, visits to Ireland by British monarchs had been rare, although excursions outside London became an increasing feature of royal life in the nineteenth century. In 1821, William IV had visited Dublin. A visit by Victoria to Ireland had been the subject of speculation for a number of years and the demand had intensified in the wake of her stay in Scotland in 1842 and her clear affection for that country.[89] However, a personal lack of interest in Ireland, combined with political agitation and the consequences of the potato blight led to repeated postpone-ments. A trip planned for 1848 was also deferred due to political unrest both in Ireland and throughout Europe, the result of which had been the overthrow of a number of royal houses.[90] The actions of the Young Irelanders led one Belfast newspaper to blame the further delay on the actions of the 'plotters of rebellion in Ireland'.[91]

In June 1849 Dublin Castle confirmed that Victoria would visit the country later in the year, probably in early August.[92] On the Prime Minister's recommendation, it was to be a private rather than a state visit, on the grounds that the latter would 'lead to ill-timed expenditure and inconvenience to her subjects', a situation regarded as inappropriate due to 'the general distress uniformly still prevalent in Ireland'.[93] The visit was to be confined to three major ports on the east coast – the Cove of Cork, Dublin and Belfast – with a few days in Dublin and only a few hours in the other centres. The royal party was to journey around the coast rather than overland, with the royal family – Victoria, Albert and four of their children – sailing in a yacht, the *Fairy*. Sir George Grey, the Home Secretary, rather than the Prime Minister was to escort the Queen. Following the visit to Belfast, the royal party would then travel directly to Scotland.[94]

Although Victoria's stay in Ireland was to be brief, the government viewed it as important in terms of propaganda. Since the harvest of 1847, leading members of the British government had been declaring that the Famine was over and the visit was to be a confirmation that this was the case. At the same time, it was hoped that the visit would bring increased British capital into Ireland and thus help rebuild the economy on more commercial lines. The fact that the visit occurred so soon after the attempted uprising in 1848 was regarded by the Belfast press as significant, demonstrating that the repeal movement was dead and the Union with Britain remained firm.[95]

Throughout July extensive preparations were made in the three designated ports. In Belfast, the activities were especially intense, as the dominant groups in the town prided themselves on having a special relationship with the British monarchy. Moreover, the Queen would be the first royal visitor since 1690, when William of Orange had passed through on his way to the Boyne. The fact that Victoria, like William III, would stay only a few hours did not deter local newspapers from devoting many column inches to arrangements for the visit. At the same time, the town councillors kept a watchful eye on the welcome preparations being made by the corporations of Cork and Dublin.[96]

Security arrangements during the visit were stringent. Additional troops and constabulary were deployed to each of the three centres in the itinerary. In Dublin, tents were erected in the Phoenix Park to accommodate additional troops brought from Naas for the duration of Victoria's stay in the Vice-Regal Lodge.[97] An extra 300 constables were placed in Belfast. In addition, battalions from the 13th Light Dragoons from Dundalk, two companies of the 9th Regiment from Newry, two companies of the 51st Regiment from Enniskillen and the 13th Regiment were stationed in the town.[98]

Immediately following confirmation of Victoria's forthcoming visit, the Belfast Town Council convened a meeting to appoint a committee to coordinate arrangements for the royal reception. At the first sitting, the committee resolved to greet the Queen 'in a manner which shall evince the loyalty of the inhabitants of the borough'. They also decided to invite other local public bodies to join the preparations and prepare suitable addresses for presentation to the Queen.[99] At the end of July, an additional committee was appointed by the Council for the purpose of preparing an official address on its behalf. Loyalty and commercial enterprise were to be the key themes of the several addresses. A variety of other local organizations also stated their eagerness to present official greetings. Copies of all the messages were forwarded to the Home Office in London for approval. The addresses came from a wide range of institutions, including the Belfast Harbour Commissioners, the General Assembly of the

Presbyterian Church, the Royal Belfast Academical Institution, the Royal Society for the Promotion of Flax in Ireland, the Teetotal Association of Belfast and the Ulster Society for the Education of the Deaf and Dumb.[100]

For the most part, the addresses adhered to the advice of *The Times*, which had recommended that they be 'devoid of all allusions to political or ecclesiastical opinion', although loyalty to the Union and monarchy was regarded as an acceptable sentiment.[101] For example, the address presented by the 'loyal inhabitants of County Down' described the visit as an 'auspicious event which may lead to dispel the gloom and despondency unhappily at this present time pervading our land'.[102] One of the dignitaries chosen to present it to the Queen was Lord Roden, the local landlord who recently had been disgraced over the conduct of some of the Orange Order at Dolly's Brae.[103]

The consensus within Belfast Council was less evident elsewhere. Dublin Corporation, for example, was split as to whether the address should refer to its demand for legislative independence (whilst maintaining that links with the monarchy should be retained).[104] Limerick Corporation, for its part, saw the visit as an opportunity to seek a royal pardon for prisoners associated with the uprising in the previous year.[105] The Mayor of Cork, who was a supporter of repeal, was asked to include in his address to the Queen, an appeal on behalf of 'Mr Smith O'Brien and his associates', but he declined to do so.[106] In general, newspapers sympathetic to repeal believed that Victoria's visit should be used as an opportunity to ask for an amnesty for those men involved in the 1848 uprising.[107]

A few notes of discord were also apparent in Belfast. The Rev. Dr Thomas Drew, a virulently anti-Catholic Anglican clergyman, issued a public warning that his loyalty to the Queen was 'conditional' and would be withdrawn if she visited the new university college in Belfast – an objection based on the absence of religious education in the college.[108] The Queen had also accepted an invitation to visit the premises of the Ulster Society for the Education of the Deaf and the Dumb. However, this agreement was reversed when it was pointed out to the royal party that the institute was exclusively Protestant and opposed to non-denominational education.[109] Instead, at the last minute, it was decided that Victoria and Albert would pass by the Society but not go inside.[110] This resolution caused considerable embarrassment to the institute's managers, who had made elaborate arrangements for meeting the Queen, including the hiring of a band.[111] The decision not to visit the Deaf and Dumb Institute was in line with a recent policy which stated that royal support and patronage would be withheld from institutions in Ireland which were exclusively Protestant – a decision which caused considerable annoyance to many Protestants in Ireland, who felt that Catholics were being unreasonably favoured.[112]

Throughout July elaborate preparations were made for the royal visit to Belfast, although the route had not been finalized and the date of arrival was still uncertain. A pavilion was erected at the end of High Street where Victoria was to land and a triumphal arch was constructed opposite Prince's Street which was to be covered with flowers and banners, including the traditional Irish greeting *Céad Mile Fáilte*. Along the anticipated route the buildings were painted and seating was provided for approximately 5,000 spectators. The platforms erected by the Town Council were to be rented at 5 shillings each, although members of the council were each to receive seven free seats.[113] It was estimated that the proceeds of the sale of the seats would raise in the region of £1,143 15s, which was to be donated to the General Hospital. The Town Council was accused of parsimony over their decision not to organize a 'general illumination' similar to the one in Dublin. They responded by saying that such a display would have been out of place in view of the brevity of the visit, but they did hire an 'eminent pyrotechnicist' to provide fireworks on the newly named Queen's Island. An arch was also constructed on the Island and seats erected for spectators to obtain the first view of the royal party sailing up the channel.[114] A charge was to be made for the seats and for watching the display on the island, the proceeds to be given to the General Hospital.[115]

The Royal Squadron left England on 1 August and sailed first to the Cove of Cork.[116] During her subsequent stay in Dublin, the Queen was the guest in the Vice-Regal Lodge of the Lord Lieutenant, Lord Clarendon. A number of Ulster dignitaries, including the Marquises of Abercorn and Downshire, the Earl of Enniskillen, Lord Massareene, Lord Dufferin and Lord Roden travelled to the capital to take part in the various official functions. To commemorate Victoria's arrival in Dublin, Lord Clarendon asked the Mendicity Institute to provide a dinner for 1,000 poor people, including the inmates of the institute.[117] Victoria left Kingstown harbour near Dublin on the evening of 10 August and travelled overnight, arriving in Belfast the following morning. The journey was rough, with both Victoria and Albert experiencing sea-sickness.[118] The Town Council had provided the Copelands Lighthouse with a telegraph to enable them to be informed of the arrival of the Royal Squadron.[119] A large number of vessels, many of which had been hired specially for the occasion, sailed up Belfast Lough to greet the royal party. Amongst the craft was *Erin's Queen*, hired by the Young Men's Total Abstinence Society Band, which welcomed the visitors with a selection of music.[120] Shortly

after 9 o'clock, various officials were received on board the royal
yacht. Amongst the first were the Mayor, William Johnston, and
other town dignitaries who officially welcomed the royal party to
Belfast and presented the mace of the borough to the Queen.
Members of the Council wore especially made costumes
comprising cloaks trimmed with ermine and waistcoats
embroidered with shamrocks, roses and thistles. A series of
welcoming addresses were then delivered to the royal couple. The
Town Council, when welcoming the Queen to 'the capital of [her]
Northern province' averred that:

> in no part of your dominions do you possess a more loyal and
> attached community than that of the town on which you have
> conferred the distinguished favour of honouring it by your Royal
> presence, on this your first visit to Ireland.

Following the greetings, the Mayor was knighted before the
assembled company of the yacht.[121] Other addresses made to the
Queen whilst on board the *Fairy* similarly emphasized the loyalty
and commercial enterprise of Ulster. The Town Council's address
also maintained that:

> notwithstanding the agricultural and commercial difficulties of
> the times, [Belfast] will be found in a state of rapid
> improvement, and affording the most satisfactory evidence of
> the national advantages derivable from the legislative Union of
> the Empire – advantages which are duly appreciated by a
> peaceful, industrious, enterprising and loyal population.[122]

The address of the General Assembly of the Presbyterian
Church compared the visit by William of Orange in 1690 with the
present occasion, stating that 'Your Royal predecessor came to
assert the public liberties in a time of war; your Majesty comes to
perpetuate them in a time of peace.'[123] The address described the
legislative Union between Ireland and Britain as 'one of the best
securities against political jealousies and best preservatives of
national prosperity and peace'.[124]

Few welcomes referred to the Famine. One of the few was that
of the Catholic clergy of Down and Connor who, after professing
that 'we yield to no class or portion in warm attachment to your
Majesty's person, or devoted loyalty to your Majesty's throne',
then thanked God for placing on the throne at a time of
'commotions abroad and unparalleled distress in some portions of
our afflicted country, a Queen tender of the feelings and compas-
sionate of the wants of all'.[125] Clearly, both the political agitation
and distress of the previous years were being construed as
problems that had existed outside Belfast.

The royal couple did not disembark until almost 3 o'clock in the afternoon; their children remaining on board the yacht. Thousands of sightseers had crowded into the town, which was estimated to contain double its usual population. Special trains were in operation on the newly opened routes from Armagh, Richhill, Portadown, Lurgan, Moira, Lisburn and Dunmurry.[126] In Armagh, many shopkeepers agreed to close for the day to allow their assistants to travel to Belfast to witness the historic occasion and 'express their loyalty' to the Queen.[127] Such gestures of wholehearted support were considered by the local press as demonstrating 'the moral worth of the community'.[128]

In honour of the occasion, a triumphal arch was erected and a special pavilion positioned at the quayside end of High Street for the sovereign and local dignitaries. Five galleries were also erected at various points in High Street to accommodate nearly 4,000 spectators. After passing through the pavilion, the royal couple commenced their tour of the town in the carriage of the Marquis of Londonderry. As they travelled down High Street, the band of the 9th Regiment played the National Anthem. During the long wait for the royal party to appear, various bands along the route kept the spectators entertained with stirring tunes.[129]

In keeping with the commercial nature of Belfast, one of the highlights of the Queen's tour was a visit to the White Linen Hall. Inside, the various stages of linen production were demonstrated and samples of the finished articles were displayed. Of particular interest was work produced by women trained by the Ladies' Association for the Relief of Destitution in Connaught and samples of lace made by women from the Fisherwick Place Lace School, which had been established in 1847 to provide employment for destitute mill workers.[130] The tour was conducted by the Marquis of Londonderry, a patron of the Linen Hall, together with his wife and daughter. It lasted for approximately 45 minutes. The *Belfast News-Letter*, describing the tour, stated that whilst Belfast had little architectural heritage, the town possessed other qualities which were 'characteristic of national greatness and prosperity – great and noble, commercial and benevolent institutions – splendid and capacious harbours – and an industrious, independent, legal and peaceable population'.[131]

The royal party then passed by the workhouse, where numbers of children were positioned outside, 'dressed in humble attire but scrupulously clean and neat'. The fact that the planned visit to the Deaf and Dumb Institute was excluded from the itinerary meant that the royal party next visited the Botanic Gardens. At the new university college, Victoria and Albert left the coach and entered the building 'for a few minutes'. The coach also passed the premises of the Belfast Charitable Society in North Queen Street, where a number of boys formed a brass band and struck up the National Anthem as the royal party passed. On the return journey to town, a poor woman was said to have jumped out of the crowds, exclaiming: 'Oh, the Lord love her purty face, for goodness is in her ... God save your Majesty and the whole of yez – hurra.'[132]

Along the royal route, numerous buildings had been freshly painted for the occasion, with many festooned with flags and flowers. There was also a number of more unusual displays. The turnpike on the old Dublin Road, for example, was decorated with a crown made of new potatoes, whilst potatoes still in their stalks were draped on a house in Donegall Street. Underneath this embellishment was a banner with the inscription 'Good Times'. The most striking decoration was a house adorned with Mexican drapes and ostriches, which were placed between two stuffed tigers brought from Panama. Two colourfully dressed attendants waved flags as the Queen's coach passed.[133]

At 6 o'clock in the evening the royal party left Belfast, having been in town for little over three hours. The Mayor was thanked for his hospitality, to which Sir George Grey responded with the comment that 'the arrangements in all respects were most creditable to Belfast'. The festivities in the town continued after the Queen's departure, with firework displays lasting until midnight. On the same evening also, the Mayor gave a sumptuous banquet for a number of dignitaries in the Donegall Arms. The rural areas around Belfast joined in the celebrations by lighting bonfires on the hillsides.[134]

Despite the brevity of the visit, the *Belfast News-Letter* described the event as 'the most auspicious and memorable that has occurred in the metropolis of the North, since it began to deserve the honourable epithet'.[135] Lord Dungannon suggested that a monument be erected in Belfast to commemorate the royal visit, Belfast having as yet no public monuments.[136] The success of the Queen's visit also pleased the government. The official letter of thanks by Sir George Grey, written on board the royal yacht on behalf of the Queen, referred to:

> The heartfelt satisfaction which she has derived from her reception in that portion of the United Kingdom, from the time of Her Majesty's arrival in Cork to that of her departure from Belfast, of warm and devoted loyalty and attachment to her throne and person.[137]

The Lord Lieutenant believed that the visit had strengthened the Union with Britain, and said of the visit to Belfast:

> Everything appears to have gone off to our hearts' desire ... and the Queen's presence has united all classes and parties in a

manner incredible to those who know the distance at which they have hitherto been kept asunder ... Even the ex-Clubbists who threatened broken heads and windows before the Queen came, are now among the most loyal of her subjects, and are ready, according to the police reports, to fight anyone who dare say a disrespectful word of Her Majesty.[138]

In the wake of the visit, Clarendon sent £300 to the Bishop of Down and Connor on behalf of Her Majesty for distribution amongst the poor of Belfast. However, Clarendon warned that:

In the allocation of this sum I am most anxious that Her Majesty's name should not, even in the remotest manner, be mixed up with political or sectarian discussions, and that no interruption should take place of that harmony and goodwill which characterized all parties during the recent visit of the Queen.

Clarendon requested that this money should go to the Belfast General Hospital, which had the support of all classes. Consequently, all the monies collected during Victoria's visit to Belfast were given to that institution. *The Times*, commenting on this action, described it 'as indicative of the Royal resolve to discourage sectarianism of every hue'.[139]

The *Banner of Ulster* also regarded the visit as strengthening the Union by offering further proof that 'the intoxicating idea, cherished by so many, that there was strength in the Roman Catholic portion of Ireland to resist successfully the British power has proved to be a delusion'.[140] Other Belfast newspapers, however, took offence at an article which appeared in the London-based *Morning Chronicle*, which described the population of Belfast as being a 'mixed breed'. It went on to say that:

There is a want of the fun, the vivacity, the careless good humour, so delightfully characteristic of the more Southern parts of Ireland. The people have, comparatively, a sour, cantankerous look. Besides I have seen more drunken men here than I saw during a fortnight's stay in the South.[141]

The *Banner* attributed the tone of the article to the fact that the correspondent had come to Belfast already prejudiced against the 'Black Northerners'.[142]

Other notes of discord had been expressed regarding the visit. The three Catholic Archbishops (Archbishop Crolly of Armagh had died in April) privately disagreed about an address to the Queen; Archbishops Slattery and MacHale believing that she was indifferent to the suffering of the poor caused by the Famine and that the address did little to remind her of its continuation. Some of the press in Dublin also believed that the associated celebrations were ill-timed and inappropriate, one article comparing them to 'illuminating a graveyard'.[143] In Belfast, however, there was less discord amongst the local press or the Catholic hierarchy regarding the visit. Religious and political grievances were overlooked as the hierarchies of the three main Churches vied in their declarations of loyalty. Yet, whilst the itinerary in Belfast reflected the determination of the government not to allow the Queen to be associated with sectarian institutions, Lord Roden, who had been censured publicly for his part in a sectarian conflict only a few weeks earlier, was chosen by his fellow landlords to officially welcome the Queen to both Dublin and Belfast.

Overall, the royal visit was judged in both Westminster and Dublin Castle to have been a major success. In Belfast, the visit had provided an opportunity for the predominantly Protestant town to reaffirm its allegiance to the Crown and Constitution. These declarations contrasted with the situation only a few months earlier, when taxpayers throughout Ulster had threatened open rebellion and warned of the lasting damage to the Union if the Rate-in-Aid tax was introduced. During the brief visit of the Queen to Belfast, this antagonism appeared to evaporate. The *Banner of Ulster* summed up the town's amnesia when it concluded that 'The loyalty of the North has never been doubted; but on Saturday last it burst forth in a blaze of irresistible devotion.'[144]

By the end of 1849, therefore, the Famine appeared to be over finally in Belfast, whilst the uprising in 1848 and the Queen's visit in 1849 confirmed that the loyalty of the local population to the Union was stronger than ever. Yet, between 1845 and 1849 fresh pressures had emerged in Belfast society which had been grafted onto existing tensions. As a consequence, although Belfast's recovery from the Famine was rapid compared with many other parts of the country, poverty, proselytism, political divisions and Protestantism had changed the town in a way that was to have reverberations into the following century.

CHAPTER 8

Aftermath. 'A Hell Below a Hell'

A good harvest in 1849 and the steady revival of local industry meant that demand for poor relief continued to fall. The Belfast Guardians were thus able to face the new decade with optimism having weathered the difficulties triggered by the potato failure of 1845 and successive years. However, the impact of the Famine on the town had left a number of long-term legacies. Although demand for relief in Belfast continued to decrease after 1849, recovery was slow for the poorest classes. Notwithstanding improved conditions in the Union in 1849, the number of people dependent on poor relief remained high. In 1841, the Belfast workhouse had been built for 1,000 paupers but in July 1849, the number of people receiving relief inside the various workhouse buildings was 2,643; 2,034 in the main workhouse, 145 in the fever hospital, 170 in the College Hospital in Barrack Street, and 294 in the old House of Correction in Victoria Street.[1] Despite the changes in the Poor Law in 1847, which had permitted outdoor relief, none had been provided in the Belfast Union. Instead, the Guardians preferred to provide indoor relief only, extending accommodation in order to make this possible. In October 1849, a new building for the use of pauper children was completed. As a consequence, the auxiliary workhouses at the former House of Correction and the College Hospital were closed.[2] By the end of the year, all the temporary buildings erected on the site of the main workhouse had been removed.[3] Yet the numbers receiving relief remained higher than had been envisaged in 1841. Alternative survival strategies were also used to deal with poverty. In 1841, the town had contained 43 pawnbrokers; by 1851, the number had grown to 55.[4]

Even into the 1850s, demand for poor relief continued to be higher than it had been prior to 1845. In December 1851, the workhouse contained 1,749 able-bodied inmates and 443 sick paupers.[5] By 1854, the average daily number of paupers in the workhouse was 2,008, with only the Cork, Dublin and Limerick Unions providing more relief. On average, however, paupers remained in the Belfast workhouse for 61 days, which was one of the lowest periods of stay in the country. This figure suggests either a greater availability of work outside the workhouse or that the deterrent aspect of workhouse life was particularly well applied

in Belfast.[6] The Belfast Guardians were also one of the few Boards
that did not avail themselves of the provisions introduced in 1849
to assist workhouse inmates to emigrate.[7] The demand for relief
continued to fall in Belfast until 1859 when it rose as a
consequence of three consecutive bad harvests.[8] By 1863, demand
had again stabilized and the average daily number of paupers in
the workhouse had fallen to 1,523. In this year also, one person
was given outdoor relief in the Belfast Union.[9] In addition to the
fall in pauper numbers, overall expenditure on poor relief fell in the
Union. This trend was repeated throughout Ireland. Since 1850,
the cost of poor relief in all Irish Poor Law Unions had fallen
drastically and, as a result, was far lower than in Unions in
England, Wales or Scotland.[10]

The post-Famine recovery and the revival in the town's
industries did not bring to an end the extreme poverty experienced
by some of Belfast's population. In 1853, the Rev. O'Hanlon
published an account of his *Walks Among the Poor of Belfast*. He
admitted to being shocked by the 'deplorable condition of the poor
who inhabit the back streets, courts and alleys of our rapidly
extending and populous town'.[11] He described the areas around
Brady's Row, Green Court, Henry Square, Johnny's Entry and
Grattan Court – which lay close to the city centre – as being
'crowded with human beings in the lowest stage of social
degradation'.[12] In Brady's Row, he found one house which
contained a family of seven who lived and slept in the same room
'without windows and open in all directions', the wretchedness of
which was 'utterly impossible to describe'.[13] At the same time, he
believed that poverty and squalor were contributing to the spread
of vice in the town which, in turn, meant that there existed
'numbers of houses of ill-fame found in the lower streets of our
town – the worst description of brothels – for even here within the
lowest depth, a lower deep still opens – a hell below a hell'.[14]

An on-going source of grievance for Poor Law Guardians in
Ireland was the operation of the British Laws of Settlement and
Removal, which continued to disadvantage Unions situated in the
east of Ireland. Their continuation in the late nineteenth century
dominated the administration of the Irish Poor Law and was a
source of grievance between the Irish Poor Law Commissioners
and the British government, and between the Irish and British
boards of Guardians.[15] The Irish Commissioners repeatedly asked
for British laws to be abolished, describing removal as 'an
interference with the personal liberties of the [Irish] poor,
unknown, we believe, in any other part of Europe'.[16]

The nature of poverty was also changing after 1850, and was
increasingly caused by disease or unemployment rather than crop

failure. In the post-Famine years, a higher proportion of paupers were unhealthy when admitted to the workhouse, demonstrating the increasing importance of the institution as a hospital for the sick poor.[17] In 1854, in recognition of the shifting balance between sick and healthy paupers, the Belfast Guardians provided additional infirmary accommodation.[18] In 1862, an amendment was made to the Poor Law which allowed Guardians to provide medical relief in the workhouse infirmaries to all sick persons within the Union rather than only to pauper inmates, which had previously been the case.[19] This regulation was widely utilized in the Belfast Union and in 1863, 5,002 sick persons received treatment within the workhouse's infirmaries.[20] In the same year, approximately 40 per cent of paupers admitted to the workhouse were already ill.[21] Since 1850, however, infectious disease had been declining throughout Ireland. In Belfast, the number of fever cases declined drastically following the Famine and industrial accidents became one of the main causes of ill health.[22] In 1870 there was a smallpox epidemic in Belfast which contributed to a demand for workhouse relief.[23] As a consequence, the average number of daily inmates rose by approximately 50 per cent to 2,426.[24]

In the late nineteenth century, therefore, the workhouse continued to be the main resource of the poor for both relief and medical assistance. But the demand for poor relief continued to be disproportionately high amongst Catholics; in general one in every two inmates was Catholic despite the fact that they accounted for less than a third of the town's population.[25] In contrast, the administrators of the Poor Law and the workhouse staff remained overwhelmingly Protestant. In 1846, out of the 55 staff employed in workhouses in the Belfast area, only three positions were held by Catholics.[26] In 1892, of the 94 workhouse staff in Belfast, three were Catholic and the other 91 were Protestant.[27]

The social composition of Belfast had also changed during the Famine decade. Employment in the textile and associated industries had expanded rapidly. In 1841, they had employed 13,296 people and by 1851, the total had grown to 18,996. Much of the growth had been in female employment, women and girls accounting for two-thirds of all employees in 1851.[28] The general health of mill and factory workers in Belfast remained poor. An inadequate diet, overcrowded accommodation, long working hours, together with high levels of pollution in the town, meant that in the second half of the nineteenth century Belfast had one of the highest death rates within the United Kingdom. Death from tuberculosis was particularly high in Belfast, and by 1891, it was responsible for one in every six deaths in the city.[29] The Medical

Officer of Health, Dr Whitaker, attributed the prevalence of the disease not only to poor living conditions, but also to pollution within the textile factories due to lack of ventilation. Urging further government regulation, he argued that 'It is a great error to suppose that nothing can be done and that this poisoning of the air is an inevitable feature of certain trades.'[30]

Migration and emigration were two of the most enduring legacies of the Famine years. Changes in linen production and the emergence of Belfast as the linen capital of Ireland meant that thousands of people from rural areas sought employment in the mills and factories of the town. Demand for labour could not keep pace with supply, and in the immediate aftermath of the Famine, there was a shortage of hand-loom weavers. As a consequence, between 1849 and 1853 the wages of these workers rose between 20 and 30 per cent.[31]

Large-scale emigration even after good harvests returned to Ireland was one of the most significant consequences of the Famine and was a major contributor to the continued decline of the Irish population. Although the whole province of Ulster experienced population loss in the second half of the nineteenth century, the greatest decline occurred in counties Cavan, Fermanagh and Monaghan. In stark contrast, the town of Belfast continued to grow; in 1841, the population had been 75,000, by 1851 it had reached 98,000, and by 1901, it was 387,000.[32] Much of the growth of Belfast in the post-Famine decades was due to migration to the town, especially from the neighbouring counties of Down and Antrim, but a small number of migrants to Belfast came from the distant counties of Cork and Kerry (see Appendix VIII). But the overall increase in the population of Belfast disguised the considerable losses experienced by some local areas during the Famine years. Whilst the town itself experienced a population growth, some of the outlying districts which were part of the Belfast Union underwent a decline. Significantly, between 1841 and 1851 the population of Ballyhackamore fell from 1,979 to 1,534; Castlereagh from 1,524 to 1,304; Dundonald from 1,151 to 933, and Holywood from 3,066 to 2,783.[33]

A disproportionate number of famine migrants to Belfast were Catholic. The impact of this was to change the religious composition of the town. At the beginning of the nineteenth century only 10 per cent of Belfast's population had been Roman Catholic. In 1861, due to Famine and post-Famine immigration, the number of Catholics peaked at 34 per cent. After this date, the proportion began to decline. The Famine immigrants usually settled in the poorest districts alongside their co-religionists, which served to reinforce denominational divisions along economic and geographic lines. Due to their rural background, Catholic immigrants generally possessed few industrial skills and were willing to take the lowest paid jobs. For unskilled workers, especially in the linen industry, wages remained low in comparison with other urban areas in the United Kingdom.[34] Increasingly also, some employers practised a policy of discrimination in order to keep the more skilled and higher paid jobs for Protestant workers.[35] Consequently, migration to Belfast became an attractive prospect for rural Protestants rather than for Catholics. By the end of the century, Catholics accounted for 24 per cent of the town's population.[36] Significantly, despite the growing prosperity of Belfast, 'the new industrial city became the setting for old sectarian battles'.[37]

There had also been an increase in the number of religious ministers in Belfast during the Famine decade. Between 1841 and 1851, the number of ministers in the three main Churches had increased, although the growth was most marked in the Presbyterian Church. The number of ministers in the Anglican Church had increased from eleven to 16; the number of Roman Catholic clergy from five to eight, and the number of Presbyterian ministers from 18 to 31.[38] Protestantism within the town continued to be characterized by evangelical fundamentalism, which had been revitalized during the Famine. Much of the evangelical theology preached in Belfast was grounded in the threat posed by Catholicism to Protestantism, mutual mistrust keeping the Churches apart.[39] A similar feature of the main Catholic and Protestant Churches was that they tended to be authoritarian and conservative. Increasingly also, they emphasized the differences between the Churches which also contributed to an atmosphere of antipathy and intolerance.[40] At the same time, as the Home Rule agitation increased, for Ulster Protestants religious identity became an essential part of British identity, driven by the fear that a Dublin government would transform them from being part of a majority within the United Kingdom to being part of a religious minority within Ireland. During the third Home Rule debate in 1912, for example, the Synod of the Church of Ireland declared: 'We cannot accept any assurances that either the property of our Church or our civil and religious liberty may be safely entrusted to a Parliament in which we should be outnumbered by men who are dominated by traditions and aspirations wholly different from our own.'[41]

Whilst the growing prosperity of the town had benefited the Catholic middle classes, Protestants continued to dominate official positions, including the Council and the Board of Guardians.[42] In 1857, when Catholics accounted for approximately one-third of the town's population, out of a total membership of 332 public and voluntary bodies in Belfast, Catholics held only 29 positions.

These figures included two Poor Law Guardians out of a total of
12, one Town Councillor out of 40, and eight Council Members
out of 194.[43] Overall, Catholics within the town continued to be
under-represented in local politics, education and employment.
Denominational differences, therefore, were increasingly
reinforced by economic, political and social ones, which were
further compounded by separation in employment and in housing.
One consequence was sporadic outbursts of sectarian violence in
the town.

The poverty and economic dislocation of the late 1840s also
continued to leave a number of other legacies.

Immigrants often brought with them the sectarian conflicts of
the countryside, thus contributing not only to the social problems
already evident within Belfast but adding a new dimension to the
existing sectarian tensions within the town. Whilst there had been
sectarian clashes in the first half of the nineteenth century, relationships between Catholics and Protestants in Belfast
deteriorated further in the wake of the clash at Dolly's Brae in
1849.[44] Although political processions had been made illegal in
1850 as a result of the conflict, a number of processions continued
to take place. On 12 July 1867, an Orangeman, William Johnston,
flaunted the ban by leading a procession from Newtownards to
Bangor. Johnston was imprisoned for two months for this action.
However, his defiance of the law made him a hero to many
working-class Protestants and he was elected to Westminster as
an Independent Orange candidate for south Belfast. In his capacity
as an MP he was responsible for having the Party Processions Act
repealed in 1872.[45]

Following the Famine, sectarian riots became both more
frequent and more violent with substantial riots occurring in 1857,
1864, 1872, 1880, 1884, 1886 and 1898. Sectarian clashes
generally took place in west Belfast which was the interface
between working-class Protestants and Catholics.[46] Until 1865,
Belfast maintained its own police force financed from local
taxation. It was frequently accused of being partisan and in the
wake of the 1864 riots, it was abolished. Consequently, Belfast
was brought in line with the rest of Ireland and policed by a
centralized, armed, professional force which was under the control
of Dublin Castle.[47] In recognition of the potential for conflict, after
1864 the police presence in Belfast was increased substantially and
in the second half of the nineteenth century the town was one of
the most densely policed areas in the United Kingdom. In 1886,
there was one policeman for every 337 inhabitants in the town,
compared with one for every 778 people in England and one for
every 914 people in Scotland.[48]

The riots of 1886 were some of the most serious experienced in the town. They were triggered by a quarrel between Catholic and Protestant dockworkers although they coincided with William Gladstone's first attempt to introduce a Home Rule Bill into parliament. The riots lasted intermittently from June until September. During these months, 32 deaths occurred, the majority being caused by police fire. The fact that a number of Protestants were included in the casualties particularly angered the local Protestant community who had traditionally regarded the police as being sympathetic to them. On the anniversary of the twelfth of July, rioting became particularly intense and 400 troops were used to support the police. In October, the government appointed a Riots Commission. They attributed much of the blame for the disturbances to the inflammatory speeches of clergymen and politicians who had proposed that violence should be used to oppose Home Rule. The police were also criticized for the way in which they handled the disorder.[49]

By Irish standards, the growth of Belfast was unique. It was also in stark contrast to the national trend of demographic decline, which had been set in train during the Famine. Moreover, Belfast's remarkable expansion made it one of the fastest growing economies in the United Kingdom. It also meant that whilst there was a general haemorrhaging of people from other parts of Ireland, in Ulster 'Belfast acted as a dam holding back the outflow'.[50] By the end of the century, the population of Belfast was larger than that of Dublin. At the same time, Belfast was recognized as the main industrial centre in Ireland, engineering and shipbuilding joining linen as generators of wealth and economic growth. As a consequence of Belfast's success, the east of Ulster became a major industrial centre within the United Kingdom. In recognition of Belfast's progress, in 1886, the town was designated a city. The late nineteenth century also coincided with the zenith of British imperial success. Increasingly, economic prosperity was regarded as being dependent on remaining as part of the Union and the wider British Empire.[51]

The economic and social success of Belfast gave Ulster Protestants a renewed confidence and determination not to change the political status quo. At the same time, the wealth of Belfast was viewed by those who opposed Home Rule for Ireland as a weapon for keeping Ireland as part of the United Kingdom. In 1910, the *Spectator* recommended that Protestants in the northeast demand separation from the rest of Ireland on the grounds that nationalists would have to back down as the country would face bankruptcy if she was no longer able to tax 'the rich city of Belfast'.[52]

The riots in Belfast in the late nineteenth century were one manifestation of wider divisions that had become evident within Ulster politics following the Famine. In the wake of the 1848 uprising and the conflict at Dolly's Brae, Belfast became a cockpit within which sectarianism became the overarching concern of both the working and the middle classes. Selective employment policies which favoured Protestant workers reinforced these divisions. Consequently, in the late nineteenth century, 'Catholicity coupled with residential and workplace [segregation] was central to a communal sense of ethnic difference.'[53] Clearly, within Belfast even poverty and unemployment were apportioned on religious lines.

In the post-Famine period, religious and political identity became largely indistinguishable. By the time of the first Home Rule bill in 1886, party politics had become polarized along Unionist and Nationalist lines which, in turn, were based on denominational divisions. For the majority of Belfast Protestants, their supremacy depended on remaining part of the United Kingdom and the British Empire. The resultant antagonisms and confrontations which dominated Belfast politics in the late nineteenth century paved the way for the eventual partition of Ireland in 1921.[54] These divisions had not been inevitable but were a tragic by-product of the religious, political and social conflicts which had become amplified as a result of the Famine.

Appendices

APPENDIX I

Townlands and Electoral Divisions in the Belfast Poor Law Union

Townlands	Electoral Divisions	Guardians
Townparks	Belfast	10
Edenderry		
Malone Lower		
Greencastle	Greencastle	1
Ballyaghugard		
Lowwood		
Skegoneill		
Old Park		
Ballysillan Lower		
Legoniel	Ballygomartin	1
Ballygomartin		
Altigarron		
Divis		
Ballymagarry		
Blackmountain		
Hannah's Town		
Ballymurphy	Ballymurphy	1
Ballydownfine		
English Town		
Ballymoney		
Tom-o-the Tae End		
Ballygammon		
Whitehouse	Whitehouse	1
Whiteabbey		
Monkstown		
Jordanstown		
Croghfern		
Dunaney		
Drumnadrough		
Ballygolan		
Carnmoney	Carnmoney	1
Carnmoney Bog		
Carnmoney Glebe		
Ballybowne		
Ballyduff		
Ballyhenry		
Ballycraigey		
Ballyvesey		
Glengormley		
Collinward		
Ballywonard	Ballysillan	1

continued

Townlands	Electoral Divisions	Guardians
Ballyhought		
Ballyvaston		
Ballysillan Upper		
Ballyuroag		
Molusk		
Ballymacarrett	Ballymacarrett	2
Ballynafoy		
Ballymacunaghy		
Castlereagh	Castlereagh	1
Multyholy		
Ballyrushnoy		
Lisnasharragh		
Carnamuck		
Cregagh		
Slatady		
Braniel		
Knock		
Tullycarnet		
Gortgrib		
Gilnahirk		
Ballymiscaw	Dundonald	1
Killeen		
Ballyregan		
Churchquarter		
Dunlady		
Carrowreagh		
Ballybeen		
Holywood	Holywood	1
Ballykeel		
Ballymenagh		
Ballycultraw		
Craigavad		
Ballygrainey		
Ballyrobert		
Ballydavey		
Ballyhackamore	Ballyhackamore	1
Strandtown		
Ballycloghan		
Ballymisert		
Ballymaghan		
Killeen		
Knocknagoney		

The first Guardians to be elected in the Belfast Union, 24 January 1839:

Belfast division (ten members)
　　James McNamara, JP, 89 Donegall Street, Gentleman
　　Samuel Graeme Fenton, 9 College Square North, Linen merchant and bleacher
　　James Blair, 12 Wellington Place, Gentleman
　　Valentine Whitla, 4 Donegall Square South, Exporter and shipping merchant
　　William Webb, 11 Commercial Court, Muslin and shawl manufacturer
　　John Clarke, 12 College Square East, Gentleman
　　James McTier, Hazelbank, Merchant and shipping agent
　　Charles Thomson, 36 Upper Arthur Street, Merchant
　　Daniel Davis, Donegall Street, Merchant
　　John Getty, 16 York Street, Gentleman

Ballymacarrett (two members)
  John Young, Shamrock Lodge, Partner in Lagan Foundry
  Robert McKibbin, Henryville, Mill owner

Greencastle (one member)
  John Ferguson, 20 Donegall Place, Linen merchant

Ballygomartin (one member)
  Samuel Nelson, Monkshill farm, West India merchant

Ballymurphy (one member)
  Lewis Redford, Beechmount, General merchant

Whitehouse (one member)
  Thomas Hughes, no details given

Carnmoney (one member)
  Alexander Halliday, Clifden, Holywood, Barrister and gentleman

Ballysillan (one member)
  Joseph Bigger, 1 Great Georges Street, Provision merchant

Castlereagh (one member)
  Robert McConnell, Castlereagh, Gentleman

Dundonald (one member)
  Hugh McCutcheon, Ballybeen, Gentleman

Holywood (one member)
  Robert Blackwell, Prairie, Holywood, Gentleman

Ballyhackamore (one member)
  William Harlin, Strandtown, Gentleman

APPENDIX II

Number of Dung Heaps in Belfast Recorded in the *Banner of Ulster*, 13 November 1846

Academy St	13
Caxton St	8
Charlotte Place	3
Charlotte St	5
Church St	4
Cooley's Court	6
Cromac St	152
Cullingtree St	31
Donegall St	341
Edward St	6
Gardner St	9
Gordon St	10
Grattan St	6
Green St	12
Hamill St	8
Hercules St	79
Hill St	7
King St	69
Lettuce Hill	7
Little Edward St/ Townsend St	146
Little Howard St	8
Lynas Lane	11
Marquis St	6
Mawhinney's Row	20
Melbourne St	16
Millfield	181
Mustard St	26
Peter's Hill	44
Queen's St	3
Robert St	6
Smithfield	13
Stanley/Albert St	8
Stephen St	17
Talbot St	8
Waring St	95
West St	11
William St	11
Total	1,392

APPENDIX III

Recorded Deaths and Burials in Various Institutions in Belfast

1. Deaths in the Belfast Poor House

Year	No. of Deaths
1840	208
1841	211
1842	206
1843	164
1844	181
1845	224
1846	293
1847	1,484
1848	291
1849	246
1850	224

2. Burials in Belfast Poor House in 1847

Month	No. of Burials
January	39
February	45
March	81
April	117
May	151
June	249
July	255
August	229
September	141
October	74
November	50
December	47

3. Deaths in the High Street Hospital, the College Hospital, the Workhouse Hospital and the Camp Hospital, June to September 1847

Week Ending	Total Deaths
19 June 1847	89
27 June	n/a
3 July	81
10 July	92
17 July	84
24 July	79
1 August	n/a
7 August	n/a
14 August	64
21 August	91
28 August	66
7 September	63
14 September	n/a
21 September	54

Sources: Banner of Ulster, News-Letter.

APPENDIX IV

Number of Births, Deaths and Marriages in Various Churches in Belfast, c.1840–50

Ballymacarrett, Church of Ireland

Year	Baptisms	Marriages	Burials
1841		incomplete	
1842	85	13	
1843	61	5	
1844	89	25	
1845	104	13	
1846	79	20	
1847	73	11	
1848	109	11	
1849	117	28	
1850	104	26	

Christ Church, Church of Ireland

Year	Baptisms	Marriages	Burials
1840	66		3
1841	89		2
1842	88		1
1843	95		5
1844	102		4
1845	127		7
1846	138		11
1847	88		2
1848	85		1
1849	109		1
1850	126		0

Holywood, Church of Ireland

Year	Baptisms	Marriages	Burials
1840	20		5
1841	19		2
1842	9		6
1843	18		7
1844	16		3
1845	13		4
1846	28		14
1847	10		4
1848	20		4
1849	11		7
1850	16		6

Knockbreda, Church of Ireland.

Year	Baptisms	Marriages	Burials
1840			41
1841			23
1842			25
1843			18
1844			22
1845			15
1846			41
1847			67
1848			32
1849			57
1850			31

May Street, Presbyterian

Year	Baptisms	Marriages	Burials
1840	57	31	
1841	61	19	
1842	44	12	
1843	20	4	
1844	49	10	
1845	39	15	
1846	30	18	
1847	39	11	
1848	36	23	
1849	29	26	
1850	32	34	

St Anne's Church of Ireland, Shankhill

Year	Baptisms	Marriages	Burials
1840	32		5
1841	39		5
1842	28		13
1843	21		9
1844	31		11
1845	5		26
1846	34		2
1847	34		10
1848	25		4
1849	18		5
1850	24		5

St John's Presbyterian, Malone

Year	Baptisms	Marriages	Burials
1840	69	11	
1841	15	11	
1842	29	8	
1843	31	15	
1844	38	9	
1845	52	8	
1846	40	7	
1847	18	5	
1848	27	8	
1849	31	3	
1850	incomplete		

St Patrick's Catholic Church, Donegall Street

Year	Baptisms	Marriages	Burials
1840	807	170	
1841	957	121	
1842	1,088	239	
1843	1,383	211	
1844	1,259	262	
1845	1,217	238	
1846	1,514	206	
1847	995	156	
1848	1,210	229	
1849	1,005	221	
1850	1,292	279	

Ballymacarrett, St Patrick's Church of Ireland

Year	Baptisms	Marriages	Burials
1840	73	6	
1841	92	2	
1842	56	2	
1843	64	1	
1844	59	7	
1845	78	8	
1846	56	10	
1847	42	1	
1848	46	4	
1849	74	5	
1850	81	8	

York Street, Presbyterian

Year	Baptisms	Marriages	Burials
1840	52		
1841	60		
1842	65		
1843	66		
1844	84		
1845	69		
1846	75		
1847	59		
1848	82		
1849	64		
1850	74		

APPENDIX V

Admissions to Belfast Fever Hospitals

Date	Admissions
1846 September	20
October	28
November	24
December	31
1847 January	55
February	50
March	83
April	172
May	350
June	524
July	603
August	404
September	276
October	199
November	151
December	110
1848 January	79
February	74
March	59
April	44
May	43
June	34
July	28
August	31
September	23

The above figures are probably an underestimate. Dr Seaton Reid calculated that due to the overcrowding in the hospitals, at least one-fourth more people were treated in their homes.
Source: Appendix to Fever Report on Ulster, *The Dublin Quarterly Journal of Medical Science*, vol. vii, Feb/May 1849, p. 289.

APPENDIX VI

Emigrants from Belfast who Died in Quarantine Hospital

Grosse Isle between 8 May 1847 and 21 July 1847

Name	Age	Vessel
Thomas Brown	1	*Lord Seaton*
John Horinger	4	
Est Horinger	34	
John Ryan	4 months	
Catherine McAver	5	
Daniel Grant	2	
Mary Morrow	58	
George Graham	2	
Stephen McKenna	40	
Robert Ward	21	
Mary Devlin	30	
Catherine Mulholland	30	
Sarah Allen	24	
Richard Bowyer	48	
M.A. Humphreys	9 months	
Eliz Jamison	12	
R. Fisher	24	*Constitution*
Ellen Brown	1	
John Greenaway	11 months	
John Jackson	24	
William Morrison	4 months	
John Woodside	5 months	
Mary Toal	1	
Michael Harry	6	
Michael O'Hara	2 months	
Mary Greenaway	7	
Mary Greenaway	17	
William Lahin	1 month	*Caithness-Shire*
Ann Barrie	21	
Daniel Nicholson	4	
Mary Bradsby	25	
Mary Mack	50	
Edward Rice	18	
Catherine Hanley	3	
Mary Loughlin	24	
Margaret Agnew	30	
John Redmond	26	*Lady Gordon*
Hannah Good	20	
David Deece	23	
James Johnson	40	
Catherine Howard	40	

Source: *Banner of Ulster*, 21 September 1847

Grosse Isle between 21 July 1847 and 21 August 1847

Name	Age	Vessel
Mary Horan	29	*Huron*
Pat Harne	37	
Denis Hynes	30	
Mrs Fettus	40	*Independence*
Thomas Quinn	40	
Robert Quinn	3	
Mary Stromacks	2	
Mary Quinn	12	
Charles Quinn	20	
Frances Collins	22	*Caithness-Shire*
William McBurnie	19	
James Connor	21	*Marquis of Bute*
Sally Blade	60	
Mary McKernan	26	*Lord Seaton*
Mary Brown	9	
Catherine Slaney	14	*William Pirie*
George Gamell	21	*Sir H. Pottinger*
Fanny Carney	47	
Mary Maher	8	
William Bradshaw	25	
Mary Kelly	13	
Alex Baukes	22	
Brid Barott	18	*Constitution*

Source: Ibid., 5 October 1847.

Grosse Isle between 12 September 1847 and 19 September 1847

Name	Age	Vessel
Timothy Barry	24	*Sir H. Pottinger*
William Jones	18	
Sarah O'Hare	48	
John Griffin	24	
Martha Delmoge	18	

Source: Ibid., 22 October 1847.

APPENDIX VII

Number of cases of cholera, and deaths, as reported to the Central Board of Health, in the principal towns

Town	No. of Cases	No. of Deaths	% Mortality
Belfast	2,750	969	35.8
Cork	3,176	1,329	41.8
Dublin	3,813	1,664	43.6
Galway	897	426	47.4
Limerick	1,500	746	49.7
Waterford	522	294	56.3

Source: Report of the Commissioners of Health, Ireland, on the Epidemics of 1846 to 1850 (Dublin, 1852). Appendix B No. 6, p. 79.

APPENDIX VIII

Immigrants to Belfast by County, 1851–55

County	1851	1852	1853	1854	1855
Carlow	1	3	1	0	6
Dublin	7	7	42	60	108
Kildare	0	1	9	5	2
Kilkenny	1	3	3	3	3
King's	22	78	61	24	30
Longford	25	95	122	57	65
Louth	9	41	65	105	183
Meath	8	24	78	33	39
Queen's	10	1	11	1	6
Westmeath	7	36	40	36	26
Wexford	0	0	4	5	2
Wicklow	0	2	4	13	7
Clare	34	72	50	72	17
Cork	0	5	16	12	16
Kerry	0	5	3	7	0
Limerick	4	6	10	26	13
Tipperary	1	11	12	35	45
Waterford	2	8	5	9	20
Antrim	3,203	3,222	4,385	3,942	5,858
Armagh	694	1,150	1,323	1,248	2,094
Cavan	237	556	724	424	498
Donegal	11	20	27	35	39
Down	1,428	2,450	3,220	3,212	4,580
Fermanagh	303	525	426	314	201
Derry	532	797	1,084	763	1,083
Monaghan	324	657	790	475	893
Tyrone	702	1,445	1,693	1,353	1,583
Galway	7	14	18	7	28
Leitrim	66	165	227	121	217
Mayo	2	13	25	18	45
Roscommon	60	136	165	78	141
Sligo	6	13	29	10	19
N/S	189	13	12	2	2
Total	7,890	11,574	14,684	12,496	17,809

Source: Appendix to General Report. Census of Ireland for 1851, PP, 1856, xxviii–lxvii.

Notes

Abbreviations

CHA   City Hall Archives, Belfast
DDA   Dublin Diocesan Archives
LHL   Linen Hall Library, Belfast
NAD   National Archives, Dublin
PLC   Poor Law Commissioners
PP   Parliamentary Papers
PROL   Public Record Office, London
PRONI   Public Record Office, Belfast
RLFC   Relief Commission Papers, NAD

Introduction

1. Patrick Lynch and John Vaisey, *Guinness's Brewery in the Irish Economy, 1759–1876* (Cambridge University Press, 1960) p. 166.
2. Roy Foster, *Oxford History of Ireland* (Oxford University Press, 1989) p. 167.
3. Brian Walker, *Dancing to History's Tune. History, Myth and Politics in Ireland* (Belfast, 1996) p. 18.
4. Liam Kennedy, 'The Rural Economy', in Liam Kennedy and Philip Ollerenshaw (eds) *An Economic History of Ulster 1820–1939* (Manchester University Press, 1985) p. 30.
5. *Belfast Protestant Journal* (hereafter *Protestant Journal*) 17 July 1847.
6. Cathal Poirteir, *Famine Echoes* (Dublin, 1995) p. 15.
7. Tony Blair's statement was read on 31 May 1997 at a Famine event in Cork. Unionist politicians who objected included Ian Paisley Jr. and Sammy Wilson of the DUP, and John Taylor, deputy leader of the UUP. See *Belfast News-Letter*, 4 February 1997, 2 June 1997; *Irish News*, 4 February 1997; *Belfast Telegraph*, 4 February 1997.
8. Stephen Rea, *Belfast Telegraph*, 16 November 1998.
9. Mr M. McDowell, Parliamentary Debates of *Dail Eireann*, vol. 456, no. 5, col. 1219, 5 October 1995.
10. Mary Daly quoted in Gerard Mac Atasney, *This Dreadful Visitation. The Famine in Lurgan/Portadown* (Belfast, 1997) p. xv.
11. For example, two recent comparative studies of the Irish Famine, Margaret Kelleher, *The Feminization of Famine. Expressions of the Inexpressible?* (Cork, 1997) and Cormac Ó Gráda, *Black '47 and Beyond. The Great Irish Famine in History, Economy and Memory* (Princeton, 1999) hardly mention the impact of the Famine on Belfast, although Ó Gráda includes a chapter on Dublin.
12. Patrick Campbell, *Death in Templecrone. An Account of the Famine Years in North West Donegal* (New Jersey, 1995); Mac Atasney, *This Dreadful Visitation. The Famine in Lurgan/Portadown* (Belfast, 1997).
13. Christine Kinealy and Trevor Parkhill, *The Famine in Ulster* (Belfast, 1997).
14. *Belfast Vindicator*, 22 April 1846.
15. *Belfast News-Letter* (hereafter *News-Letter*) 23 February 1849.

16. Mac Atasney, *This Dreadful Visitation*, pp. 12–17.

17. Brenda Collins, 'The Linen Industry and Emigration to Britain during the mid-Nineteenth Century', in E. Margaret Crawford (ed.) *The Hungry Stream. Essays on Emigration and Famine* (Belfast, 1997) pp. 156–8.

18. Ibid., p. 159.

19. Poorer Classes Enquiry, PP. 1836, xxxii, pp. 279–86.

20. Mr and Mrs S.C. Hall, *Ireland, Its Scenery, Character and History* (first published in 1844 in three vols, reprinted London, 1984) p. 343.

21. Thackeray quoted in B. Walker, 'Ulster Society and Politics', in C. Brady, M. O'Dowd and B. Walker (eds) *Ulster. An Illustrated History* (London, 1989) p. 163.

22. For example, during the economic crisis in 1826, apart from soup kitchens being established, an emigration committee was also set up in Ballymacarrett, *News-Letter*, 12, 19 May, 12 September 1826.

23. Jonathan Bardon, *A History of Ulster* (Belfast, 1992) p. 326.

24. Jacqueline Hill 'National Festivals, the State and Protestant Ascendancy in Ireland 1790–1829', in *Irish Historical Studies*, xxiv, no. 93 (May 1984).

25. Michael H. Gould, *The Workhouses of Ulster* (Belfast, 1983) p. 18.

26. Evidence of Edward Senior, Select Committee of the House of Lords on the Irish Poor Laws, 1849, xvi.

27. *Northern Whig* (hereafter *Whig*) 13 May 1847.

28. *Protestant Journal*, 20 March 1847.

29. Ibid., 14 November 1846.

30. *Banner of Ulster* (hereafter *Banner*) 13 April 1847.

31. *Transactions of the Central Relief Committee of the Society of Friends during the Famine in Ireland in 1846 and 1847* (Dublin, 1852) pp. 190–2.

32. For discussion of mortality rates, see Cormac Ó Gráda, *Ireland before and after the Famine: Explorations in Economic History* (revised edn Manchester, 1993); and Joel Mokyr, *Why Ireland Starved. An Analytical and Quantitative History of the Irish Economy, 1800–1850* (London, 1985).

33. See, for example, *News-Letter*, 23 April 1847, 30 April 1847, 7 May 1847, 25 May 1847, 28 May 1847, 8 June 1847, 11 June 1847.

34. For more on Rate-in-Aid, see Christine Kinealy, *A Death-Dealing Famine. The Great Hunger in Ireland* (London, 1997) pp. 141–6; also see Chapter 6.

35. *Freeman's Journal*, 11 January 1847.

36. Linda Colley, *Britons, Forging the Nation 1707–1837* (Princeton, 1992) pp. 18–19; John Wolffe, *The Protestant Crusade in Britain, 1829–60* (Oxford, 1991).

37. For contemporary Protestant interpretations of the Famine, see Hugh McNeile, *The Famine, a Rod of God; its Provoking Cause, its Merciful Design* (Liverpool, 1847); Asenath Nicholson, *Annals of the Famine in Ireland* (first printed New York, 1851, reprinted Dublin, 1998, ed. M. Murphy) p. 177. Many Catholics also viewed the Famine as a judgment of God, see, for example, Nicholson, *Annals*, pp. 163–4; Sermons of the late Most Reverend Daniel Murray, Archbishop of Dublin (Dublin, 1859).

38. Donal Kerr, *A Nation of Beggars? Priests, People and Politics in Famine Ireland, 1846–52* (Oxford, 1994) p. 207.

39. The enduring legacy of the accusations of proselytism was evident during the Famine commemorations in 1995 when in a number of articles, writers in the *Church of Ireland Gazette* appealed for a reappraisal of the role of their Church during the Famine years. For example, Dr Robert McCarthy argued: 'This is perhaps the moment to face squarely the charge of "souperism" which is still levied against the Church of Ireland' (11 August 1995); and Dr Ken Milne, historiographer of the Church, averred: 'One hopes for an end to such canards as those referring to Victoria as the Famine Queen ... More especially towards the Church of Ireland one looks forward to an end

to blanket dismissal of landlords as callous perpetrators of eviction and of clergy as dispensers of soup at a price' (1 September 1995).

40. *Belfast Vindicator*, 6 January 1847.
41. *News-Letter*, 14 March 1848.

Chapter 1

1. Liam Kennedy and Philip Ollerenshaw (eds) *An Economic History of Ulster, 1820–1939* (Manchester, 1985) preface.
2. A.C. Hepburn, *A Past Apart. Studies in the History of Catholic Belfast 1850–1950* (Belfast, 1996) p. 4.
3. W.E. Vaughan and A.J. Fitzpatrick, *Irish Historical Statistics* (Dublin, 1978) pp. 48–68.
4. Hepburn, *Catholic Belfast*, p. 3.
5. William Maguire, *From Town to City* (Belfast City Council on the Internet, www.belfastcity.gov.k/hist1.htm).
6. Samuel Lewis, *A Topographical Dictionary of Ireland*, Vol. one (London, 1837) p. 194.
7. Ibid.
8. Cormac Ó Gráda, *A New Economic History 1780–1939* (Oxford, 1994) p. 276.
9. Ollerenshaw, 'Industry 1820–1914', in Kennedy and Ollerenshaw, *Economic History*, p. 66.
10. Ibid., p. 69.
11. Ibid., p. 70.
12. Ibid., p. 69; Ó Gráda, *New Economic History*, p. 278.
13. Ollerenshaw, 'Industry', p. 72.
14. Ibid., p. 88.
15. Ó Gráda, *New Economic History*, p. 296.
16. Lewis, *Topographical Dictionary*, p. 194.
17. Ibid.
18. Ollerenshaw, 'Industry 1820–1914', p. 64.
19. Ibid., p. 88.
20. Ibid.
21. W.A. McCutcheon, 'Transport 1820–1914', in Kennedy and Ollerenshaw, *Economic History*, pp. 120, 130.
22. Jonathan Bardon, *Ulster*, p. 260.
23. *News-Letter*, 4 May 1826.
24. Ibid., 11 July 1826, 12 September 1826.
25. Ibid., 9 May 1826.
26. Ibid., 12 May 1826, 19 May 1826, 23 May 1826.
27. Ibid., 19 May 1826.
28. Ibid., 9 June 1826.
29. Ibid., 1 August 1826, 8 September 1826.
30. Bardon, *Ulster*, p. 260.
31. Ibid., pp. 260–1; Kennedy and Ollerenshaw, *Economic History*, pp. 5–6.
32. Evidence of C.S. Courtney, *First Report of the Commissioners for Inquiring into the Condition of the Poorer Classes in Ireland* (hereafter, *Poorer Classes Inquiry*), 1835 (369) xxxii, Supplement to Appendix C., p. 54.
33. Ibid.
34. Ibid., evidence of Rev. Samuel Smythe, Supplement to Appendix D, p. 261.
35. Ibid., evidence of the Committee of the Holywood Mendicity Society, Supplement to Appendix D, p. 326; ibid., evidence of J.P. Blackiston, p. 328; ibid., evidence of Rev. William Finlay, Supplement to Appendix E, p. 326.

36. Ibid., evidence of Rev. William Bruce, Supplement to Appendix C, p. 50.
37. Ibid., Supplement to Appendix D, pp. 261, 279, 326, 328.
38. Ibid., evidence of Rev. Thomas Hincks, Supplement to Appendix C, p. 49; ibid., evidence of Rev. J. Kinahan, Supplement to Appendix D, p. 328.
39. *Valuation Field Books*, PRONI, Val.1B/76/13. No. 66, 23 June 1837.
40. Ibid., No. 70, 24 June 1837; ibid., No. 37, 14 June 1837.
41. *Poorer Classes Inquiry*, Supplement to Appendix A, p. 276.
42. A.G. Malcolm, *The Sanitary State of Belfast with Suggestions for its Improvement* (Belfast, 1852) pp. 6–8.
43. *Poorer Classes Inquiry*, Supplement to Appendix C, p. 49.
44. Malcolm, *Sanitary State of Belfast*, p. 27.
45. Ibid., pp. 4–5.
46. *Poorer Classes Inquiry*, Supplement to Appendix E, pp. 261, 263, 279, 326, 328; evidence of Rev. R.M. Dillon and Rev. William Finlay; evidence of Richard Blackiston and the Holywood Mendicity Society, p. 326.
47. Ibid., evidence of Holywood Mendicity Society, p. 326.
48. Ibid., evidence of Rev. J. Kinahan, p. 328.
49. Ibid., Supplement to Appendix C, pp. 7, 49–54; ibid., Supplement to Appendix D, pp. 261, 263, 279, 326, 328.
50. Ibid., Supplement to Appendix B, Part II, p. 252.
51. Ibid., p. 234.
52. Ibid., Supplement to Appendix D, pp. 49–58, 163–9, 171, 195–6, 209.
53. Ibid.
54. Report from Commissioners, *Poor Law Inquiry* (Scotland) 1844, Part IV, vol. xxiii, pp. 175b–180b.
55. *Poorer Classes Inquiry*, Supplement to Appendix C, pp. 11, 52.
56. Ibid., p. 7.
57. Ibid., evidence of John Rowan, Supplement to Appendix D, p. 261.
58. Ibid., p. 328.
59. Ibid., Supplement to Appendix C, pp. 19–20.
60. Ibid., Supplement to Appendix F, pp. 261, 263, 279, 326, 328.
61. Letter from Rev. Thomas Drew to James E. Tennant and George Dunbar, MPs, LHL, 1838, p. 4.
62. W.A. Maguire, 'Lord Donegall and the Sale of Belfast; A Case History from the Encumbered Estates Court', in *Economic History Review*, xxix, 1976, pp. 570–84.
63. *The Belfast Monthly Magazine*, no. 11. vol. 2, 30 June 1809, pp. 436–7; Extracts from *Orderly Book of the Belfast Charitable Society*, 1803–1820, LHL, pp. 13–23; *Belfast News-Letter* (hereafter *News-Letter*) 8 December 1817, 28 December 1817, 4 January 1818, 9 January 1818, 13 January 1818; R.W.M. Strain, *Belfast and its Charitable Society. A Story of Urban Social Development* (London, 1961) p. 5.
64. *Poorer Classes Inquiry*, Supplement to Appendix F, pp. 261, 263, 279, 326, 328.
65. Remarks on the Third Report of the Poor Inquiry Commissioners, by G.C. Lewis, 1837 [91] li, pp. 10–31.
66. George Nicholls, *A History of the Irish Poor Law* (London, 1856) pp. 118–40.
67. Ibid., p. 159.
68. Derek Fraser, *The New Poor Law in the Nineteenth Century* (London, 1976). For a comparison between Poor Laws in England, Ireland, Scotland and Wales, see Christine Kinealy, *A Disunited Kingdom, England, Ireland, Scotland and Wales 1800–1949* (Cambridge University Press, 1999), pp. 68–81.
69. Report by George Nicholls to His Majesty's Secretary of State for the Home Department, on Poor Laws, Ireland, 1837 [69] li.
70. Nicholls, Irish Poor Law, pp. 176–7.
71. *News-Letter*, 13 February 1838.

72. Ibid., 13 March 1838.
73. Ibid.
74. Ibid.
75. Ibid., 16 March 1838.
76. Ibid.
77. Ibid., 17 April 1838.
78. Ibid., 24 April 1838.
79. Poorer Classes Inquiry, Supplement to Appendix C, p. 13.
80. *News-Letter*, 19 October 1838.
81. Ibid., 25 September 1838, 19 October 1838, 20 November 1838.
82. Ibid., 19 February 1839.
83. Seventh Annual Report of Poor Law Commissioners (hereafter PLC) 1841, Appendix E, no. 10, pp. 188–9.
84. *News-Letter*, 1 January 1839, 4 January 1839.
85. Ibid., 12 February 1839.
86. Seventh Annual Report of PLC, 1841, Appendix E, No. 13, pp. 206–9.
87. *News-Letter*, 6 November 1838.
88. Ibid.
89. Ibid., 9 February 1841, 12 February 1841, 2 March 1841.
90. Ibid., 4 June 1841.
91. Seventh Annual Report of PLC, 1841, Appendix E, No. 13, pp. 208–9.
92. Christine Kinealy 'The Introduction of the Poor Law to Ireland' (unpublished PhD thesis, Trinity College, Dublin, 1984) pp. 56–61.
93. Tenth Report of PLC, Appendix A, No. 30, pp. 410–11.
94. *News-Letter*,15 January 1841, 19 January 1841, 8 October 1841.
95. Ibid., 9 March 1841.
96. Eighth Annual Report of PLC, 1842, pp. 5–9.
97. Halls, *Ireland*, p. 343.
98. Henry Cooke, quoted in J.L. Porter, *The Life and Times of Henry Cooke* (London, 1871) p. 412.
99. Report from the Assistant Handloom Weavers' Commission, PP, 1840, xxiv, p. 674.
100. William Thackeray quoted in B. Walker, 'Ulster Society and Politics', in C. Brady, M. O'Dowd and B. Walker (eds) *Ulster. An Illustrated History*, p. 163.
101. Throughout 1841 the *News-Letter* provided weekly details of workhouse statistics.
102. Ibid., 14 April 1842, 19 April 1842.
103. Ibid., 3 May 1842, 6 May 1842.
104. Ibid., 19 April 1842.
105. Ibid., 28 June 1842.
106. Ibid.
107. Ibid., 1 July 1842.
108. Ibid.
109. Ibid.
110. Ibid., 22 July 1842, 29 July 1842.
111. Ibid., 1 July 1842, 29 July 1842.
112. Ibid., 29 July 1842.
113. Ibid.
114. Ibid., 1 July 1842.
115. The population of the Ballymacarrett electoral division in 1841 was 1,105 (Eighth Annual Report of PLC for 1842).
116. *News-Letter*, 30 July 1842, 19 August 1842.
117. Ibid., 2 August 1842.
118. Ibid., 3 May 1842, 6 May 1842.
119. Ibid., 1 July 1842, 29 July 1842, 2 August 1842, 9 September 1842.

Chapter 2

1. *Gardner's Chronicle and Horticultural Gazette*, 16 August 1845.
2. *Analysis of the Loss of the Potato Crop in 1845–46*, Christine Kinealy, *This Great Calamity. The Irish Famine 1845–5* (Dublin, 1994) pp. 360–2.
3. Ibid., pp. 31–70.
4. Brenda Collins, 'The Linen Industry and Emigration to Great Britain during the mid-Nineteenth Century', in E. Margaret Crawford (ed.) *The Hungry Stream. Essays on Emigration and Famine* (Belfast, 1997), p. 156.
5. Ibid. p. 157.
6. *The Times*, 16 November 1846.
7. *Vindicator*, 10 September 1845.
8. *News-Letter*, 12 September 1845; *Whig*, 16 September 1845.
9. *Whig*, 27 September 1845, 14 October 1845.
10. Ibid., 28 October 1845.
11. Ibid., 21 October 1845.
12. *Vindicator*, 15 October 1845.
13. Ibid., 1 November 1845.
14. Walter Lowry, Resident Magistrate (R.M.) to Relief Commissioners, NAD, RLFC, second series, Box 2/441/18, 21 October 1845.
15. Report of Mansion House Committee on the Potato Disease, LHL, Synopsis nos. I & II (Dublin, 1846).
16. William Radcliffe to Lord Lieutenant, NAD, RLFC, 2/441/18, 5 November 1845.
17. Ibid., Lord Donegall to Lord Lieutenant, 20 November 1845.
18. Ibid., James Burns to Lord Lieutenant, 28 October 1845.
19. Ibid.
20. *News-Letter*, 31 October 1845.
21. Ibid., 4 November 1845.
22. *Whig*, 4 November 1845.
23. *Vindicator*, 12 November 1845, 26 November 1845.
24. Kinealy, *A Death-Dealing Famine*, p. 56.
25. Christine Kinealy, 'Peel, Rotten Potatoes and Providence: The Repeal of the Corn Laws and the Irish Famine', in Andrew Marrison (ed.) *Free Trade and its Reception*, Vol. 1 (Routledge, 1998) pp. 63–81.
26. Sir Robert Peel to Sir James Graham, C.S. Parker, Sir Robert Peel. From his Private Papers (London, 1899, 2nd edn) 13 October 1845, p. 223.
27. *Whig*, 6 November 1845.
28. *Vindicator*, 10 December 1845.
29. *Whig*, 27 November 1845.
30. Ibid., 29 November 1845.
31. Ibid., 25 November 1845.
32. James Burns to Lord Lieutenant, RLFC, 2 2/441/18, 28 October 1845.
33. Ibid.
34. *Whig*, 25 November 1845.
35. *Vindicator*, 8 November 1845.
36. Ibid., 29 October 1845.
37. Twelfth Annual Report of PLC, 1844, Appendix B, No. 26, pp. 270–1.
38. *Banner*, 10 February 1846.
39. *Whig*, 18 September 1845.
40. *Vindicator*, 26 November 1845.
41. *Banner*, 27 March 1846.
42. Ibid.
43. Ibid., 31 March 1846.
44. Ibid., 3 April 1846.
45. Ibid.

46. Ibid.
47. *Whig*, 9 April 1846.
48. *Vindicator,* 22 April 1846.
49. Rev. Charles Courtney, Mount Pottinger, to J. Kennedy Esq., NAD, RLFC, 1140, 1 April 1846.
50. *News-Letter* and *Banner* 10 April 1846.
51. *Banner*, 10 April 1846.
52. Ibid.
53. Ibid., 17 April 1846.
54. Ibid., 21 April 1846.
55. Bardon, *Ulster,* p. 314.
56. *Whig*, 7 April 1846.
57. Ibid., 28 May 1846.
58. Ibid., 27 June 1846.
59. Various Constabulary Reports, NAD, RLFC, 4 2/441/13, for Dundonald, 29 May 1846, 2 June 1846; for Holywood, 2 June 1846; for Ballymacarrett, 1 June 1846; for Knockbreda, 2 June 1846.
60. Rev. Charles Courtney, Ballymacarrett to Relief Commissioners, NAD, RLFC, 3/1/269, 29 May 1846; Ibid., Edward Clarke to Relief Commissioners, 3/1/3077, 10 June 1846.
61. Ibid., Edward Clarke to Relief Commissioners, 3/1/3077, 10 June 1846.
62. *Banner* and *Whig*, 21 July 1846.
63. Edward Clarke to Relief Commissioners, NAD, RLFC, 3/1/4885, 31 July 1846.
64. *Ulster Times*, 21 July 1838, 29 July 1838, 27 November 1838.
65. Ibid., 29 November 1838.
66. Ibid., 27 November 1838.
67. Ibid., 20 November 1838.
68. *Protestant Journal*, 11 July 1846.
69. *Ulster Times*, 20 November 1838.
70. *Protestant Journal*, 21 March 1846.
71. Ibid.
72. Ibid., 11 July 1846.
73. Ibid.
74. Ibid., 4 July 1846.
75. Ibid.
76. Ibid., 18 July 1846.
77. Ibid., 11 July 1846.
78. Ibid., 18 July 1846.
79. Ibid.
80. Ibid.
81. Ibid.
82. Ibid., 18 July 1846.
83. Ibid., 11 July 1846.
84. Ibid., 17 July 1846.
85. Ibid., 14 November 1846.

Chapter 3

1. Randolph Routh to Trevelyan, NAD, Chief Secretary's Office Registered Papers, O.549, 9 July 1846.
2. Kinealy, *Death-Dealing Famine*, pp. 66–91.
3. The various pressures influencing the new *Whig* administration have been explored in R.J. Montague, 'Relief and Reconstruction in Ireland, 1845–49. A Study in Public Policy during the Great Famine' (unpublished DPhil

thesis, Oxford, 1976); and Peter Gray, 'British Politics and the Irish Land Question 1843–50' (unpublished DPhil thesis, Cambridge, 1992).

4. *Banner*, 17 July 1846.
5. Ibid., 21 July 1846.
6. *Whig*, 4 August 1846.
7. 'Returns Relating to the Potato Crop in Ireland' in Thirteenth Annual Report of Poor Law Commissioners (hereafter PLC), Appendix A, No. 9. pp. 180–91.
8. *Whig*, 13 August 1846.
9. *News-Letter*, 11 August 1846, 8 September 1846.
10. Ibid., 8 September 1846.
11. Ó Gráda, *Black '47*, p. 173; *News-Letter*, 2 October 1846.
12. *Banner*, 13 November 1846, 17 November 1846.
13. Ibid., 3 November 1846.
14. *News-Letter*, 27 October 1846.
15. *Vindicator*, 24 October 1846.
16. *News-Letter*, 11 December 1846.
17. *Banner*, 10 November 1846.
18. *News-Letter*, 3 November 1846.
19. Diary of James MacAdam, PRONI, D/2930/7/6, 13 November 1846, p. 151.
20. *Banner*, 10 November 1846.
21. *Banner* and *News-Letter*, 20 November 1846, 11 December 1846.
22. *Banner*, 17 November 1846.
23. *News-Letter*, 18 December 1846.
24. Petition of Richardson Bros and Co., Belfast, Merchants, and response, Irish University Press, Famine Papers, vol. v, 26 August 1846, pp. 455–6.
25. Edward Clarke to W. Stanley, NAD, RLFC, 3/2/1/9, 19 December 1846.
26. Ibid., reply from Stanley, 24 December 1846.
27. *Banner* and *News-Letter*, 22 December 1846.
28. *Banner*, 22 December 1846.
29. See, Andres Eiriksson 'Food Supply and Food Riots', in Cormac Ó Gráda (ed.) *Famine 150* (Dublin, 1997) pp. 67–93, although he concentrates mostly on counties Clare and Limerick.
30. *Whig*, 19 December 1846.
31. *Whig*, 17 December 1846.
32. *Banner* and *News-Letter*, 25 December 1846.
33. *Whig*, 26 December 1846.
34. *Banner*, 8 January 1847.
35. *Banner* and *News-Letter*, 8 January 1847.
36. Christine Kinealy, 'Food Exports from Ireland', in *History Ireland*, vol. 5, no. 1. Spring 1997, pp. 32–6.
37. *Vindicator*, 2 January 1847.
38. *Banner*, 12 January 1847.
39. Committee on Police Affairs, Minute Book, CHA, 17 February 1847.
40. John Rowan to W. Stanley, RLFC, 3/2/16, 19 January 1847.
41. *Banner*, 22 January 1847.
42. Barney Tedford to Mr Lowry, Oakley, Strandtown, Recollections of B. Tedford, PRONI, T.515, c.1920, pp. 8–9.
43. Henry Henderson to Sir Randolph Routh, Incoming Letters, NAD RLFC, 3/2/8/53, 29 January 1847.
44. Notice of Holywood Soup Kitchen, NAD RLFC 3/2/8/12 and 2/44/42, 11 December 1846.
45. Ibid., Holywood Dispensary Report for 1846, by R.O. McKittrick, Surgeon, January 1847.
46. Dorothea Kennedy to Archbishop Crolly, Correspondence of Archbishop Crolly, Down and Connor Diocesan Archives, C.45/3, 9 April 1846.

47. Henry Henderson to Sir Randolph Routh, RLFC, 3/2/8/53, 29 January 1847.
48. *News-Letter*, 26 February 1847.
49. Ibid., 26 February 1847.
50. *Whig*, 4 February 1847.
51. Application to Central Relief Committee of the Society of Friends by Bally-macarrett Relief Committee, Papers of Society of Friends, NAD, U.B 299, 10 May 1847.
52. John Boyd to Relief Commissioners, NAD, RLFC 3/2/8/9, 27 January 1847; *Whig*, 4 February 1847.
53. Ibid., Boyd to Relief Commissioners, NAD, RLFC, 27 January 1847.
54. *Banner*, 5 February 1847.
55. Ibid., 8 January 1847.
56. Application to Central Relief Committee of the Society of Friends by Bally-macarrett Relief Committee, Papers of Society of Friends, U.B 299, NAD, 10 May 1847.
57. *Banner*, 2 March 1847.
58. *News-Letter*, 26 January 1847.
59. *Banner*, 22 January 1847.
60. Committee on Police Affairs, Minute Book, CHA, 13 February 1847.
61. Ibid., 11 March 1847.
62. *News-Letter*, 26 February 1847.
63. For further information about the work of the various charitable bodies in Belfast, see Chapter 5.
64. *Banner* and *News-Letter*, 16 February 1847.
65. *Whig*, 16 February 1847.
66. Ibid., 18 February 1847.
67. Ibid., 16 February 1847.
68. Ibid., 4 March 1847.
69. Ibid., 16 March 1847.
70. *Banner*, 19 February 1847.
71. The PLC Annual Report for 1841 gave the population figures for the electoral division of Ballymacarrett as 1,105.
72. Edward Clarke to W. Stanley, NAD, RLFC 3/2/1/9, 22 February 1847.
73. *Banner*, 23 February 1847; *News-Letter*, 26 February 1847, 5 March 1847.
74. *News-Letter*, 19 March 1847.
75. *Vindicator*, 27 March 1847.
76. *Whig*, 4 March 1847.
77. *News-Letter*, 26 February 1847, 5 March 1847; *Whig*, 2 March 1847.
78. *Vindicator*, 17 April 1847.
79. *Whig*, 9 March 1847.
80. *Vindicator*, 3 March 1847.
81. Ibid., 11 November 1846.
82. *Banner*, 5 March 1847.
83. Kinealy, *Death-Dealing Famine*, pp. 98–100.
84. *Banner*, 2 March 1847, 5 March 1847.
85. Ibid., 19 March 1847.
86. Ibid., 13 April 1847.
87. Ibid.
88. Ibid.
89. *News-Letter*, 18 May 1847.
90. *News-Letter*, 23 February 1847.
91. Ibid., 12 March 1847.
92. Ibid., 13 April 1847; *Vindicator*, 14 April 1847.
93. *News-Letter*, 13 April 1847.
94. *Banner* and *News-Letter*, 12 March 1847.

95. *Banner*, 23 April 1847.
96. Ibid., 16 April 1847; *News-Letter*, 16 April 1847; *Vindicator*, 17 April 1847.
97. *News-Letter*, 16 April 1847.
98. *Banner*, 5 November 1847.
99. Ibid., 30 March 1847.
100. Ibid., 16 April 1847, 4 May 1847.

Chapter 4

1. Sixth Report of the Board of Public Works, PP 1847–48 (983) xlxvii.
2. R.S. Allison, *The Seeds of Time. A Short History of Belfast General and Royal Hospital 1850–1903* (Belfast, 1972) p. 9.
3. *Whig*, 22 April 1847, 29 April 1847.
4. Ibid., 11 May 1847.
5. Dublin Medical Press, 29 May 1850, quoted in Ó Gráda, *Black '47 and Beyond*, p. 173.
6. Quoted in Frank Neal, 'The Famine Irish in England and Wales', in P. Sullivan, *The Meaning of the Famine*, pp. 74–5.
7. Minutes of Belfast General Hospital Committee, PRONI, Mic. 514/1/1/5, 17 October 1846.
8. Minutes of Belfast Board of Guardians (hereafter bg), PRONI bg.7 a.5. p. 16, 20 October 1846.
9. Ibid., p. 60, 17 November 1846.
10. Ibid., p. 42, 3 November 1846.
11. Ibid., p. 60, 17 November 1846.
12. Ibid., p. 73, 24 November 1846.
13. Ibid., p. 107, 15 December 1846; pp. 114–15, 22 December 1846.
14. Ibid., pp. 149–50, 12 January 1847.
15. Ibid., p. 96, 18 December 1846; p. 128, 29 December 1846; pp. 157–8, 19 January 1847.
16. Ibid., p. 170, 26 January 1847.
17. Ibid., p. 171.
18. Ibid., p. 175.
19. Ibid., p. 176.
20. Ibid., p. 136, 5 January 1847; p. 169, 26 January 1847; p. 183, 2 February 1847.
21. Ibid., p. 183, 2 February 1847.
22. Ibid., p. 201, 9 February 1847.
23. Ibid., p. 218, 23 February 1847; p. 238, 2 February 1847; p. 246, 9 March 1847.
24. Ibid., p. 228, 2 March 1847.
25. Ibid., p. 249, 9 March 1847; Minutes of General Hospital Committee, PRONI, Mic. 514/1/1/5. 27 February 1847, 6 March 1847, 8 March 1847.
26. Minutes of Belfast Guardians, bg.7.a.5. p. 256, 16 March 1847; p. 278, 23 March 1847.
27. Ibid., p. 243, 9 March 1847.
28. Ibid., p. 197, 9 February 1847.
29. Ibid., p. 275, 23 March 1847.
30. Ibid.
31. Ibid., p. 277, 23 March 1847; Minutes of General Hospital Committee, PRONI, Mic. 514/1/1/5, 20 March 1847.
32. Minutes of Belfast Guardians, bg.7.a.5. p. 278, 23 March 1847.
33. Ibid., pp. 298–9, 30 March 1847.
34. Ibid., p. 301.
35. Ibid., p. 300.

36. *News-Letter*, 20 April 1847.
37. John Boyd to Relief Commissioners, NAD, RLFC 3/2/8/9, 27 January 1847.
38. *News-Letter*, 6 April 1847.
39. Minutes of Belfast General Hospital Committee, PRONI, Mic. 514/1/1/5, 2 April 1847; *Banner* 9 April 1847.
40. Minutes of Belfast Guardians, bg.7.a.5. pp. 307–8, 3 April 1847.
41. *Banner* and *News-Letter*, 6 April 1847.
42. Ibid., 6 April 1847.
43. *News-Letter*, 23 April 1847.
44. Ibid.
45. *Vindicator*, 21 April 1847.
46. *Banner*, 30 April 1847.
47. Minutes of Belfast Guardians, bg.7.a.5. p. 302, 25 March 1847; p. 345, 27 April 1847.
48. Annual Report of Belfast General Hospital for the year ending 31 March 1848, quoted in Allison, *Seeds of Time*, p. 10.
49. Ibid., p. 326, 13 April 1847.
50. Police Committee Minute Book, CHA, 28/4, 30 June 1847.
51. Minutes of Belfast Guardians, bg.7.a.5., pp. 328–9, 13 April 1847.
52. Police Committee Minute Book, CHA, 28/4, 11 May 1847.
53. Minutes of Belfast Guardians, bg.7.a.5. p. 315, 6 April 1847; p. 327, 13 April 1847; Minutes of Belfast General Hospital, PRONI, 514/1/1/5, 10 April 1847.
54. Minutes of Belfast Guardians, bg.7.a.5., pp. 318–19, 6 April 1847.
55. Ibid., p. 340, 20 April 1847; p. 367, 4 May 1847.
56. Ibid., p. 353, 27 April 1847.
57. Ibid.
58. *Banner*, 30 April 1847.
59. Ibid.
60. *News-Letter*, 30 April 1847.
61. *Banner* and *News-Letter*, 4 May 1847.
62. Letter written by E. McCormack, 81 North Queen Street, *Banner*, 1 May 1847; ibid., 4 May 1847.
63. *News-Letter*, 7 May 1847.
64. Minutes of Belfast General Hospital, PRONI, Mic. 514/1/1/5, 7 May 1847; Minutes of Charitable Society, PRONI, Mic. 61/6/32, 8 May 1847, 15 May 1847.
65. *News-Letter*, 7 May 1847.
66. Ibid., 25 May 1847.
67. Minutes of Belfast Guardians, bg.7.a.5. p. 380, 4 May 1847.
68. *News-Letter*, 11 May 1847.
69. Minutes of Charitable Society, PRONI, Mic.61/6/32, 1 May 1847.
70. *Whig*, 3 June 1847.
71. Diary of James MacAdam, PRONI, D/2930/7/6, 13 June 1847.
72. *Whig*, 8 June 1847.
73. Diary of MacAdam, 8 March 1847.
74. *News-Letter*, 25 May 1847.
75. Ibid., 28 May 1847.
76. *News-Letter*, 7 May 1847.
77. Ibid. 8 June 1847.
78. Ibid., 20 July 1847.
79. Ibid., 25 May 1847, 28 May 1847.
80. *Banner*, 23 April 1847.
81. *Banner*, 4 June 1847.
82. *News-Letter*, 8 June 1847.
83. *Banner* and *News-Letter*, June 1847, passim.

84. Unlike England, where civil registration of births, deaths and marriages was made compulsory in 1837, similar legislation was not introduced into Ireland until 1864.
85. *News-Letter*, 25 June 1847.
86. *Banner*, 14 May 1847.
87. *News-Letter*, 18 June 1847.
88. Minutes of Belfast Guardians, bg.7.a.5. p. 132, 5 January 1847.
89. Ibid., pp. 159–61, 19 January 1847.
90. Ibid., p. 192, 9 February 1847.
91. Ibid., p. 280, 23 March 1847; p. 303, 30 March 1847.
92. Ibid., p. 247, 9 March 1847.
93. Correspondence Relating to the State of Union Workhouses in Ireland, PP. 1847 (863) iv, pp. 5–23.
94. Minutes of Belfast Guardians, bg.7.a.6. p. 5, 25 May 1847.
95. Minutes of Belfast General Hospital, PRONI, Mic.514/1/1/4, 27 March 1847.
96. Ibid., 10 April 1847; Minutes of Charitable Society, PRONI, Mic.61.6.32, 10 April 1847.
97. Minutes of Belfast Guardians, bg.7.a.6. pp. 86–7, 14 July 1847; p. 97, 21 July 1847.
98. Ibid., bg.7.a.6. p. 7, 25 May 1847; p. 41, 15 June 1847.
99. *News-Letter*, 2 July 1847.
100. Minutes of Charitable Society, PRONI, Mic/61/6/32, 9 July 1847.
101. *Banner* and *News-Letter*, 16 July 1847.
102. *News-Letter*, 16 July 1847.
103. Minutes of Belfast Guardians, bg.7.a.6. pp. 106–7, 28 July 1847.
104. *News-Letter*, 23 July 1847.
105. Diary of MacAdam, 5 March 1847.
106. Report of A.C. Buchanan, Chief Agent, Government Emigration Office, Quebec, PRONI, T/3168/3, 11 May 1847.
     Ships Departing Belfast on 12 April 1847:

Vessel	Passengers
Lord Seaton	299
Caithnesshire	240
Chieftain	245
Lady Gordon	206

107. Minutes of Belfast Guardians, bg.7.a.6. p. 68, 30 June 1847.
108. *News-Letter*, 29 June 1847.
109. Ibid., 13 August 1847.
110. Ibid., 30 July 1847.
111. *Banner*, 17 August 1847.
112. Diary of MacAdam, 30 April 1847.
113. *News-Letter*, 18 May 1847.
114. Diary of MacAdam, 30 January 1847; *Banner*, 1 May 1847.
115. *Banner* and *News-Letter*, 25 June 1847.
116. *Banner*, 6 July 1847.
117. *Banner* and *News-Letter*, 20 July 1847, 31 August 1847.
118. *News-Letter*, 20 August 1847.
119. *Banner* and *News-Letter*, 24 August 1847.
120. *Whig*, 3 August 1847.
121. *News-Letter*, 9 July 1847, 23 July 1847.
122. Ibid., 25 May 1847.
123. *Banner*, 23 July 1847.
124. Ibid., 9 July 1847.
125. Ibid., 27 August 1847.
126. Ibid.

127. *Banner* and *News-Letter*, 7 September 1847, 19 October 1847.
128. *Banner*, 21 September 1847.
129. *News-Letter*, 5 October 1847.
130. *Banner*, 2 November 1847.
131. *Whig*, 28 October 1847.
132. *Banner*, 28 December 1847.
133. Ibid., 9 November 1847.
134. *News-Letter*, 16 November 1847.
135. Evidence of Edward Senior, Select Committee of the House of Lords on the Irish Poor Laws, 1849, xvi; First Annual Report of PLC for Ireland, 1848, pp. 10–13.
136. *News-Letter*, 2 November 1847; *Banner*, 7 December 1847.
137. *Whig*, 25 December 1847.
138. *News-Letter*, 29 June 1847.
139. Ibid., 9 July 1847.
140. Ibid., 29 June 1849.
141. Ibid.
142. Walter Maloney, R.M., to Under Secretary, Dublin Castle, NAD, Outrage Papers for Co. Antrim, 8 July 1847.
143. *Protestant Journal*, 17 July 1847.
144. Ibid.
145. Walter Maloney, R.M., to Under Secretary, Dublin Castle, Outrage Papers for Co. Antrim, NAD, 14 July 1847.
146. *News-Letter*, 13 July 1847.
147. *Banner*, 16 July 1847.
148. *Protestant Journal*, 17 July 1847.

Chapter 5

1. Kinealy, *Calamity*, pp. 136–74.
2. The longevity of the memory of proselytism can be gauged from an article in the *Church of Ireland Gazette*, by Dr Robert McCarthy, the Rector of Galway Parish and the Provost of Tuam, who stated 'This is perhaps the moment to face squarely the charge of "souperism" which is still levied against the Church of Ireland in relation to its actions during the famine period ... the great majority of clergy of the Established Church were successful in resolving any tension which arose from both Protestant ministers and resident gentlemen. They tried to keep their identities in balance and when they did so, they were seldom accused of either proselytism or "souperism". Rather they were respected as men who brought direct, temporal and indirect spiritual blessings to the Irish countryside', 11 August 1995.
3. *Whig*, 13 May 1847.
4. Minutes of Belfast Guardians, bg.7.a.6., 30 June 1847.
5. *News-Letter*, 29 June 1847, 7 July 1847.
6. Minutes of Belfast Guardians, bg.7.a.6. p. 304, 15 December 1847.
7. Ibid.
8. Ibid., bg.7.a.7, pp. 3–5, 16 February 1848.
9. Ibid., bg.7.a.7, p. 114, 26 April 1848; p. 205, 28 June 1848.
10. Ibid., bg.7.a.7, pp. 282–3, 6 September 1848.
11. Ibid., bg.7.a.8, p. 29, 13 December 1848.
12. For example, the Bradford Guardians removed all Irish paupers irrespective of their length of residence, D. Ashford, 'The Urban Poor Law', in Derek Fraser (ed.) *The New Poor Law in the Nineteenth Century* (London, 1976) p. 146.

13. Minutes of Belfast Guardians, bg.7.a.8, p. 29, 13 December 1848.
14. Ibid., bg.7.a.7, p. 85, 12 April 1848.
15. Ibid., bg.7.a.7, p. 113, 26 April 1848.
16. Ibid., bg.7.a.7, pp. 124–6, 3 May 1848.
17. Ibid., bg.7.a.7, pp. 158, 24 May 1848; p. 186, 14 June 1848.
18. General Hospital Minutes, PRONI, Mic.514/1/1/5, 12 September 1848, 16 September 1848.
19. Ibid., 23 September 1848, 7 October 1848.
20. Minutes of Belfast Guardians, bg.7.a.8, p. 160, 7 March 1849.
21. Rob Goodbody, *A Suitable Channel. Quaker Relief in the Great Famine* (Bray, 1995).
22. Christine Kinealy, 'Potatoes, Providence and Philanthropy: The Role of Private Charity during the Irish Famine', in Patrick O'Sullivan, *The Meaning of the Famine* (Irish World Wide Series, vol. 6, Leicester University Press, 1996) pp. 114–71.
23. Northern *Whig*, quoted in Flann Campbell, *The Dissenting Voice. Protestant Democracy in Ulster from Plantation to Partition* (Belfast, 1991) p. 206.
24. *Banner* and *News-Letter*, 5 January 1847.
25. David Hempton and Myrtle Hill, *Evangelical Protestantism in Ulster Society 1740–1890* (London, 1992) p. 117.
26. *Banner* and *News-Letter*, 19 January 1847.
27. *Banner*, 5 February 1847.
28. Ibid., 12 February 1847.
29. *News-Letter*, 26 February 1847.
30. Ibid., 26 February 1847.
31. Kinealy, *Death-Dealing Famine*, pp. 98–106.
32. Seventh Report of the Relief Commissioners, PP, 1847–48, xxix.
33. *Banner* and *News-Letter*, 23 March 1847.
34. *Whig*, 23 March 1847.
35. *Banner* and *News-Letter*, 23 March 1847.
36. *Whig*, 1 April 1847.
37. *Banner*, 30 April 1847.
38. Ibid.
39. *Banner*, 12 February 1847; *News-Letter*, 5 March 1847, 26 March 1847, 6 April 1847.
40. Final Report of General Belfast Fund, in *Banner*, 5 January 1849.
41. Annals of Christ Church, by Rev. Abraham Dawson, PRONI T.2159, p. 110.
42. *Banner* and *News-Letter*, 1 January 1847.
43. Asenath Nicholson, *Annals of the Famine in Ireland* (first published 1851, reprinted Lilliput Press, 1998, ed. Maureen Murphy) p. 211.
44. First Report of Belfast Ladies' Association for the Relief of Irish Destitution (Belfast, 6 March 1847) pp. 4–6.
45. Nicholson, Annals, p. 57.
46. *Whig*, 24 April 1847.
47. Roscommon and Leitrim Gazette, 9 January 1847, 10 July 1847.
48. *Banner* and *News-Letter*, 16 February 1847.
49. First Report of Ladies' Association, pp. 12–38.
50. Ibid., p. 36.
51. Ibid., p. 37.
52. Ibid, p. 18.
53. *Whig*, 24 April 1847.
54. Report of the Irish Work Society, PRONI, D.1558/7/1/3, undated, c. 1847.
55. *News-Letter*, 2 April 1847.
56. Trevelyan to Ladies' Relief Associations in Ireland, PROL, HO 45 1942, 10 October 1847.

57. *News-Letter*, 17 April 1847, 20 April 1847.
58. Goodbody, *A Suitable Channel*, p. 67.
59. John Wolffe, *The Protestant Crusade in Great Britain, 1829–1860* (Oxford, 1991).
60. Irene Whelan, 'The Stigma of Souperism', in Cathal Poirteir, *The Irish Famine* (Cork, 1995) p. 136.
61. Peter Grey, *Famine, Land and Politics. British Government and Irish Society 1843–50* (Dublin, 1999) pp. 96–106.
62. Donal Kerr, *A Nation of Beggars? Priests, People and Politics in Famine Ireland 1846–52* (Oxford, 1994) p. 207.
63. *News-Letter*, 20 July 1847.
64. George Ensor, *The New Reformation. Letters showing the Inutility and Exhibiting the Absurdity of what is rather Fantastically termed 'The New Reformation'* (Dublin, 1828).
65. Whelan, 'The Stigma of Souperism', p. 139.
66. Hempton and Hill, *Evangelical Protestantism*, p. 91.
67. Rev. John Edgar, *A Voice from Ireland*, vol. 1 May 1850, p. 9.
68. Report of Dundee Ladies' Association on Behalf of the Presbyterian Church in Ireland, p. 1.
69. *News-Letter*, Report of Rev. Dr Edgar, Honorary Secretary of the Home Mission of the Irish Presbyterian Church, 17 August 1847.
70. Ibid. Report of Home Mission Committee read at Synod of Free Church of Scotland.
71. *Banner*, 26 October 1847.
72. *Voice from Ireland*, p. 4.
73. *News-Letter*, 18 May 1847.
74. *Banner*, 18 September 1846.
75. *Banner* and *News-Letter*, 25 September 1846.
76. Appeal and Report of Belfast Ladies' Relief Association for Connaught, p. 1.
77. Ibid., pp. 11–17.
78. *Banner*, 19 January 1847, 24 January 1847.
79. *Banner*, 1 January 1847.
80. Appeal of Association for Connaught, p. 2.
81. Ibid., p. 21.
82. Ibid., pp. 1–2.
83. *Vindicator*, 16 December 1846.
84. Ibid., 19 December 1846.
85. *Voice from Ireland*, p. 4
86. *Weekly Freeman's Journal*, 25 September 1847.
87. Rev. John Edgar, *The Women of the West. Ireland Helped to Help Herself*, p. 3.
88. Father Peter Hart, P. P. to Archbishop Murray, DDA, Murray Papers, File 32/4, 19 June 1848.
89. Ibid, p. 4.
90. Ibid, pp. 18 and 49.
91. W.D. Killen, *Memoir of J. Edgar*, p. 200.
92. *Banner*, 12 January 1849.
93. Ibid.
94. Ibid.
95. *Banner* and *News-Letter*, 8 January 1847.
96. *News-Letter*, 8 January 1847.
97. Ibid.
98. *Banner*, 8 January 1847.
99. *Whig*, 7 January 1847.
100. *Vindicator*, 13 January 1847.
101. *Dublin Evening Packet*, 9 January 1847.
102. *Whig*, 14 January 1847.

103. Ibid., 13 February 1847.
104. *News-Letter*, 2 February 1847.
105. Ibid.
106. Ibid., 23 January 1847.
107. *News-Letter*, 16 March 1847.
108. *Protestant Journal*, 18 March 1848.
109. Kerr, *Nation of Beggars*, p. 210.
110. *Banner*, 2 February 1847.
111. Ibid., 9 January 1849.
112. Ibid.
113. Ibid.
114. John Edgar D.D., 'Ireland's Mission Field', A paper read at the Sixth Annual Conference of the British Organisation, August 1852.
115. *Banner*, 23 January 1849; Nicholson, *Annals*, pp. 182–3.
116. Recollections of Mrs Lennox, Hollywood, in Cathal Poirteir, *Famine Echoes* (Dublin, 1995) p. 173.
117. Kerr, *Nation of Beggars*, pp. 210–12.
118. See Chapter 6 for the 1848 Uprising and Chapter 7 for the incident at Dolly's Brae.
119. Hempton and Hill, *Evangelical Protestantism*, p. 94.
120. Kerr, *Nation of Beggars*, pp. 324–5.
121. Whelan, 'The Stigma of Souperism', pp. 135–54.
122. Bardon, *Ulster*, pp. 306–7.
123. Hempton and Hill, *Evangelical Protestantism*, pp. 124–5.

Chapter 6

1. Kerr, *Nation of Beggars*, pp. 206–7.
2. Kinealy, *Great Calamity*, pp. 232–6.
3. *Banner*, 14 September 1849.
4. Ibid., 5 January 1849.
5. Ibid.
6. Minutes of Belfast Guardians, bg.7.a.7, p. 24.
7. Ibid., p. 335.
8. Ibid., p. 342.
9. Ibid., bg.7.a.8, p. 6.
10. Ibid., p. 8.
11. Ibid., p. 19.
12. Ibid., bg.7.a.6, p. 369.
13. Ibid., bg.7.a.8, p. 29.
14. Ibid., pp. 137, 147, 157, 171,181, 201.
15. *Banner*, 16 February 1849.
16. Ibid., 16 January 1849.
17. *News-Letter*, 28 March 1847.
18. Minutes of Belfast Guardians, bg.7.a.8, p. 92.
19. Ibid., p. 119.
20. Ibid., p. 456.
21. Ibid., bg.7.a.9, p. 86.
22. Bardon, *Ulster,* pp. 308–10.
23. *Glasgow Herald*, 11 June 1847.
24. C. Kinealy, 'Irish Immigration into Scotland in the Nineteenth and Twentieth Centuries', in *European Immigration into Scotland: Proceedings of the Fourth Annual Conference of the Scottish Association of Family History Societies* (Glasgow, 1992) p. 11.
25. *News-Letter*, 24 December 1846.

26. *Armagh Guardian* quoted in *Roscommon and Leitrim Gazette*, 24 April 1847.
27. *Banner*, 21 September 1847.
28. *Downpatrick Recorder*, 14 April 1847.
29. Dr Morgan, Moderator, Report of Presbyterian General Assembly, printed in *News-Letter*, 9 July 1847.
30. Rev. John Edgar D.D. 'Ireland's Mission Field', a paper read at the Sixth Annual Conference of the British Organisation (August 1852).
31. Instruction to Poor Law Inspectors from Poor Law Commissioners, 7 March 1848, Second Annual Report of Poor Law Commissioners, 1849.
32. See Chapter 7.
33. An Act to Make Further Provision for the Relief of the Destitute Poor in Ireland, 10th and 11th Vict., Cap. 31.
34. Tenth Annual Report of the Colonial Land and Emigration Commissioners, PP, 1850, xiii, pp. 3–5.
35. Frank Neal, *Sectarian Violence: The Liverpool Experience 1819–1914* (Manchester, 1987).
36. *Illustrated London News*, 3 April 1852.
37. Frank Neal, 'The Famine Irish in England and Wales' in Sullivan, *Famine*, p. 66.
38. Minutes of Belfast Guardians, bg.7.a.8, p. 36.
39. Ibid., p. 119.
40. *News-Letter*, 19 January 1849.
41. Ibid., 5 January 1849.
42. *Warder*, 7 March 1849.
43. *Belfast Vindicator*, 6 January 1847.
44. Bardon, *Ulster*, pp. 255–7.
45. *Protestant Journal*, 11 July 1846, 18 July 1846.
46. Ibid., 13 April 1847.
47. *Freeman's Journal*, 29 April 1845.
48. Charles Gavan Duffy, *Four Years of Irish History 1845–1849* (London, 1883) p. 439.
49. Ibid. pp. 438–40.
50. *Protestant Journal*, 13 November 1847.
51. Ibid., 20 November 1847.
52. Ibid.
53. *Whig*, 16 November 1847.
54. Thomas Verner, S.M. to Chief Secretary, Dublin Castle, NAD, Outrage Papers for Co. Antrim, 18 November 1847.
55. *Whig*, 16 November 1847.
56. Thomas Verner S.M. to Chief Secretary, Dublin Castle, Outrage Papers for Co. Antrim, 1847, NAD, 18 November 1847.
57. *Protestant Journal*, 20 November 1847.
58. Davis, *Revolutionary Imperialist: William Smith, O'Brien* (Dublin, 1998), p. 233.
59. *Protestant Journal*, 20 November 1847.
60. Thomas Verner S.M. to Dublin Castle, NAD, Outrage Papers for Co. Antrim, 1847, 19 November 1847.
61. *Protestant Journal*, 20 November 1847.
62. Duffy, *Four Years*, p. 440.
63. *Nation*, 22 January 1848.
64. *News-Letter*, 14 March 1847.
65. Ibid., 17 March 1847.
66. Ibid., 21 March 1847.
67. Ibid., 28 March 1847.
68. Richard Davis, *Revolutionary Imperialist*. p. 251.

69. George Suffern, Mayor of Belfast, to Chief Secretary, Dublin Castle, NAD, Outrage Papers for Co. Antrim, 1848, 8 April 1848.
70. *Protestant Journal*, 17 July 1847.
71. George Suffern, Town Hall, Belfast, to Redington, Dublin Castle, NAD, Outrage Papers for Co. Antrim, 1848, 15 April 1848.
72. Memorial of Inhabitants of Belfast to Lord Lieutenant, PROL, HO45 OS2488, 15 April 1848.
73. Ibid., Lord Lieutenant to Belfast Delegation, 20 April 1848.
74. Ibid., Sir George Grey to Lord Lieutenant, 2 May 1848.
75. Petition from Loyal Orange Lodge No. 356, Outrage Papers, Co. Down, NAD, 29 July 1848.
76. Ibid.. H. Ellis, Belfast to Lord Lieutenant, Dublin Castle, 11 April 1848.
77. Davis, *Revolutionary Imperialist*, p. 247.
78. *Nation*, 29 July 1848.
79. Ibid., 13 May 1848, 20 May 1848.
80. *Warder*, 10 July 1848.
81. Ibid.
82. *News-Letter*, 11 July 1848.
83. *Warder*, 10 July 1848.
84. Ibid., 17 July 1848.
85. *News-Letter*, 12 July 1848.
86. Town Clerk, Belfast to Chief Secretary, Dublin Castle, NAD, Outrage Papers for Co. Antrim, 1848, 26 July 1848.
87. Ibid., Belfast Petty Sessions to Chief Secretary, 26 July 1848.
88. Ibid., George Bentinck, R.M., Belfast to Dublin Castle, 29 July 1848.
89. Ibid.
90. John Rea's arrest without charge resulted in him being nicknamed 'the Kilmainham spy', Brian Griffin, *The Bulkies. Police and Crime in Belfast 1800–1865* (Dublin, 1997) p. 127.
91. John Burnett, JP, to Dublin Castle, NAD, Outrage Papers for Co. Antrim, 1848, 16 August 1848.
92. *Nation*, 29 July 1848.
93. *Banner*, 20 February 1849.
94. *Armagh Guardian*, 16 July 1849.
95. *The Warder*, 14 July 1849.
96. Kinealy, *Great Calamity*, Chapter 6.
97. Lord John Russell to Lord Clarendon, Clarendon Papers, Bodleian Library, 24 February 1849.
98. *Banner*, 20 February 1849.
99. Evidence of Edward Twistleton, Select Committee on Irish Poor Law (hereafter Poor Law) PP, 1849, xv, pp. 699–714.
100. Sir Robert Peel to Sir James Graham, in Charles Stuart Parker (ed.) *Sir Robert Peel from his Private Letters* (London, 1899) 20 January 1849, p. 501.
101. Evidence of Edward Senior, *Poor Law*, pp. 103–4.
102. *Hansard*, col. 295, 6 March 1849.
103. Ibid., col. 204, 5 March 1849.
104. Ibid., J.Reynolds, col. 81, 1 March 1849.
105. Ibid., J. Reynolds, col. 171, 5 March 1849.
106. Quoted in James Grant, 'The Great Famine and the Poor Law in Ulster: The Rate-in-Aid Issue of 1849', in *Irish Historical Studies*, vol. xxvii, no. 105, p. 38.
107. *Newry Telegraph*, 6 March 1849.
108. *Banner*, 15 February 1849.
109. First Report of the Commissioners for Inquiring into the Number and Boundaries of Poor Law Unions and Electoral Divisions in Ireland, PP, 1849, xxiii.

110. *Banner*, 22 May 1849.
111. *Warder*, 6 January 1849, 7 March 1849.
112. *Whig*, 10 March 1849, 17 March 1849.
113. Quoted in the *Whig*, 17 March 1849.
114. *Warder*, 7 March 1849.
115. *Banner*, 10 May 1849.
116. *Whig*, 24 May 1849.
117. Accounts showing the total sum assessed as Rate-in-Aid in Ireland under the Act 12 Vict. c.24 ... bearing the date 13 day of June 1849 and 23 day of December 1850, respectively, PP, 1852, xlvi.
118. For example, in 1937–38, the N.I. Department of Education refused to cooperate with a national study of Famine folklore, see, Poirteir, *Famine Echoes*, p. 151; Ruth Dudley Edwards' sympathetic and partisan account of the Orange Order, *The Faithful Tribe. An Intimate Account of the Loyal Institutions* (London, 1999), does not mention the Famine years.

Chapter 7

1. *Banner*, 14 September 1849.
2. *Northern Whig*, 13 July 1848.
3. Barton, *History of Ulster*, p. 264.
4. *News-Letter*, 13 July 1849.
5. *Banner*, 13 July 1848.
6. Ibid., 6 April 1849.
7. Ibid., 27 July 1849.
8. Ibid., 10 August 1849, 21 August 1849.
9. *The Times*, 30 August 1849.
10. *Banner*, 14 September 1849.
11. *The Times*, 18 July 1849.
12. *Dublin Evening Post*, 19 December 1848, 21 December 1848; Minutes of Belfast Guardians, 17 January 1849, 24 January 1849.
13. Ibid., 7 February 1849.
14. Ibid., 18 April 1849.
15. *Banner*, 30 March 1849.
16. Minutes of Belfast Guardians, 9 May 1849.
17. E. Senior to Guardians, Minutes of Belfast Guardians, 31 May 1849.
18. Ibid., 6 June 1849.
19. Home Office to Governor of South Australia, PROL, HO45 2252, 17 February 1847.
20. See, T. Parkhill, 'Permanent Deadwood. Emigration from Ulster Workhouses during the Famine', in M. Crawford (ed.) *The Hungry Stream. Essays on Emigration and Famine* (Belfast, 1997) pp. 87–100.
21. Trevelyan to Clarendon, PROL, T.64.367. C/1, 29 January 1848.
22. Minutes of Evidence of Surgeon Superintendent Douglass, Minutes of Enquiry, NAD, CSORP, 0.9048.
23. Report of Poor Law Commissioners, printed in *Banner*, 17 July 1849, 27 July 1849.
24. Minutes of Belfast Guardians, 13 December 1848.
25. Dr Phelan to PLC, 18 January 1849, Report of the Commissioners of Health, Ireland (Dublin, 1852) p. 39.
26. Minutes of Belfast Guardians, 10 January 1849.
27. Minutes of Belfast Guardians, bg.7.a.7, p. 6.
28. Ibid., p. 43.
29. Minutes of General Hospital, 16 January 1849.
30. Minutes of Belfast Guardians, bg.7.a.8, p. 52.

31. Ibid., p. 38.
32. Ibid., pp. 60, 62.
33. Ibid., p. 59.
34. Ibid., p. 373.
35. Ibid., pp. 141, 253.
36. Ibid., 7 February 1849.
37. Ibid., 5 January 1849.
38. Minutes of Charitable Society, PRONI, Mic.61/6/32, 30 December 1848.
39. Ibid., 20 October 1849.
40. *Banner*, 20 February 1849.
41. Ibid., 20 February 1849.
42. Ibid., 6 April 1849.
43. Minutes of Belfast Guardians, bg.7.a.8, p. 224.
44. Ibid., p. 72.
45. Ibid., p. 191.
46. Ibid., pp. 211, 252–3.
47. Ibid., p. 372.
48. Ibid., 11 July 1849.
49. *Banner*, 27 July 1849.
50. *The Times*, 17 August 1849.
51. Minutes of Belfast Guardians, bg.7.a.9, p. 33.
52. *Banner*, 14 September 1849.
53. Summary of Returns showing the Number of Cases of Cholera and the Number of Deaths in the Principal Towns in Ireland, *Epidemics, 1846–50*, p. 79.
54. H. Ellis, Belfast to Lord Lieutenant, Outrage Papers for Co. Antrim, 11 April 1848.
55. *News-Letter*, 14 March 1848.
56. Ibid., 28 April 1848.
57. Ibid., 14 March 1848.
58. Warder quoted in *Armagh Guardian*, 10 July 1848.
59. *Northern Whig*, 13 July 1848.
60. *News-Letter*, 14 July 1848.
61. *Nation*, 29 July 1848.
62. *Armagh Guardian*, 19 March 1848.
63. *Northern Whig*, 13 July 1848.
64. Ibid., 13 July 1848.
65. George Suffern, Mayor, to Lord Lieutenant, Outrage Papers for Co. Antrim, NAD, 12 July 1848.
66. *Warder*, 6 January 1849.
67. *Banner*, 22 January 1849.
68. Memorial of Roman Catholic Inhabitants of Belfast and vicinity, Outrage Papers for Co. Antrim, NAD, 5 February 1849.
69. *Warder*, 24 March 1849.
70. *Banner*, 27 March 1849.
71. *Weekly Vindicator*, 24 March 1849.
72. *The Times*, 12 July 1849.
73. Ibid., 2 July 1849.
74. J. Dyas R.M. to Under Secretary, Dublin Castle, Outrage Papers for Co. Antrim, NAD, 4 July 1849.
75. *Warder*, 14 July 1849.
76. J. Graves, R.M., to Under Secretary, Dublin Castle, Outrage papers for Co. Antrim, NAD, 13 July 1849.
77. Ibid., 13 July 1849.
78. Ibid., 14 July 1849.
79. Ibid., 14 July 1849.

80. Ibid., 17 July 1849.
81. *Banner*, 14 September 1849.
82. *Warder*, 21 July 1849.
83. Ibid.
84. Ibid., 14 July 1849.
85. *Banner*, 24 July 1849.
86. *Hansard*, 1849, c.1129.
87. Clarendon to Lewis, quoted in Kerr, *Nation of Beggars*, p. 202.
88. There are many songs commemorating the 'victory' at Dolly's Brae which continue to be sung.
89. Kinealy, *Disunited Kingdom*, p. 115.
90. *Armagh Guardian*, 10 July 1848, 17 July 1848.
91. *Northern Whig*, 13 July 1848.
92. Clarendon to Sir George Grey, PROL, HO45 OS 2522, 29 June 1849.
93. Lord John Russell to Clarendon, 29 June 1849, in Arthur Christopher Benson and Viscount Escher (eds), *The Letters of Queen Victoria* (London, 1907) p. 265.
94. Ibid., Queen Victoria to Russell, 19 July 1849, p. 266.
95. *Liverpool Mercury*, 7 August 1849.
96. *Banner*, 24 July 1849.
97. Ibid., 3 August 1849.
98. *Liverpool Mercury*, 17 August 1849.
99. Mayor of Belfast to Under Secretary, Dublin Castle, PROL, HO45 OS 2522, 2 July 1849.
100. *Banner*, 27 July 1849.
101. Queen's Visit to Ireland File, PROL, HO45 OS 2522, July, 1849.
102. *The Times*, 30 July 1849.
103. Address from Loyal Inhabitants of Co. Down, PROL, HO45 OS 2522, 21 July 1849.
104. *Banner*, 24 July 1849.
105. *The Times*, 18 July 1849.
106. Ibid., 16 July 1849.
107. *Banner*, 7 August 1849.
108. *Weekly Vindicator*, 14 July 1849.
109. *Banner*, 3 August 1849.
110. Daniel McPheron, Belfast, to Sir George Grey, PROL HO45 OS 2522, 1 August 1849.
111. *Liverpool Mercury*, 17 August 1849.
112. *Banner*, 14 August 1849.
113. Memorial of Dublin Protestant Association, PROL HO45 OS 2764, 29 September 1849.
114. *Banner*, 31 July 1849, 3 August 1849.
115. An illustration of the arch is provided in, Eileen Black, *The People's Park. The Queen's Island and Belfast 1849–1879* (Belfast, 1988) p. 10.
116. Ibid., p. 9; *Banner*, 3 August 1849.
117. *Liverpool Mercury*, 7 August 1849.
118. *Banner*, 3 August 1849.
119. *Liverpool Mercury*, 17 August 1849.
120. *Banner*, 3 August 1849.
121. Ibid., 14 August 1849.
122. Ibid., 7 August 1849.
123. *News-Letter*, 14 August 1849.
124. Ibid.
125. Ibid.
126. *Banner*, 14 August 1849.
127. Ibid., 10 August 1849.

128. Ibid.
129. *News-Letter*, 14 August 1849.
130. Ibid.
131. *Banner*, 21 August 1849.
132. *News-Letter*, 14 August 1849.
133. Ibid.
134. Ibid.
135. *Banner*, 14 August 1849.
136. *News-Letter*, 14 August 1849.
137. *Banner*, 17 August 1849.
138. Ibid., 21 August 1849.
139. Clarendon to Sir George Grey, 14 August 1849, Benson and Escher, *Letters*, pp. 268–9.
140. *The Times*, 30 August 1849.
141. *Banner*, 17 August 1849.
142. Ibid.
143. Ibid.
144. *Banner*, 14 August 1849.

Chapter 8

1. *Banner*, 27 July 1849.
2. Minutes of Belfast Guardians, bg.7.a.8, p. 456.
3. Ibid., bg.7.a.9, p. 86.
3. Collins, *The Hungry Stream*. p. 159.
4. Table of Occupations in Town of Belfast, 1841 Census, p. 290 and Table of Occupations, 1851 Census, p. 416.
5. Minute Books of Belfast Guardians, 5 December 1851; Annual Reports of Poor Law Commissioners for 1850 to 1860.
6. Ninth Annual Report of PLC, 1856, Appendix B, pp. 92–3.
7. Ibid., 1856 p. 123.
8. Seventeenth Annual Report of PLC, 1864, p. 5.
9. Ibid., p. 87.
10. Ninth Annual Report of PLC, 1856, p. 15.
11. Rev. W. O'Hanlon, *Walks Among the Poor of Belfast*, (Belfast, 1853), LHL, p. 1.
12. Ibid., pp. 2–3.
13. Ibid., p. 4.
14. Ibid., p. 5.
15. Twenty-Fourth Annual Report of PLC, 1871, p. 23.
16. Nineteenth Annual Report of PLC for 1866, p. 14.
17. Christine Kinealy, 'The Administration of the Irish Poor Law, 1838–62' (unpublished PhD Thesis, Trinity College, Dublin, 1984).
18. Minute Books of Belfast Guardians, 31 May 1854.
19. An Act to Amend the Laws in Force for the Relief of the Destitute Poor In Ireland, 25 & 26 Vict. Cap. 83.
20. Appendix B., Seventeenth Annual Report of PLC, p. 159.
21. Ibid., p. 154.
22. Allison, *Seeds of Time*, p. 59.
23. Twenty-Fourth Annual Report of PLC, 1871, p. 27.
24. Ibid., p. 175.
25. Paddy Devlin, *Yes We Have No Bananas* (Belfast, 1981) p. 22.
26. *Vindicator, 11* April 1846.
27. Devlin, *No Bananas*, p. 23.

28. Table of Occupations in Town of Belfast, 1841 Census, pp. 288–90 and Table of Occupations, Census for Ireland in the Year 1851, PP, 1856, pp. 414–16.
29. Allison, *Seeds of Time*, pp. 160–1.
30. Ibid., p. 162.
31. Collins, 'Linen Industry', in *Hungry Stream*, p. 159.
32. Vaughan and Fitzpatrick, *Historical Statistics*, p. 16. the boundaries of Belfast did change; in 1853, the industrial suburb of Ballymacarrett was included in the town.
33. Emigrants to Belfast, Appendix to General Report, Census of Ireland for 1851, pp. lxxviii–lxxxvii. Census for 1851, Population in Counties Antrim and Down, pp. 7–11, 163–5, 184.
34. Henry Patterson, 'Industrial Labour and the Labour Movement', in Kennedy and Ollerenshaw, *Economic History*, pp. 166–7.
35. Ibid., Clarkson, 'Population Change', p. 154.
36. Vaughan and Fitzpatrick, *Historical Statistics*, pp. 49–69.
37. Clarkson, 'Population Change', in Kennedy and Ollerenshaw, *Economic History*, p. 154.
38. Table of Occupations in Town of Belfast, 1841 Census, pp. 288–90 and Table of Occupations, Census for Ireland in the Year 1851, PP, 1856, pp. 414–16.
39. Thomas Bartlett, 'Ulster 1600–2000: Posing the Question?', in Bullan, 1996, p. 15.
40. Walker, Ulster Society, pp. 172–3.
41. Meeting of General Synod of Church of Ireland, 16 April 1912, quoted in Patrick Buckland, *Irish Unionism 1885–1923. A Documentary History* (Belfast 1973) pp. 80–1.
42. Brian Walker 'Ulster Society and Politics, 1801–1921' in Brady et al., *Ulster*, pp. 170–1.
43. *News-Letter*, 27 October 1857.
44. Kerr, *Nation of Beggars*, p. 211.
45. Walker, *History's Tune*, p. 94.
46. Mark Radford, 'Closely Akin to Actual Warfare. The Belfast Riots of 1886 and the RIC', in *History Ireland*, vol. 7, no. 4. Winter 1999, pp. 27–9.
47. Griffin, *The Bulkies*, p. 6.
48. Radford, *Belfast Riots*, p. 28.
49. Ibid., pp. 29–31; Edward Royle, *Modern Britain. A Social History 1750–1985* (London, 1990) p. 218.
50. L.A. Clarkson, 'Population Change and Urbanization 1821–1911', in Kennedy and Ollerenshaw, *Economic History*, p. 153.
51. Bartlett, 'Ulster 1600–2000', pp. 8–10.
52. Liz Curtis, *The Cause of Ireland. From United Irishmen to Partition* (Belfast, 1995) p. 212.
53. Hepburn, *Catholic Belfast 1850–1950*, p. 130.
54. Brian Walker, *Ulster Politics. The Formative Years, 1868–86* (Belfast, 1989).

Further Reading

Between 1994 and 1997, there was an outpouring of books concerned with the Great Famine in Ireland to coincide with the 150th anniversary of catastrophe. This surge of research and writing was particularly welcome in view of the historiographical silence which had been evident in the preceding period. However, a number of areas, such as the impact of the Famine on Belfast, have tended to be underrepresented in the literature.

Amongst the most useful of the recent studies are: E.M. Crawford (ed.), *The Hungry Stream. Essays on Emigration and Famine* (Belfast, 1997); Peter Gray, *Famine, Land and Politics. British Government and Irish Society 1843–1850* (Dublin, 1999); Margaret Kelleher, *The Feminization of Famine. Expressions of the Inexpressible?* (Cork, 1997); Donal Kerr, *A Nation of Beggars? Priests, People and Politics in Famine Ireland, 1846–52* (Oxford, 1994); John Killen, *The Famine Decade. Contemporary Accounts 1841–1851* (Belfast, 1995); Christine Kinealy, *This Great Calamity. The Irish Famine 1845–52* (Dublin, 1994); Christine Kinealy, *A Death-Dealing Famine. The Great Hunger in Ireland* (London, 1997); Christine Kinealy and Trevor Parkhill (eds), *The Famine in Ulster* (Belfast, 1997); Gerard Mac Atasney, *This Dreadful Visitation. The Famine in Lurgan and Portadown* (Belfast, 1997); Joel Mokyr, *Why Ireland Starved. A Quantitative and Analytical History of the Irish Economy 1800–1850* (London, 1983); Cormac Ó Gráda, *Black '47 and Beyond. The Great Irish Famine in History, Economy and Memory* (New Jersey, 1999); Patrick O'Sullivan (ed.), *Patterns of Migration* (Vol. One of 'The Irish World Wide. History, Heritage, Identity', Leicester University Press, 1992); Patrick O'Sullivan (ed.), *The Meaning of the Famine* (Vol. Six of 'The Irish World Wide. History, Heritage, Identity', Leicester University Press, 1997); Cathal Poirteir (ed.), *The Great Irish Famine* (Dublin, 1995).

For a greater understanding of Belfast's history, the following are valuable: Jonathan Bardon, *A History of Ulster* (Belfast, 1992); Paddy Devlin, *Yes We Have No Bananas* (Belfast, 1981); Brian Griffin, *The Bulkies. Police and Crime in Belfast 1800–1865* (Dublin,

1997); A.C. Hepburn, *A Past Apart: Studies in the History of Catholic Belfast 1850–1950* (Belfast, 1996); W.A. Maguire, *Belfast* (Keele, 1993); Eamon Phoenix, *Northern Nationalism. Nationalist Politics and the Catholic Minority in Ireland 1890–1940* (Belfast, 1994); B.M. Walker, *Ulster Politics. The Formative Years 1868–86* (Belfast, 1989).

Index